THE UNITED STATES OF TRUMP

THE UNITED STATES OF TRUMP

How the President Really Sees America

BILL O'REILLY

ST. MARTIN'S GRIFFIN
NEW YORK

Published in the United States by St. Martin's Griffin, an imprint of St. Martin's Publishing Group

THE UNITED STATES OF TRUMP. Copyright © 2019 by Bill O'Reilly. All rights reserved. Printed in the United States of America. For information, address St. Martin's Publishing Group, 120 Broadway, New York, NY 10271.

www.stmartins.com

Designed by Kelly S. Too

Library of Congress Control Number: 2019948930

ISBN 978-1-250-23722-4 (hardcover)
ISBN 978-1-250-23721-7 (ebook)
ISBN 978-1-250-77033-2 (trade paperback)

Our books may be purchased in bulk for promotional, educational, or business use. Please contact your local bookseller or the Macmillan Corporate and Premium Sales Department at 1-800-221-7945, extension 5442, or by email at MacmillanSpecial Markets@macmillan.com.

First published in the United States by Henry Holt and Company

First St. Martin's Griffin Edition: 2020

D 10 9 8 7 6 5 4 3

This book is dedicated to my sister, Janet,
and to my nephew, Brandon Ricci.
Both solid patriots.

FOREWORD

MANHASSET, NEW YORK

VALENTINE'S DAY, 2019

DUSK

This book was a bear to write. Almost as difficult as *Killing Jesus*, which required methodical research to separate myth from reality. Same thing here—the Trump myth collided with the Trump reality, and getting to the truth was no easy matter.

That's because much of what has been written and said about President Trump is false, stated through a prism of disdain and, on the other side, adulation. Either way, there is so much garbage floating around the Trump story, I felt more like a sanitation worker than a reporter.

But report I did, without fear or favor.

If you despise Donald Trump, this book may frustrate you. It tells the truth about the man, both good and bad. It is not pro- or anti-Trump. It is history.

I was in a good position to work on the project because I've known the president for more than thirty years. I attended one of his weddings, and I even double-dated with him. (I think you'll enjoy that story.)

But I am not a close friend of his because he doesn't have many of those, and there is a reason for this, which we'll examine.

I once said on television that the election of Donald Trump to the presidency was the most stunning political story of my lifetime. I wasn't pandering; what I said is absolutely true.

It is 2014, and Trump and I are sitting in Madison Square Garden watching the Knicks lose another one. We are talking about the news business when Donald suddenly turns to me and says, "I'm thinking about running for president."

To which I reply, "Of what country?"

Now, Trump had flirted with a presidential run back in 2011. But that went nowhere. He shrugged off my wise-guy comment and went on to recite a litany of things that needed to be done in America. Some of his ideas were good, others less so. But I never delved into the most important question: *Why* does Donald Trump believe what he believes?

Hopefully, this book will explain the why behind the power. The why behind the bluster. The why behind the hatred he absorbs and sometimes dishes out. And most important, the key question: HOW ON EARTH did he get to the Oval Office?

To travel down that pathway, you have to ask another question: How exactly does President Trump see his country? As another business to be run? Or as a special place that should set a shining example for the rest of the world?

Luckily, I was able to speak with the president about America in a personal way. In truth, he did not want to have that conversation. But I badgered him until he finally gave in.

During the interview he was at times charming, distracted, transported back to another time, teed off.

Here's one of my favorite exchanges, which came after we discussed the war in Vietnam:

PRESIDENT TRUMP: **This is a lot of work.**

O'REILLY: **You want a break?**

PRESIDENT TRUMP: It's a lot of work. You know I want to give the perfect answer.

O'REILLY: It's going to be a great book.

PRESIDENT TRUMP: I'm doing this for you, Bill, I'm not doing this for me. I'm just saying as I'm answering these very intense questions that maybe I've never been asked before . . .

O'REILLY: They're good, though.

PRESIDENT TRUMP: Maybe that's why you're the best. But I'm saying it's a lot of work . . . I'm doing this to make you happy. Well, let's go forward. How much longer do you think it will be?

Thank God we were sitting on Air Force One so he couldn't bolt out the door.

The reality is it was the president's fault it was so much work. He's a complicated man who is not prone to introspection, nostalgia, or patience.

TTT

THERE WILL BE no armchair psychoanalysis in this book. No cheap shots. No speculation. No anonymous sources—a fact that will crush the national media.

Also, this is not a policy book or an investigation into the Trump finances. My goal is simple because I am a simple man: show the president as a real person, not some caricature created by haters, phonies, or flatterers.

What there *will* be in this book is an honest narrative with the intent of finding out President Trump's view of America—why he thinks what he thinks. After you read these pages, I hope you will understand more about the most powerful man on the planet and how he achieved that status.

If you don't, I'm sorry. I tried my best. I tackled, almost literally, a very elusive subject.

And at least this time, I don't kill anybody.

THE UNITED STATES OF TRUMP

PART I

CHAPTER ONE

ABOARD AIR FORCE ONE

FEBRUARY 1, 2019

5:15 PM

The president of the United States, Donald J. Trump, is not happy. Sitting behind a large wooden desk in his spacious airborne office, he asks that his wife, Melania, be brought into the room immediately. In less than a minute, she appears, immaculately groomed and flashing her bright smile.

"Can you believe Bill?" the president says to his confused wife while nodding toward me. "He's grilling me just like he used to do on television. I need to relax! All day I've been talking: CBS interview, meetings. My voice is shot!"

The First Lady says nothing. Just looks at us smiling. All of a sudden, she simply vanishes.

It is four days before the State of the Union address, and the Trumps are flying to their retreat in Palm Beach for some rest and relaxation. But an intruder is delaying that state of mind. For months, I have been trying to secure a sit-down with the president to talk with him. I want to know how Donald Trump's view of America was formed and how it has changed since he became the most powerful person in the world.

Now, for a man who relishes competition and achievement, that kind of introspection is annoying. The only reason Donald Trump consented to the Q-and-A in the first place was legacy. He trusts that I will treat him fairly, which I always have. But clearly, flying over the East Coast of the United States, the president wants to get this over with.

"Can I get a few more questions in?" I say as he finishes his shrimp salad. Still wearing his suit jacket, he loosens his bright red tie. "I'd only do this for you, Bill. But you have to give me a break. These questions are so intense; let's get it over with."

And so, we did.

Interviewing Donald Trump on television is much easier than for print. On TV, he is hyperfocused, ready for rhetorical battle, locked into the moment. TV is action, immediate gratification, the high wire. The president loves TV.

And that's my problem aboard Air Force One, the finest flying machine in the world. On the wall directly facing the president is a huge screen silently beaming Fox News into the room. This distracts Donald Trump, especially when the chyron indicates the discussion is about him.

"What do you think of Bret Baier?" the president asks me while handing his empty plate to an attendant.

"Nice pocket hankies," I say, attempting to deep-six the topic. I'm trying to zero in on how the president has changed his opinion about his country since taking office. I've got to get him refocused.

I succeed. Somewhat. And you will read his musings in the upcoming chapters. The president's words were sincere, I have never known him to be phony with me, and we've had hundreds of conversations. You might not like what Mr. Trump has to say, but it's genuine, and there's a fascinating history behind his thought process.

After I wrap up the questioning, the president relaxes and begins grilling me about his enemies and possible opponents in the upcoming election. I answer honestly, and he takes notes. Throughout my forty-five-year career in journalism, I have spoken off the record with some of the most powerful people on earth, and I always answer honestly because, as my first-grade teacher Sister Mary Lurana told me, "Honesty is the best policy."

President Trump likes short answers with no nuance. Go longer than thirty seconds, and he'll become impatient. He wants the point, not the posture. He is a man used to getting his way, and what he wants is action—even in conversation. When I brought him back to his childhood by asking how his view of America was formulated, he gave me a look that said, "Who cares?" He answered the question, but I know he hated the entire exercise.

However, it was important—that is, if you want to understand what motivates the president. If you simply want to hate him, you don't care. But if you want some insight into the most unlikely political phenomenon in our lifetimes, you'll get it here.

After Donald Trump defeated Hillary Clinton, I said that the two most stunning political stories I had ever witnessed were the assassination of President Kennedy and the election of President Trump. I actually predicted on TV a few days before the vote that Trump would win. I came to that conclusion after analyzing Secretary Clinton's failure to connect with working Americans on the campaign trail. Watching her work a Waffle House was brutal.

Incredibly, the billionaire mogul Trump did connect with the folks, and I know why (which we'll also deal with in these pages). But I wanted to explore some history, so I sought to find out when and how he had formulated his view of our country, a view that convinced more than 60 million Americans to vote for him. That I did not know. Thus, I verbally tortured the president trying to find out.

As we are leaving the airborne office, I thank Donald Trump for the interview. I doubt he'll ever do anything like this again, but he doesn't seem to be annoyed anymore. The plane is descending into West Palm Beach, and soon the president will be socializing at his Mar-a-Lago resort; the next day, he is set to play golf with Tiger Woods and Jack Nicklaus. There will be action and competition on the links.

And that's what Donald J. Trump lives for: action and competition. It is on his mind always. Because of his vast power, that mindset directly affects the lives of individual Americans and the welfare of the entire world.

It does—whether we like it or not.

CHAPTER TWO

———

JAMAICA HOSPITAL

QUEENS, NEW YORK

JUNE 14, 1946

MIDDAY

Fred Trump has another mouth to feed, and little does he know how prominent that mouth will one day become. The forty-year-old house builder and his wife, Mary Anne, already have three young children, and baby Donald John Trump will make four.

The Trumps are an upper-middle-class family deeply embedded in the world of New York City real estate. In fact, Fred has been building small homes and apartments for white working-class people since 1925.

During World War II, Fred Trump escaped the draft because he was past age thirty-five, with children to support. But Fred was involved with wartime activities in private business, building barracks for naval personnel in Virginia and Pennsylvania. He then prospered after the war as American military people arrived home to get married and start families. The New York City boroughs of

Queens and Brooklyn were teeming with recently arrived young adults.

They all needed housing.

But Fred Trump had a problem. He was of German descent, his father and mother born and raised in Kallstadt, a village in what is now southern Germany. Because many of Fred's customers were Jewish, this was not optimal in 1946, when anti-German feeling in America still ran high. But Fred came up with a very simple solution: he said he was Swedish.

Many in Stockholm were stunned.

Baby Donald's mother, Mary Anne MacLeod Trump, had come a long way since arriving in America from Scotland in 1930, the year after the Great Depression shattered the world. She had two sisters in New York City, so at age nineteen, she made the journey from her small village of Tong to join them in the United States.

Before meeting Fred Trump at a dance, Mary Anne described herself as a maid. Now she is a homemaker and busy mother who will take her new baby to a nice house in Jamaica Estates, far from her cold and windy birthplace.

Built by Fred Trump, the family home at 85-15 Wareham Place is modest by today's standards: a Tudor with small front and back lawns, and just a few yards separating it from neighboring houses on both sides.

Queens in 1946 is composed of segregated neighborhoods, the borough being mostly ethnic white with strong Irish, Italian, and German enclaves. There is a heavy Jewish component as well. Those in each group tend to cluster together.

Jamaica Estates is a safe neighborhood with easy access to Manhattan by train or car. Donald Trump will soon have plenty of playmates as the Baby Boom generation explodes and urchins are everywhere. The streets of Queens become vast playgrounds where children compete in sports and games. Few kids stay inside; outside is where life unfolds, mostly without parental supervision.

Although there is no record of it, Baby Donald is likely driven home from the hospital in his father's luxury car. Fred Trump has

Donald Trump's childhood home in the Jamaica Estates neighborhood of Queens.

been making good money for twenty years but is essentially a frugal man. His single luxury is a navy-blue Cadillac with a vanity license plate: FCT. He replaces the car every three years with a new Caddy in the same color.

Five years later, in 1951, Fred and Mary Anne Trump have to move. They now have five children, and their house is too tight. Fred could have purchased a large home with acres of property in Nassau County, a few miles away, but he did not. Firmly planted in Queens, he moved the family exactly one block away, to a half-acre plot.

The new house is larger and will eventually have a pool, a tremendous status symbol in Queens. Fred and Mary Anne will live at 85-14 Midland Parkway for the rest of their lives.

TTT

AS THE YEARS pass, Donald and his four siblings don't see much of their father, who works like a madman. Nevertheless, Donald idolizes

Donald Trump's mother, Mary Anne MacLeod
Trump, with baby Elizabeth.

him. Today in the Oval Office, a picture of Fred and Mary Anne
Trump is prominently displayed on a side table near the Resolute
desk.

But getting President Trump to speak about his childhood is tougher
than getting him to compliment Senator Chuck Schumer, whom he
loathes. The president sees little advantage in describing what happened in the 1950s at the Trump family dinner table.

"Were you a conservative family?" I ask.

"In those days, you didn't even talk in terms of conservative
or anything else. You talk more in terms of Republican or Democrat . . . but I would certainly say my parents had conservative
values."

"How did they impart those to you?"

"Only through osmosis. They didn't say you should do this or

Real estate mogul Fred Trump on the lawn of
Trump Village in 1983.

you should do that." The president takes a sip of diet soda, his eyes
wandering to the TV screen.

"Who in the family was the political person?" I ask, trying to
refocus the conversation.

"My mother was a very interesting woman. She loved ceremony.
She came from Scotland, not a rich family, but she loved anything to
do with the royal family. She always had an affection for the Queen,
who I got to know recently. Spending time with the Queen was quite
something. My father was political only as it pertained to his business, where he was doing his building. So, I wouldn't say either was
overtly political, but of the two, my mother loved the ceremony and
my father loved the nitty-gritty."

What Donald Trump is saying there is that his father supported
local politicians who helped him get building permits and variances.

Fred Trump apparently had little interest in party politics or individual politicians on a national level.

The same was true for my grandfather John O'Reilly, a New York City police officer who likely patrolled the same Brooklyn neighborhoods where Fred Trump was building homes in the 1930s. Pop, as I called him, considered most politicians corrupt nitwits. As a member of the "Lost Battalion" in World War I, John O'Reilly was as tough as the nails Fred Trump bought in buckets.

"So, you and your brothers and sisters are sitting at the dinner table in Queens in the 1950s," I say. "Dwight Eisenhower was president. Did it ever come up in conversation that Dwight Eisenhower's doing this or that?"

The president shakes his head. "You're asking me to go back a long way, and it was certainly not anything that I was thinking about at the time. That was not a conversation that we would have very much."

TTT

SITTING AT THAT dinner table, the young Donald Trump would converse with his sisters Maryanne, nine years his senior, and Elizabeth, four years older. His brother Fred Jr. was eight years ahead of Donald, leaving only baby brother Robert, younger by two years.

As he got older, sports (and the competition they brought) dominated Donald's attention. Baseball was number one with him as he played first base. Fred Trump knew the value of education and sent Donald to the private Kew-Forest School, a haven for affluent Queens families. But Donald was restless in school, a subject he's not fond of recalling.

"When I look at what's going on today, I think I was a beautiful child, a perfect child. What I did was a different level of misbehavior than what you see today—I would say really rambunctious as opposed to really big misbehaving."

Suddenly, disaster strikes—an aide appears in the Air Force One office with a "Make America Great Again" hat. Bye-bye childhood discussion.

PRESIDENT TRUMP: Did you ever see anything like this? So, is that hat one of the great symbols? You understand.

O'REILLY: Sold a lot of them.

PRESIDENT TRUMP: Millions. Are you surprised by that?

O'REILLY: No, I mean you marketed well. You have a lot of fans. That's just going to happen.

PRESIDENT TRUMP: And that came right out of me. That was like one of your book titles, right?

O'REILLY: Yeah.

PRESIDENT TRUMP: Somebody said it was Reagan. I said no. He said, "Let's Make America Great." He didn't use it much . . . But it wasn't "Make America Great Again." That's just a wonderful phrase to use. And by the way, I don't know if you want to use this, but for the next campaign, we've really lifted things up, created trillions of dollars in stock market value. Let me ask you a question: Would you keep this incredible MAGA phrase?

O'REILLY: I'd just change it to "keep."

PRESIDENT TRUMP: You'd change it to "*Keep* America Great"?

O'REILLY: I'd say "keep." You should move it forward.

PRESIDENT TRUMP: My new phrase would be "Keep America Great"? You like that better?

O'REILLY: I do. Let's get back . . .

PRESIDENT TRUMP: It's awfully hard to get rid of that phrase [MAGA] because it's so good.

O'REILLY: But you might sell more hats.

At this point, I had completely lost the president on the look back. The hat thing had obliterated his childhood in Queens and how his early family life had shaped him. I had to jar him with something from his past to refocus him on how his upbringing had affected his political thinking.

But how could I do that when the most powerful man in the

world was now looking at a gigantic television screen, homing in on a cable news program? We were about halfway to Palm Beach, and my interview time was slipping away. I had to think of something fast. Then it hit me.

Military school!

CHAPTER THREE

NEW YORK MILITARY ACADEMY
CORNWALL-ON-HUDSON, NEW YORK
SEPTEMBER 1959

The soft life that thirteen-year-old Donald Trump was leading in Queens is over. Sensing a need for discipline, his parents pack up the Cadillac and drive their tall, good-looking son about sixty miles north from Jamaica Estates to a strict, expensive boarding school in the shadow of West Point. The mission: shaping the kid up.

The adolescent Donald was growing increasingly restless and defiant, something common in late 1950s America. It was the age of the greaser, when rebels like Elvis Presley, James Dean, and Marlon Brando made indelible impressions on young people with their sneering disregard for the conformity and convention that had taken deep root in America since the end of World War II.

In researching exactly why Fred and Mary Anne Trump decided their son needed to be shipped out of the home, I came upon a number of incredibly mean-spirited articles in publications like the New York *Daily News* and London's *Daily Mail*, which despise Donald Trump and will say just about anything to hurt him and his family.

But here's the truth as far as I can ascertain it. Donald was an aggressive, competitive child who did not bend easily to the rules. But I found no malice in his childhood. He did tease his shy younger brother, Robert, who was the opposite of Donnie, as they called him. But President Trump told the truth when he stated that he was rambunctious, not malevolent. However, he might have stretched it when he described himself as a "perfect" child.

▼▼▼

THE TIPPING POINT for his parents seemed to be disobedience. Donald did not ask permission to go into Manhattan, where he was attracted to the garish streets of Times Square. Apparently, he bought some switchblade knives on his clandestine trips to the city, which he then hid in his room.

Fred Trump, in particular, was not happy upon the discovery of the knives. A stern father who insisted on formality, often wearing a tie in his leisure time, Fred expected good behavior from his children, and basically got it from the older three and the youngest. But the energetic Donald needed consistent discipline, which Fred could not supply because of his rigorous work schedule.

▼▼▼

FOUNDED IN 1889, the New York Military Academy held that a strict structure provided the best environment for academic achievement. That meant cadets would do as they were told, or suffer punishment. The academy was all male, students could not leave on most weekends, and they could never be alone with a girl on campus.

Donald Trump spent five years there, almost his entire teenage life.

More than six decades later, as the Trump political story unfolded, NPR ran a report on his military school experience. Here is a partial transcript:

> *Back in Trump's day, cadets would wake up near the crack of dawn, hurry into uniforms, and march in formation to breakfast. First-year cadets had to eat their meals squared off—lifting*

their forks in a right angle into their mouths. And after break-
fast, they'd scurry back to clean their rooms for inspection.

T T T

SITTING BACK IN his desk chair on Air Force One, President Trump acknowledges that his parents were worried about his behavior and believes they made the right decision. Military school, he says, shaped his view of the world.

"It has a tremendous influence. So, I had a lot of tough military people at that school. There were ex-drill sergeants . . . They were very, very strong people out of central casting.

"And they were able to whip people into shape. And it was a very interesting period of time because I had never dealt with people like this before, so you had to acclimate. But we had some very rough military people there, and I really learned to respect the military very much."

"Were they physical with you?"

"A little bit. Sometimes it was physical. That was not the age where pushing your weight around in a truly physical way would be unthinkable. Yeah, I would say they were physical. They were power- ful people physically and emotionally and really mentally. They were strong people."

"Did you resent that?"

"No, I didn't resent it. I had to figure a way out of it. I had to figure out a way around it, and I ended up having a lot of friendships with those people."

"So, you bought into the system and thought this was good for you?"

"I was able to buy into the system, and I did well militarily. It was a very different life for me, but I ended up doing well militarily from the standpoint of cadet captain."

T T T

IN HIS SENIOR year at the New York Military Academy, Donald Trump did achieve the status of cadet captain, a high honor. He was also captain of the baseball team, playing first base. He played soccer as well.

By all accounts, the teenage Donald Trump succeeded at NYMA because he was ferociously competitive and focused on achievement. On October 12, 1963, the school's student body marched in New York City's annual Columbus Day Parade, with the young Trump leading the way. As the parade passed St. Patrick's Cathedral, on Fifth Avenue, Donald Trump was greeted by Cardinal Spellman, the first of many encounters with powerful people.

In 1964, the school yearbook portrayed Cadet Trump as a solid leader and a "Ladies' Man." The latter assumption was based on his parents having brought some girls Donald knew on weekend visits to see him. Apparently, he enjoyed squiring the ladies around campus, but the rule stood: they could never be alone together.

And so it was that Donald Trump graduated from high school a far different person than he was before entering. He had succeeded outside the family home, using guile, determination, and discipline. Now he would prepare for a career.

As his sister Maryanne, a recently retired federal judge, once said of her much younger brother, "[I] knew better even as a child than to even attempt to compete with Donald."

Judge Trump's words contain an explicit warning—one that many now wish they had heard.

CHAPTER FOUR

QUEENS, NEW YORK

SUMMER 1963

DINNER HOUR

To understand Donald Trump's view of America, it is instructive to know about his early environment and family history. Much of that takes place outside the protective enclave of Jamaica Estates. In fact, one of Trump's roots extends all the way to the Klondike.

In 1885, sixteen-year-old Friedrich Trumpf sails to America from Germany. Young Friedrich has had a tough life—at age eight his father died, leaving the Trumpf family deeply in debt. Friedrich's mother literally could not support her six children so she sent him to a nearby town to apprentice with a barber. Friedrich hated it, saved some of his meager earnings, and eventually booked passage on a ship in order to live with his sister in New York City.

There he stayed for six years, but barbering did not cut it for young Friedrich. So, in 1891 he moved west to seek his fortune. The German immigrant was now twenty-two years old and wound up in the Wild West town of Seattle, where he purchased a share in a restaurant. The establishment was called the Poodle Dog and was located smack in the middle of Seattle's notorious red-light district. Here the situation gets murky—some believe the Poodle Dog provided rooms for prostitutes. But there is no direct proof of that.

Anyway, Friedrich Trumpf made a pile of money in Washington State, which had just entered the union. Then, opportunity presented itself in the Yukon.

In the late 1890s, gold was discovered in northwest Canada. Friedrich Trumpf arrived there in 1898, almost immediately opening the Arctic Restaurant and Hotel. The establishment proved to be very popular, but again there are varying dispatches as to why. One Canadian reporter describes Trumpf's property this way: "For single men the Arctic has excellent accommodations, as well as the best restaurant . . . but I would not advise respectable women to go there to sleep, as they are liable to hear that which would be repugnant to their feelings— and, uttered to, by the depraved of their own sex."

Perhaps based on that report, the Canadian authorities began to look at Trumpf's enterprises and, in 1901, there was a crackdown on prostitution in the Yukon. Soon after, Friedrich sold his interests to a business partner. Subsequently, the Canadian Mounties seized control of the Arctic for past taxes due.

Gathering up his wealth, Friedrich returned to Kallstadt, in the Kingdom of Bavaria, where he married a young woman named Elizabeth Christ. The couple then moved back to New York City, changing their last name to Trump.

In 1905, Donald Trump's father, Fred, is born in Queens. Thirteen years later, the flu pandemic, which killed perhaps as many as 650,000 Americans, strikes Friedrich Trump, who dies at the age of forty-nine.

In his will, Friedrich leaves his wife and family $31,640—the equivalent of $919,000 today. With that cash, Elizabeth enters the real estate business along with Fred, who apparently harbors a strong desire to make money just as his father had.

Thus, the Trump business dynasty is born.

T T T

FROM THE BEGINNING, the operation was a tight circle. With his mother signing checks, Fred Trump built mostly small, sturdy homes, then sold them to people of white, European descent. Fred also joined local organizations that disdained outsiders. His home business prospering, he started the Trump Market in Woodhaven, Queens, one of the first grocery stores in the city. Again, he made money.

But he also made enemies.

In 1927, when he was twenty-one years old and single, Fred was arrested at an anti-Catholic march in Jamaica. Members of the Ku Klux Klan were also taken into custody. Some reports had Fred Trump in KKK regalia, but the situation is unclear. At the time, many New York City police officers were Irish Catholics, and they had no use for the crew with whom Fred Trump associated.*

However, in an extensive obituary of Fred Trump, the *New York Times* does not mention the arrest, and it was apparently never spoken about in the Trump domain.

What is abundantly clear is that Fred Trump lived in a white, Protestant world at least until his operations later expanded to include Catholics and Jews. But Fred's business life was largely kept from his family. Today, his father's early activities are not a favorite topic for President Trump.

"Did you know about the Klan thing when you were a very young man?" I asked.

"No."

"You never knew about it?"

"I never knew about it. I don't think it's true, by the way."

"There were reports that he was in a group involved with an anti-Catholic demonstration. That he was involved. Did he ever raise religion or Catholics with you?"

"No, no, he wouldn't have been against any of that. You know the story was never proven to be true . . . I just knew my father. There was no chance of that."

---

* It was estimated that more than thirty thousand Ku Klux Klan members lived in the New York City area at the time.

"Was he a religious man? Your father and mother, were they religious?"

"I would say he was, modestly. My mother a little beyond modestly."

"You guys are Protestant, right?"

"Presbyterian. My father was religious, but it was not the number one thought in his life. But he had a belief in religion and a belief in God."

"And your mom?"

"Maybe a little bit more so."

"Did they get you to say your prayers when you were a little kid?"

"My mother did. Come to think of it, my mother did. That's right."

"Did you go to church?"

"Yeah, First Presbyterian Church in Jamaica, Queens."

"Every Sunday?"

"No, not every Sunday, but I went to Sunday school, actually."

"You did?"

"Yeah, we went there on a Saturday. But I would not go to church every Sunday."

"So, you were a secular family then?"

"We were a Protestant family, but we did not go to church every weekend."

T T T

THE TRUMP FAMILY also was not very political. It is the summer of 1963, and President John F. Kennedy is presiding over Camelot. In Jamaica Estates, Donald Trump has just finished his junior year in high school and is home for the summer, soaking up his father's success in business. His older siblings are now out of the house, leaving only Donald, Robert, and their parents.

Because JFK was such an icon, I wanted to discuss him with President Trump. I didn't get far.

O'REILLY: **So, Kennedy, because my mother's people came from a line of Kennedys, was big in my house. Was he big in yours?**

PRESIDENT TRUMP: No, he was not big. Respected but not big. It wasn't a topic that would be discussed much. Not because my parents didn't like him, but because he just wasn't a front-line conversation.

O'REILLY: Back then the threat of nuclear war was big news. In my school . . . the kids had to go under their desks [in drills]. We all knew about the Cuban Missile Crisis. Did that touch your family?

PRESIDENT TRUMP: It was a huge event, but I don't think even that event radiated [with my family] as much as it probably should have.

TTT

FROM WHAT I can gather, and to be completely fair, it seems that the Trump home was largely devoid of politics. It was all business—Fred's booming real estate business. Besides sports, that's what Donald Trump was drawn to as a young man. He loved his father and mother but lived independently at military school, where he competed and largely succeeded, gaining approval from his father.

Politics, religion, and current events were not "front-line" topics at home. But Fred Trump did do one consistent thing in the house: he and his wife watched the news.

"They watched the news religiously . . . they were usually tuned to CBS," the president told me.

"Walter Cronkite?"

"The great Walter Cronkite. Very hard to replace Walter Cronkite. In fact, as time went by, he looked like my father. It was almost like your father was doing the news."

"Did you watch?" I asked.

"I'd watch because my father would always watch. If I was in the room, I'd automatically be watching Walter Cronkite."

"But for you, sports was bigger [than news]."

"For me, sports was everything. I was far more interested in sports than politics."

Quietly, the seventeen-year-old was also absorbing his father's work ethic, even if it wasn't being openly discussed. Fred Trump worked hard for the money but lived rather modestly. Donald's older brother,

Donald Trump with his father, Fred C. Trump.

Fred Jr., wanted no part of real estate and eventually became a pilot for TWA. But Donald was fascinated by it.

"Was it just a profit thing for your father, or did he have another reason to build?"

"It was more than building. He would buy places in Virginia, in Brooklyn, and in Queens. He was a home builder and a good one. He was able to build things for less money. And when they were completed, they would cost less than the competitor across the street and they would look better, which is a great combination."

"So, he just used his skills?"

"He was a very skilled negotiator, and he was able to build a house for less money and make it look better."

"Did he teach you about capitalism?"

"He did. And when the person across the street couldn't sell his house, my father would buy it at a discount, spend a little money, very little money, fixing it up, and he'd sell it at a higher price. He had a great grasp of this."

"So did your grandmother."

"She was mostly not involved with the actual work. My father was fourteen years old when he started, unbelievably young. And he had to work to put his brother through MIT. His brother was a great student, Dr. John Trump . . . so he had to have my grandmother be involved with the company because he wasn't old enough to sign checks."

"So, capitalism was basically rooted in your upbringing."

"I think so, yeah."

"And you became a very successful capitalist."

"Yeah. Not because my father really wanted that, but because it was like that's all I got to see."

T T T

AND SO IT was that Donald Trump knew at a young age where his destiny would lie: in the brutally competitive real estate world of New York City. But first he had to deal with college, the looming war in Vietnam, and changing race relations in America.

The last situation is still an issue for him as he sits in the White House.

CHAPTER FIVE

LEVITTOWN, NEW YORK

SUMMER 1963

MIDDAY

At the same time seventeen-year-old Donald Trump was in Queens preparing for his senior year at the New York Military Academy, a few miles away twelve-year-old Bill O'Reilly was playing on the streets in one of the largest housing developments in America: Levittown.

Developers Abe Levitt and his sons William and Alfred eventually built 17,447 small homes in Nassau County and marketed them to working-class people, many of them veterans who wanted to get out of New York City and/or start families in houses they could afford.

Levittown was about twenty miles east of the city and approximately fifteen miles east of Jamaica Estates, where Fred Trump was competing with the Levitts for the housing dollar.

The elder Trump and the Levitts had a lot in common, including constructing military dwellings in Virginia and possessing the know-how to build homes quickly and economically. In 1951, my mother and father bought the O'Reilly family home at 11 Page Lane in Levittown for $8,000. They lived there the rest of their lives.*

The other thing Fred Trump and the Levitts agreed upon was a marketing strategy. In 1963, they were reluctant to sell to African Americans. William Levitt openly admitted it.

"As a Jew, I have no room in my heart for racial prejudice," he said. "But the plain fact is that most whites prefer not to live in mixed communities. That attitude may be wrong morally, and someday it may change. I hope it will."

But William Levitt, his father, and his brother did little to foster such a change. They made millions selling houses to whites, so they sold houses to whites—despite President John F. Kennedy signing an executive order in 1962 banning racial discrimination in homes "built, purchased or financed with federal assistance."

If racial profiling was in, that meant buyers using the GI Bill were out. The Levitts tried to fight the federal order but lost. Eventually they cashed out, selling their company in 1964 to the International Telephone and Telegraph Corporation for $90 million.

Racial prejudice has a long history in southern New York, which includes Queens. On July 4, 1924, a reported thirty thousand people attended a Ku Klux Klan rally in New Jersey during the Democratic National Convention—which was being held in Manhattan at the time. The gathering would later earn a sarcastic reference as a "Klanbake."

In many neighborhoods, real estate agents and mortgage companies simply would not deal with blacks. As the civil rights movement picked up steam behind Dr. Martin Luther King Jr. in the mid-1960s, the feds became more aggressive in bringing housing discrimination cases. But locally, the fix was in—it was very tough for black Americans to buy into white neighborhoods in Queens and the two counties to the east.

It was all about money and prejudice, of course. In 1963 Levittown, the population was one-third Catholic, one-third Jewish, and one-third Protestant. But it was nearly 100 percent Caucasian. If blacks moved in, some bigoted whites would move out, and home prices would drop. In Manhattan, ruthless real estate people would actually

* That part of Levittown eventually shifted to a Westbury post office address.

buy row houses in white neighborhoods and then turn around and sell them to blacks, hoping for "white flight" so other properties in the area could then be bought up cheap. (These people were called "block-busters.") Those fleeing integrated city neighborhoods would often move to the white suburbs, where business was brisk for the Levitts, Fred Trump, and many others.

In addition, white-only housing enclaves appreciated faster in value than mixed places. Total it all up, and you had a perfect storm of real estate discrimination. Back then, bias against blacks was called good business by just about everybody in the white real estate world. Few challenged the rigged system.

To understand Queens and Levittown post–World War II, you must know the power that white ethnicity held. My friends were mostly Irish, Italian, and Jewish. We all pretty much got along, although Hebrew school was a problem. Our stickball games were regularly interrupted because the Jewish guys departed around 4:30 on selected weekdays.

Like children all over the world, the Levittown kids aped their parents. So, many Irish kids didn't like England. The Italians didn't like anybody except other Italians. The Jewish guys didn't say much but tended to be more liberal than the Irish and Italian kids.

But we all liked sports, and I was a huge Willie Mays fan. Even though Willie had moved to San Francisco from New York in 1958, he was still tremendous to me. The Giant centerfielder was a legend in Harlem and revered in Levittown as well.

On those occasions when I heard a kid disparage blacks, I'd point to Willie Mays. That pretty much stopped the blather.

The truth is my crew never saw or discussed black people at all. They lived miles away. There was no interaction between the races. I never heard my parents speak about African Americans. They didn't say anything bad because they didn't say anything at all. My father might hammer white ethnic groups once in a while, but never blacks.

My mother liked everybody. But *her* mother didn't approve of blacks, even though she did not know any. I once asked my grandmother why she occasionally spoke harshly about African Americans. She had no answer. I then asked if she had ever spoken with one. She said no, she just didn't like them.

I finally figured it out: she was afraid. She watched the local New York City news and saw blacks routinely being arrested on the tube. She led an insulated life, in a white neighborhood where everyone thought as she did. Strangers of color were dangerous to her.

By the way, when I told that story on *The Radio Factor*, I was branded a racist by the far-left extremist movement that uses race as a club to injure its perceived ideological enemies, an obviously despicable practice.

I can safely say that most white families in my Levittown neighborhood had the same experience that I did regarding black Americans—that is, no experience. And apparently that extended to the Trump family, in Queens.

T T T

As we flew high above the East Coast on Air Force One, I brought the subject up with President Trump.

O'REILLY: Was race ever an issue or a discussion point in the Trump household?

PRESIDENT TRUMP: Literally, it wasn't an issue. It probably was for many, but it wasn't for this family. It was never an issue, and I wasn't exposed to it in a tremendous way. My father was very open-minded. I could actually say he was a man that didn't see the color of skin.

O'REILLY: Yet he was accused by some newspapers of being anti-black, not selling real estate to blacks.

PRESIDENT TRUMP: Yeah, you'd have a building in a certain area, and those areas were very different then. You would have white areas, you'd have African American areas. It was a very different kind of city then. You'd have white buildings and black buildings all throughout the city.

O'REILLY: There was segregation in the city.

PRESIDENT TRUMP: It was a societal segregation.

O'REILLY: So, race wasn't a big topic of conversation?

PRESIDENT TRUMP: Race was rarely a topic, if ever. I can't even remember talking about it. But I will tell you, in my family—and this goes for me—the color of skin was not a factor, and that was true for my father.

T T T

ONCE AGAIN, IT is hard to nail down what Fred Trump was thinking in terms of racial justice. Evidence suggests his business plan overrode any wider view of the issue, but that's just speculation.

What I can say for certain is that in thirty years, I have never heard Donald Trump say anything negative about a group of people, black or otherwise. And I'm making that statement about a man who uses negativity like a flyswatter. He'll verbally crush perceived individual or media opponents, but at least in my presence, he has never slurred anyone using race.

The Hate Trump media has branded the president a racist and repeats the vile charge on a regular basis. And in fact, there are two racially charged situations regarding Donald Trump that deserve a hearing.

In July 1972, Fred Trump's organization, Trump Management, owned about fourteen thousand apartments throughout Queens and Brooklyn. One day a black woman applied for housing at the Shorehaven Apartments in Brooklyn. She was told that no vacancies existed.

A short time later, a white woman approached the same Trump-owned building with the same request. She was shown two unoccupied units.

Both women were undercover activists.

More than a year later, the Justice Department filed a civil rights suit against Trump Management, charging that it had violated the Fair Housing Act of 1968. At the time, twenty-six-year-old Donald Trump was president of the company, his father chairman.

The Trumps fought the case hard, asserting they had not knowingly done anything wrong. They hired the notorious Roy Cohn, who had been counsel to Senator Joseph McCarthy, to defend them, and a bitter legal brawl began.

Two years later, a settlement was reached. The Trumps agreed to become more compliant with the Fair Housing Act and paid for newspaper advertisements telling minorities they were welcome to rent at Trump properties. There was no financial settlement and no admission of guilt.

Both sides claimed victory.

T T T

THE SECOND HIGHLY charged race controversy, one that has angered many African Americans, is the so-called "birther" accusation lodged against Barack Obama.

The allegation is that the former president was not born in the United States, that his Hawaii-issued birth certificate is a fraud.

To put this stupid theory to rest, my staff investigated the charge, circa 2008. We found that two Honolulu newspapers, the *Advertiser* and the *Star-Bulletin*, ran birth announcements for baby Barack shortly after his birth on August 4, 1961.

Now, that is impossible to fake or contrive. Barack Obama was born in Honolulu. Period.

But Donald Trump continued to question President Obama's birth certificate long after the issue should have been buried. I told Donald to his face on national TV that the conspiracy was total BS. Far too late, Mr. Trump issued a statement saying he had changed his mind, that he now believed Barack Obama's birth certification was real.

But no apology.

That situation is still a source of bitterness in many African American precincts. Despite the fact that the Trump economy is beneficial to blacks in general, polls show that President Trump's support among African Americans remains tepid, to say the least. Most blacks hate the birther thing.

So, why did Donald Trump do it? Perhaps the best analysis comes from his son and close adviser Donald Trump Jr.:

O'REILLY: **I scolded him for the birther stuff . . . I thought that was mean-spirited and unnecessary.**

TRUMP JR.: It's the way he fights. He will fight hard and push back.

O'REILLY: But why did he do that? He wasn't running against Obama. Why did he even bring the issue up and risk being called a racist?

TRUMP JR.: Listen, I don't think accusations that are nonsense mean anything to him ... I mean, he can dish it out and take it with the best of them, and actually enjoys some of that. I think he's seen and learned that the other side is not going to give him any quarter for admitting something. He would just rather move on and ignore it.

O'REILLY: Did you ever pull him aside and say, "Dad, the Obama birther stuff, that's not a winner"?

TRUMP JR.: I think we had conversations about some of those things. But he has an innate ability to understand things through a different lens that I don't think anyone else has. So, I can question something, but I don't second-guess because there's always a method to the madness with him.

TTT

AND THE METHOD was this: Donald Trump used the bogus birther issue to galvanize the support of those who despised President Obama. As he did with illegal immigration, Trump inflated an issue to gain approval from a select audience. No other Republican candidate swam in the waters of controversy like Donald Trump. He quickly separated himself from the pack with his outrageous claim about the birth certificate and became the "anti-Obama" candidate.

Is that racist? There is evidence that it was a pure political play, not designed to denigrate skin color.

But millions of Americans, of all colors, do not see it that way. In fact, an argument can be made that by questioning Barack Obama's nationality, you are actually denigrating his race. To this day, the debate continues to rage.

President Obama put forth the audacity of hope. President Trump replaced "of hope" with the audacity "of me."

And the audacity worked. Against all odds, he's the president.

TTT

BACK IN THE summer of '64, little did Donald Trump or anyone else know that his personal journey to the White House would soon begin when he started college.

It was an ominous time, with America still suffering from the assassination of its young president. Added to that was a distant fire just beginning to get out of control.

Vietnam.

CHAPTER SIX

THE BRONX, NEW YORK

SEPTEMBER 1964

MORNING

The drive from Donald Trump's house in Queens to Fordham University's Rose Hill campus takes about forty minutes, unless there's traffic—which there always is. It is an urban ride, across the Grand Central Parkway to the Triborough Bridge (where the toll is a quarter), then up the Deegan roadway north into the Bronx, another working-class part of the mammoth New York City landscape.

The eighteen-year-old Donald is a commuting student, preferring to live with his parents and younger brother than in the Fordham dormitories. Sometimes he rides to school with his pal Roger Gedgard, who will become his closest friend at the Jesuit-run Catholic university.

According to the 1965 *Maroon*, the school's yearbook, Donald Trump was on the squash team at Fordham and was considered a good athlete. He also joined the ROTC but did not participate in the military training program his sophomore year.

That may be because ROTC rules say students must commit to at least two years in the actual military if they participate in two years of college ROTC. With the Vietnam conflict heating up, many students had doubts about serving.

Donald Trump studied economics at Fordham and distinguished himself from other freshmen by always wearing a well-tailored suit. Jackets were required in the classroom, but suits were rare.

After Trump entered the presidential sweepstakes, the campus newspaper, the *Fordham Ram*, sent out 150 emails to alumni who had attended Fordham at the same time Donald Trump did. As it turns out, few even remembered he was on campus for two years. Those who did recall him generally said positive things, but one description stood out: loner.

Apparently, the young Trump was a B student. Fordham does not give academic transcripts to the public, citing privacy, but that seems to be the consensus. Some classmates remember him participating in classes and being an accessible guy socially, despite the expensive suits.

In his junior year, Donald Trump transferred to the University of Pennsylvania. Little is known about his time at the Wharton School, a business program within the Ivy League institution, other than that he took some real estate classes and lived in an apartment off campus.

Trying to research Donald Trump's time at Penn is just about impossible because of the hatred he now engenders there. School administrators have been ordered not to talk about him, even though he has donated major money to the university—by some accounts, more than a million dollars.

Three of his children also attended Penn: Don Jr., Ivanka, and Tiffany. The college did give Donald Trump a distinguished alumni award before he entered politics. But now the liberal campus does not embrace President Trump, to say the least.

The motivation for Donald to transfer from Fordham to Penn coincides with his decision to join his father's real estate company. Living at home full-time after five years of military school awakened Donald to the world of moneymaking. Those nice suits were just a part of it. By 1966, Fred Trump had a chauffeur and millions in the bank. His older three children wanted no part of the real estate business, but Donald did—only, not in Queens.

A number of nasty things have been said in print about how Donald Trump was actually admitted to Penn. All that seems to be bogus. From the best available evidence, Donald and his father decided that Penn offered the finest business degree in the Northeast, and the student could work for his father on selected weekends. Philadelphia is just ninety minutes from New York. I could find no evidence of anything sinister about Trump's move to the Ivy League.

Throughout Donald Trump's college career, he received deferments from the draft because he was in school. Just about every college student did. In fact, half of the twenty-seven million American men eligible to be drafted in that era got out of it one way or another.

The consequence of the deferment policy was that the draft snared kids unwilling or unable to go to college. Many of them went off to fight in the jungles of Vietnam right out of high school.

Donald Trump and his father, Fred Trump, seated, visit a tenant in one of their apartment buildings in Brooklyn, in January 1973.

In my working-class Levittown neighborhood, the war in Vietnam was at first widely supported. Home-owning vets of World War II and Korean War vintage resented the anti–Vietnam War movement early on. After liberating Europe, Asia, and South Korea for them, the military was seen as a positive. They essentially trusted President Kennedy and then Lyndon Johnson to confront the growing threat of communism in a responsible way.

In the late 1960s, the New York City area saw thousands of mostly poor and lower-middle-class kids head over to Southeast Asia after a few weeks of army basic training. When they came back home, there was shock.

Some of the guys I knew growing up returned from Vietnam radically changed. One committed suicide. A few others became addicted to heroin, something unheard of in Levittown before the mid-1960s.

In the summer, when the college guys returned home from school, some of us tried to talk with our friends who had fought in Vietnam. It was difficult. They'd often lament that things were "screwed up over there," but specifics were few. We knew some of these guys from kindergarten, and many of them had changed—for the worse.

In general, there was a somberness about the Vietnam guys. They were no longer up for hanging out at Jones Beach or going to a drive-in movie. They tended to want to be alone. There wasn't a lot of outward happiness.

And there was a lot of drinking.

My grandfather was a hero in World War I. My father was a naval officer who was part of the U.S. occupation of Japan after Hiroshima and Nagasaki. Both turned against the Vietnam War and President Johnson.

But they didn't like the Jane Fonda crowd, either.

My cousin Dickie Melton was a hero in Vietnam, walking point on patrol in the jungle near Cambodia with his German shepherd, Sarge. Dickie wouldn't tell me anything about the war after he came back, but he briefed my father.

That was it for Vietnam in the O'Reilly house.

Jamaica Estates is just twenty miles west of Levittown, and the same thing was happening there. Draftees were coming back, some in body bags, and the truth about the Vietnam experience was on vivid display. It was a chaotic situation, one where constant death loomed. And most draftees had no idea why they were being sent far away "in country."

Fred and Donald Trump had to have seen the same thing my father and I saw. But I was three years behind Donald in school, and change came rapidly once Richard Nixon was elected president in 1968. Peace negotiations with Hanoi were under way, and rumors that the draft would be abolished spread quickly across the country. Eventually, that would happen, with military service decided by a lottery system.

Nineteen sixty-eight was the same year Donald graduated from Penn and, therefore, would lose his student deferment. But Fred Trump was renting office space to a Queens doctor, a podiatrist. The man examined the now twenty-two-year-old Donald and found he had heel spurs, a calcium buildup on the bone.

Donald Trump once again received a military deferment, this time for a medical problem.

As president, Mr. Trump is an ardent supporter of the military, which has led to vicious attacks on him from Trump haters like former Democratic National Committee chair Debbie Wasserman Schultz, who has called the president a "chicken-hawk."

On Air Force One, Mr. Trump turned very serious when I brought up Vietnam.

T T T

PRESIDENT TRUMP: I didn't like the Vietnam War, even though I was very young, and I probably shouldn't have made a judgment, but I thought it was ridiculous. And that never changed. [I even apply it] to what we're doing now in the Middle East. I was against getting involved there.

O'REILLY: What is it about Vietnam, the Middle East?

PRESIDENT TRUMP: I don't think we knew what we were doing. In retrospect, you look at the seven trillion that we've spent [in the Middle East], and if anything, it's a worse situation.

O'REILLY: But that's interesting because you were in military school and they weren't against Vietnam.

PRESIDENT TRUMP: I would say that I am an absolute hawk. But that doesn't mean I'm a hawk for the wrong things. I am somebody that is very militaristic. You look at the money that I've spent on the military, seven hundred billion dollars, which is far more than the previous administration . . . but if you're going to be doing something [militarily], you've got to do the right thing. And going into the Middle East [Iraq] was a tremendous mistake.

O'REILLY: Let's go back to when you were in school and Vietnam was looming. You didn't want to go to Vietnam, right?

PRESIDENT TRUMP: No.

O'REILLY: And you made the decision based on what?

PRESIDENT TRUMP: I thought it was a ridiculous war that was so far away. Nobody ever heard of Vietnam and people were saying we had to go there.

O'REILLY: Were you a protester?

PRESIDENT TRUMP: I wasn't a protester, only inwardly. I wasn't marching [in] the streets as many people were. I said, why are we going there? So, I thought Vietnam was a bad war. Now, at the same time, I was very young and probably shouldn't be making judgments at that age. You're supposed to rely on your great leaders. But that was a big mistake for a lot of people.

T T T

DONALD TRUMP WASN'T the only one making judgments about Vietnam. Former Vice Presidents Joe Biden and Dick Cheney avoided military service in that era. So did President Bill Clinton. President Bush the Younger got into the Air National Guard.

With his Vietnam problem solved for the moment, Donald Trump received his degree from Penn and immediately joined his father at the real estate company. Now he was all business and unbridled ambition.

His father welcomed Donald into the fold, paying him well and

making sure he had projects from which he could learn, such as Swifton Village, in Cincinnati, Ohio.

In 1962, Fred Trump had bought the 1,200-unit "village" for
$5.6 million at a bankruptcy auction. It was essentially a slum. Fred
rehabbed the property using his usual frugal but effective building
strategies. Rentals picked up, but a major problem emerged: the
Trump organization was accused of not renting to black tenants.

Foreshadowing what would happen in New York a few years later,
the case was settled with no admission of wrongdoing by the Trump
company.

Young Donald was given oversight on Swifton but did not work
in the rental office. His job was quality control, and on his visits
to Cincinnati he kept busy upgrading the facility. The once-derelict
complex became very profitable. Eventually, it was sold for a $6 mil-
lion profit. The Trumps then said good-bye to Ohio.

Quickly growing in confidence, Donald Trump learned a very
clear lesson from his experience at Swifton: he didn't want to be in
Cincinnati, or in Queens.

The brash Trump had his sights set on one prime destination:
Manhattan.

CHAPTER SEVEN

MANHATTAN
NOVEMBER 3, 1968
AFTERNOON

It is Sunday, and the New York Jets are rolling again. Led by a brash young quarterback from Beaver Falls, Pennsylvania, named Joe Namath, the home team has just defeated the Buffalo Bills 25 to 21, upping their record to six wins with just two losses.

Richard Nixon will defeat Hubert Humphrey for the presidency two days from now, but in the New York City area, it is Joe Namath who is king. He will eventually lead the Jets to an eleven-win, three-loss regular season record, then drive a playoff victory over the powerful Oakland Raiders. And, finally, he will back up his shocking prediction that the Jets would defeat the Baltimore Colts in the Super Bowl by engineering that stunning upset.

Namath wears his hair long and his football shoes white. He is cocky, charming, and cunning with the media. A true prince of the city, the quarterback squires around beautiful women, has commercial endorsements all over the place, and looks like he's having a helluva good time every second of every day.

The newspapers love him.

Joe Namath is twenty-five years old. Donald Trump is twenty-two. Both are single. Both crave two things: action and adulation.

Namath has branded himself "Broadway Joe." His marketing quote is "I can't wait until tomorrow, because I get better looking every day." He will front a restaurant, Bachelors III, and pretty much owns Manhattan, figuratively speaking.

Donald Trump does not yet have a brand, but he does have a vision: he wants to own Manhattan, at least the affluent parts, literally. He sees in front of him glittering Gotham City, and how the flamboyant Broadway Joe is dominating it. The young Trump believes he can do that, too. But the real estate developer has a problem.

The problem's name is Fred.

Nineteen sixty-eight was a very turbulent year for America. In January, the Tet Offensive in Vietnam turned many American citizens against the war. About ninety days after that fight began, which American forces eventually won, President Lyndon Johnson announced that he would not seek reelection.

On April 4, Dr. Martin Luther King Jr. was assassinated in Memphis, Tennessee. That brutal incident incited race riots across the country, adding to the public acrimony over the Vietnam War.

Then, on June 5, Senator Robert F. Kennedy was shot in Los Angeles, the second Kennedy brother assassinated for political reasons. The country was reeling.

Almost three months later, in late August, the city of Chicago erupted in violence and chaos while hosting the Democratic National Convention. Protesters and police clashed violently, as the nation watched on television. Americans were angry, exhausted, and discouraged.

But back in Queens, the real estate business was good, the Trump organization making a lot of money. For a kid right out of college, Donald was being well paid, but he was already chafing. He wanted to begin buying property in Manhattan. His father did not.

TTT

"[FRED] NEVER UNDERSTOOD my father's vision," Donald Trump Jr., who is now running the Trump real estate empire, told me. "Fred had that Germanic thrift. I remember stories that he would buy a mop handle and the mop separately, then put the two together because that was a way to save money. You'd save a penny, and it mattered. He'd go around job sites collecting nails because a wasted nail was money [lost].

"He wasn't a spender at all. I mean his house was nice, probably one of the nicest homes in Jamaica Estates, Queens. But it was still Queens."

Fred Trump well understood that expanding into Manhattan meant spending an enormous amount of money getting established. He simply did not want to do it. Having graduated from the working-class Richmond Hill High School, Fred was overjoyed to be a millionaire. He didn't need to be a billionaire.

Apparently, his son did.

But Fred would not budge.

"I think no two people respected each other more than my father and his father," Don Jr. said. "But they fought."

T T T

IT IS FEBRUARY 2019, and Donald Trump Jr. and I are speaking at the lavish Trump Tower on Fifth Avenue in Manhattan. The president's oldest child is well positioned to understand how the Trump real estate dynasty evolved from his grandfather to his father, as he has experienced both the personal and business sides of both men:

O'REILLY: **Did they clash at all?**

TRUMP JR.: **Incredibly, because it was the same personality with two very different perspectives. Fred would go to job sites and ask my father, "Why are you doing that?" . . . He would go around to make sure my father was doing it right.**

O'REILLY: **To check up on your father to make sure the building was constructed correctly?**

TRUMP JR.: Right ... There was a love and a respect like you couldn't possibly understand but they [had disagreements].

O'REILLY: Was your grandfather a workaholic?

TRUMP JR.: There were a few occasions when it was like, okay, I'm going to go over and spend the weekend with my grandfather and grandmother. Now, my grandmother was the opposite of [Fred]. She had an incredible sense of humor, just an amazingly tough, funny lady. Fred was the opposite. When I was there, he'd say to me, "Let's go collect some rent!" He would do that. I was five, six years old.

O'REILLY: Collecting rent with your grandfather?

TRUMP JR.: Like in middle-income housing in Queens. He'd knock on the door and be like, "Hey, you're late with the rent." And he took me along because he literally did not know anything other than what it was like to work. His constant saying was "to retire is to expire."

T T T

So IT IS that, in late 1968, Donald Trump faced a dilemma in the early part of his real estate career. His father ran the show and was not going to expand or step aside. Donald was learning and earning, but yearning. He wanted the action of Manhattan. He wanted to have what Broadway Joe had—fame, excitement, and success, big success.

But how to make it all happen?

Donald Trump became obsessed with finding a way.

CHAPTER EIGHT

MANHASSET, NEW YORK

FEBRUARY 22, 2019

DUSK

Before Donald Trump makes his bold move into billionaire land, it is worth noting his personal philosophy of life by looking at both his actions and words. As I sit writing this chapter in my living room, I am resisting the temptation to analyze Mr. Trump because I am not qualified to do that. What I am qualified to do is impart what I have seen and learned after knowing the president for so many years.

There is no question that Donald Trump's ambition exploded after he graduated from college. And it was not driven solely by money. There were other things in play.

If you research what has been written about the businessman Trump, you will find mostly ill-informed drivel, even before he became the polarizing political figure he is today. Many articles about him are condescending and full of cheap shots. Others are puff pieces designed to flatter him. Most reportage is a total waste of time, the product of lazy reporters with agendas.

To understand the person who, against all odds, achieved the most powerful position in the world, you must listen to what he himself says. In 1990, already known to a national audience, Donald Trump gave an interview to *Playboy* magazine. That was a pretty big deal. Big celebrities were often featured in the *Playboy* Q-and-A. The magazine also put Trump on its cover, along with a nice-looking young woman. That was unusual. Women almost always commanded the covers of *Playboy* by themselves.

For much of the interview, Donald Trump is posturing, elaborating on his success in business and life. He talks about giant yachts and marble floors—the usual.

But then the conversation turns to Fred Trump Jr., Donald's elder brother by eight years.

As a boy, Donald looked up to Fred, who treated him with kindness. The elder Trump brother attended Lehigh University, married young (at twenty-four), quickly had two children, and became a pilot, eventually flying for TWA.

By his late twenties, Fred Trump Jr. had developed a drinking

Above left: Front cover of *Playboy* magazine, March 1990. *Above right:* Then presidential candidate Trump holds up a vintage *Playboy* magazine with him on the cover as he greets supporters after speaking at a campaign rally in Wilkes-Barre, Pennsylvania, April 2016.

problem, the death knell for an airline pilot. He spiraled downward, divorcing his wife and relocating to Florida to launch a commercial fishing venture.

It failed.

By the late 1970s, even as his younger brother was beginning to amass a fortune in Manhattan, Fred Jr. was back living with his parents in Queens and working for one of his father's maintenance crews.

A few years later, in 1981, Fred Jr. died from problems related to alcoholism. He was forty-two years old.

"Take one environment and it will work completely differently on different children," Donald Trump told the magazine. "Our family environment, the competitiveness, was a negative for Fred. It wasn't

Murray Zaret, right, producer of the Pet Festival and Animal Husbandry Exposition, signs a contract with Donald's brother Fred Trump Jr., left, who recently purchased the famous Steeplechase Park in Coney Island, 1966.

easy for him being cast in a very tough environment and I think it played havoc on him. I was very close and it was very sad when he died. Toughest situation I've had.

"His death affected everything . . . I think constantly that I never gave him thanks for it. He was the first Trump boy out there and I subconsciously watched his moves."

TTT

"I SAW PEOPLE really taking advantage of Fred and the lesson I learned was always to keep my guard up one hundred percent, whereas he didn't. He didn't feel that there was a reason for that, which is a fatal mistake in life. People are too trusting. I'm a very untrusting guy. I study people all the time, automatically. It's my way of life for better or worse.

"I am very skeptical about people; that's self-preservation at work. I believe that, unfortunately, people are out for themselves."

TTT

THAT KIND OF candor is a Trump trait, and to this day, I do not believe Donald Trump's philosophy of human beings has changed. He is essentially a loner, with few close friends. He can be gregarious but is rarely revealing. He's emotional but not nostalgic; nor does he regularly practice outreach to others.

He essentially lives within himself, driven by success and the anticipation of public acknowledgment of his achievements. He does not rest easy, sleeping only about four hours a night.

As his success grew, so did his lack of trust. Donald Trump even passed that along to his young children.

"We'd see him in the morning briefly before he went to work and we went to school," Don Jr. told me. "It was the daily lecture: you know, no smoking, no drinking, no drugs, and then 'Don't trust any-one.' There were a couple of times he'd follow up with a question: 'Do you trust me?' 'Of course, [I said], you're my dad!' He's like, 'Wrong! You can't trust.'"

TTT

As THE WORLD has turned meaner, led by the Twitter option that the president so much enjoys, Donald Trump's view of humanity has narrowed even further. The prism now is how every person he encounters will affect him. That's his quick study and main evaluation. Sensitive about slights, the president is always on guard, and quick to react if he senses unfairness and negativity.

As I stated, Donald Trump did not want to speak to me for this book, and he did so only because we have a long-standing relationship. I am certain he does not trust that a book of history about him will be beneficial to his life.

But even though he doesn't fully trust me, he knows that I have always treated him and his family fairly. He also understands that when he asks me a question, I will answer it honestly, whether he likes the answer or not.

The truth is that many powerful and successful human beings are egocentric and emotionally distant. Pretty much all of them are like Trump in that they lack trust and are almost devoid of concern for those who cannot help them. But most famous people hide those dubious attributes much better than Trump does.

The president is not good at hiding stuff. His moods are often on vivid display. Everyone working in the West Wing knows quickly each morning what they are in for that day.

Donald Trump has that New York thing: "Blank you and the cab you drove in on"—especially if things are not going well or if you are annoying him.

In Washington, DC, the world's center of political power, calculation is the coin of the realm, and rationalization is the bank you cash it in. That city has a long history of treachery and deceit. Abraham Lincoln was openly mocked as a hayseed when he arrived to run the country from Illinois. Ronald Reagan was looked upon by many in Washington society as a Hollywood moron.

Donald Trump did not understand Washington when he decided to run for president, and he does not understand it today. That's because he achieved his initial success in New York City, which is light years away from DC in attitude and behavior.

After his schooling, the young Donald developed into an economic hustler similar to his dad, but he incorporated a much smoother pre-sentation. And that's not necessarily a bad thing. If you want to suc-ceed in the big, tough city, you have to out-hustle your competition. You have to beat them, sometimes brutally.

If you want to succeed in Washington, it's a different story. There, you must out-ingratiate the competition, a much more mannered hustle. The rules of polite society are many in the nation's capital, and you are expected to obey them. Outsiders like the Obamas will be accepted if they behave accordingly. But some people (for example, Richard Nixon, the Clintons, and Jimmy Carter) are never accepted. It is all about pedigree.

Donald Trump is in the unacceptable category.

The only rule in the power precincts of New York is to keep a strong bank account. It doesn't matter what fork you use. In his climb to real estate royalty, Donald Trump had to accommodate cor-rupt politicians, Mafia killers, union thugs, ruthless lawyers, and dis-honest press people. And he did, sometimes gleefully.

But Trump did not temper his New York style and swagger when he rolled into Washington. His inauguration was met with wide-spread loathing, and he did little to win over the DC establishment. He simply did not understand the game because he didn't want to take the time to figure it out.

In New York, it's in your face. In Washington, it's in your back.

T T T

THE FASCINATING THING about President Trump is that despite all the excess he embraces, the working folks outside the coastal cities like him. The more extreme his presentation, the more applause he gets from the non-elite forces. It is hard to understand, but regular people accept him and overlook his faults when they don't overlook Hillary Clinton's deficits, for example. If they did, she'd be sitting in the White House right now.

Perhaps the folks see Donald Trump as genuine, which he mostly is. There is not much difference between the public and private Trump. He likes people on a casual basis. Whenever I've been with him, he

United States president Donald Trump is joined by the congressional leadership and his family as he formally signs his cabinet nominations into law, Friday, January 20, 2017, in the President's Room of the Senate on Capitol Hill in Washington. From left are Senate Majority Leader Mitch McConnell, Senator Roy Blunt, Donald Trump Jr., Vice President Mike Pence, Jared Kushner, Karen Pence, Ivanka Trump, Melania Trump, Barron Trump, Speaker of the House Paul Ryan, House Majority Leader Kevin McCarthy, House Minority Leader Nancy Pelosi.

takes time to be nice to those with whom he interacts. When he tells them they are "terrific," they beam.

The decade of the 1970s saw Donald Trump rise and begin achieving stardom, something he wanted above all else. He consolidated his success in the 1980s, but in both decades, there were bitter defeats and questionable activities. Trump can be generous but also ruthless. He engenders both loyalty and loathing. His children love him, even though he was often not there for them while they were growing up. But today, the eldest three are his best friends.

In evaluating Donald Trump's ascension to the presidency, the practical thing to do is acknowledge that he used all available advantages to build his power. He certainly did things that most people would not do. I will chronicle some of those things, but I will always give the president the presumption of innocence in unclear situations. That, of course, will anger the Hate Trump media, which is in business to destroy him.

History will record that ongoing corrupt media campaign and how it has harmed America. The country deserves honest reporting on the president, who is capable of both good and bad.

It is an undeniable fact that Donald Trump has achieved amazing things in his life. Those accomplishments were all centered on money until he entered national politics in 2015.

So, let's find out how he made that money.

CHAPTER NINE

MANHATTAN

SPRING 1978

Things have changed for Donald Trump. Now age thirty-two, he has been president of the Trump Organization for almost seven years. The company has moved its headquarters into Manhattan from Queens, even though company chairman Fred Trump prefers to remain in the outer boroughs, overseeing the fourteen thousand apartments the Trumps currently own in Queens, Brooklyn, and Staten Island.

Donald Trump is content to let his father and younger brother, Robert, now in the family business as well, sweat the small stuff. Donald wants the big stuff—and has finally latched on to a piece of it.

New York City is in the midst of its most permissive era since the Roaring Twenties. Studio 54 and a bunch of other discos are packed most nights, fueled by cocaine and lust. Sybarites such as Andy Warhol, Truman Capote, and their crews smirk in photos that dominate the city's tabloid newspapers. Life is good for the party people, and also for the street criminals.

Times Square is Sodom, a seedy marketplace where vice and petty crime go largely unchecked. But lawbreaking is a contagion that, once ignored, moves quickly into the extreme.

In 1978, there will be nearly 150,000 violent acts committed in New York City, including more than 1,800 murders and 5,200 rapes. By contrast, there were fewer than 300 murders reported in 2018 New York City, forty years later.

The city is also broke, trying to dig out from a fiscal crisis that has been going on for years. In 1975, New York City officials asked the federal government to provide funding in order to avoid the embarrassment of bankruptcy. President Gerald Ford said absolutely not, a decision that led to one of the most infamous newspaper headlines in history, the New York *Daily News* on October 30, 1975: "Ford to City: Drop Dead."

In the face of the chaos, Ed Koch, a flamboyant politician who will come to despise Donald Trump, has just been sworn in that January as mayor, winning 50 percent of the vote—more than nine points ahead of his liberal opponent, Mario Cuomo. Koch ran on a promise to clean up the city, making it great again, if you will.

But Mayor Koch and the other politicians who run New York well understand that little will change unless high-end developers begin investing in new businesses and buildings. The city needs to be revitalized economically, and only private-sector money can do it.

The powerful billionaire Harry Helmsley and his vicious second wife, Leona, are already acquiring properties in Midtown at bargain prices. With new construction and facilities come jobs and the increased business tourism the city desperately needs.

Still on the outside looking in, Donald Trump knows this.

T T T

THE COMMODORE HOTEL on Forty-Second Street is just a few blocks away from Times Square and abuts the heavily used Grand Central Station. The hotel is a squalid mess, with dingy, dimly lit hallways and rats infesting its foundation.

Built before 1920, the Commodore was owned by the bankrupt Penn Central Railroad. Sensing a distress sale, Donald Trump convinces his father to arrange a series of city tax abatements in order to

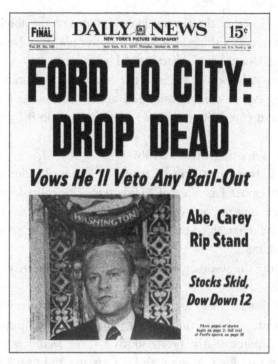

Front page of the New York *Daily News* on October 30, 1975.

buy the Commodore and some other Penn Central property near the Hudson River. Fred Trump, still smarting over the civil rights beef in 1973, agrees and becomes the silent partner in a deal that will eventually total $80 million.

Times had indeed changed in Jamaica Estates, Queens.

Donald Trump quickly allies with the Hyatt Hotel company to turn the Commodore into the Grand Hyatt Hotel. And grand it will be, with Trump demanding every modern convenience and design.

The rats are confused.

Now on a roll, the wheeler-dealer Trump sells his other Penn Central land acquisition to New York City. The land will be used to build the Jacob K. Javits Convention Center, a project the city hopes will bring in billions in new revenue.

Donald wants the new building named after his father, but the city balks. However, the Trumps make millions on the hotel and land transactions, establishing Donald as a power player in New York.

Helping Donald with the Grand Hyatt construction is his new wife, Ivana Zelnickova, a Czech national who had immigrated to Canada to escape communism. Tall and blond, Ivana is a model, designer, and competitive skier who has her eye on the good life in America.

She finds it, at least temporarily.

In 1976, Ivana met Donald Trump at Maxwell's Plum, a singles bar on the Upper East Side of Manhattan. The courtship was relatively quick, and the two were married the next year in a lavish ceremony at Manhattan's Marble Collegiate Church. Norman Vincent Peale officiated.

Attending the wedding was Abe Beame, then the mayor of New York City.

Beame, one of the worst mayors in the city's history, was a longtime associate of Fred Trump. In the late 1940s and throughout the '50s, the diminutive Abe pretty much ran the Democratic political machine in Brooklyn. Along with Fred's friend and fixer Bunny Lindenbaum, Beame set the Trump business up with excellent real estate opportunities at heavily discounted prices. Fred, Abe, and Bunny were the Supremes behind the scenes in post–World War II Brooklyn. If there was a good deal to be had in that teeming borough, these three men knew about it.

On the hunt in Manhattan, Donald Trump tapped into the Beame machine, but then actually one-upped his father, getting close to the powerful governor of New York, Hugh Carey, who ruled the state from 1975 to 1982. Carey even posed for a picture with young Donald, standing in front of an architectural drawing of the new Grand Hyatt Hotel, immediately bestowing power on the project.

In turn, Donald donated generously to Carey, who enjoyed the many pleasures of Manhattan very much.

With all that firepower behind him, Donald Trump decided to launch a blitzkrieg. Tooling around Manhattan in a silver Cadillac with the vanity license plate "DJT," he bought a number of expensive properties, including the Bonwit Teller site on Fifth Avenue, which would become ground zero for Trump Tower.

Trump was making deals constantly, aided by his own fixer, the much-feared and much-loathed Roy Cohn, the lawyer who had represented the Trumps in the 1973 federal civil rights case. Cohn had put together a vast network of informers, including police commanders, and knew much about the powerful men who ran the city. Donald Trump once told a reporter that Cohn was a bad lawyer but a "genius" in getting things done. How he got things done was usually shrouded in secrecy, but one thing was widely known: it would not be wise to cross Roy Cohn.

The short, crude Cohn became a mentor to Donald, second in influence only to his father. Cohn once told legendary reporter Cindy Adams that the young Trump would someday rule the city.

By 1980, the Trump Organization was acquiring and building real estate, and raking in tens of millions of dollars. The Trumps

Attorney Roy Cohn at home, posing with stuffed toy frogs and holding a photo of him and Donald Trump, 1984.

had secured protection and were wired into the Manhattan power structure. Even organized crime, which controlled some of the labor unions in the city, did not interfere with Donald and his dad.

Deals and offers came quickly across Donald Trump's desk. He rarely missed an opportunity. He was smart, driven, and tough—tougher, even, than his father.

At age thirty-three, Donald Trump began construction on the sixty-eight-story Trump Tower on Fifth Avenue, helped by a $140 million tax abatement. If you're going to build a skyscraper on one of the most expensive pieces of land on the planet, it helps to have friends in high places before the concrete is poured.

And Trump did.

So it is that Donald Trump finds himself a multimillionaire with a wife, a baby (Donald Jr., born in 1977), and a growing financial empire. He lives lavishly, wanting for nothing in the material world. His skills as a negotiator bring him satisfaction and staggering success.

But there is one thing that Donald Trump does not have. He is not yet Broadway Joe.

National fame still eludes him.

And he wants it.

CHAPTER TEN

TRUMP TOWER

MANHATTAN

SUMMER 1985

Life is good for Donald Trump, who has just turned thirty-nine. He sits in his office knowing that he owns one-third of perhaps the most valuable building in the world. In addition, he has now acquired a casino in Atlantic City, New Jersey, and will soon preside over the dramatic Mar-a-Lago property in Palm Beach, Florida, once the home of the famously wealthy Marjorie Merriweather Post.

Donald now has three children, who live with him and Ivana on the top three floors of this sixty-eight-story high-rise. The Trump Organization is housed with other businesses throughout the first nineteen floors.

In 1985, the average cost of a home in the United States is $96,500. But to buy even the most inexpensive apartment in Trump Tower, you would need millions. Celebrities such as Bruce Willis, Liberace, and Johnny Carson have all been buyers. The volatile Carson, however, did not stay long. As the story goes, he misplaced a coat and accused some Trump employees of stealing it. Two people were fired. Shortly after that, Carson found the coat. Shortly after that, he sold his place.

Steven Spielberg also has a residence in Trump Tower, even as he is marketing his hit film *The Color Purple*, starring Oprah Winfrey. Donald Trump is well aware of the glamour and status that are now attached to his building, where a waterfall cascades in the atrium. The Trump name has become a selling point.

As he strategizes in his office, Donald Trump may or may not be aware that a Panamanian holding company will soon purchase an apartment at Trump Tower in secret for the notorious Jean-Claude Duvalier, the deposed and despised dictator of Haiti. A man who looted hundreds of millions from the most impoverished country in the Western Hemisphere, Baby Doc, as he is known, wants the elaborate security in place at Trump Tower to protect him from avengers. While running Haiti, he used his secret police, the Tonton Macoute, to terrorize thousands. Duvalier has legions of enemies who would kill him if they could.

T T T

IT IS IMPOSSIBLE to ascertain exactly how much Donald Trump knows about what goes on inside his growing empire. He is not a leasing agent. But he is surely aware that on all major building projects in New York City, including Trump Tower, organized crime is involved.

The mayor, governor, and perhaps even President Ronald Reagan also know about mob activity inside the city's vast construction industry because it is common knowledge within the Justice Department. The FBI has been tasked with stopping the corruption.

In 1980, Donald Trump chose to have Trump Tower constructed using primarily concrete, not steel girder, the other option. Structures built with concrete go up faster. However, concrete is more expensive than steel.

In New York City, the organized crime families controlled the concrete industry through the Teamsters Union Local 282. If a developer wanted concrete poured, that union supplied the labor, and Mob-run concrete companies like Scara-Mix, in Staten Island, provided the material.

If a builder defied the union, the Hudson River beckoned.

In 1985, a mobster named Constantino "Big Paul" Castellano oversaw the concrete situation. As head of the Gambino crime family, Big Paul put his son Philip in charge of Scara-Mix, and the construction money rolled in.

Again, New York and federal authorities were aware for years that this was how the business of building was done in the city because the FBI had wiretapped Castellano's Staten Island mansion and, in early 1985, indicted him and a number of other alleged mobsters in the so-called Mafia Commission Trial.

One of Big Paul's lawyers was Roy Cohn.

A number of reporters have sought to involve Donald Trump directly with the illegalities going on in the New York City construction industry. This is grossly unfair. If Trump had been a hands-on participant, his name would certainly have surfaced on the federal wiretaps.

Evidence shows that the Trump Organization did what every other major builder did—that is, make deals with the companies and unions in place at the time. It is certainly true that Donald Trump was aware of Big Paul and his top enforcer, John Gotti, because the newspapers often covered their nefarious activities.

And then there is Roy Cohn.

So, it is likely that Donald Trump paid acute attention to the gunning down of Big Paul Castellano on December 16, 1985. Arriving at the Sparks Steak House for dinner in Manhattan, Castellano was assassinated on the order of Gotti, who resented Castellano for resisting expansion into the illegal narcotics industry.

Big Paul, out on three million dollars' bail at the time he was murdered, was denied a Catholic funeral and burial by order of the Church.

Despite the murder, nothing much changed in the city's construction industry.

▼▼▼

THE YEAR 1985 sees New York City flush as Reaganomics has finally taken hold, leaving the recession-ridden Carter administration a distant memory. On paper, Donald Trump's success over a fourteen-year period is stunning. By some estimates, the Trump Organization has amassed a billion dollars in assets and almost unlimited lines of credit from American banks.

If Donald Trump wants it, Donald Trump can buy it. And he doesn't have to use his own money. The Trump brand now opens financial lending doors everywhere.

In addition, Trump has achieved fame in New York and is gaining recognition everywhere else. His is not yet a household name like "Joe Namath" or the rising fame of "Michael Jordan," but he's on his way. His mind constantly racing, Donald Trump envisions a world-wide empire of property and products. He has the financial resources. Now all it will take is marketing. And Trump is a genius at that.

TTT

ALTHOUGH DONALD TRUMP does not know it in 1985 (but surely knows now), fame is dangerous. Wealth and recognition cause envy. Money is a magnet for grifters, blackmailers, sycophants, and deceivers.

Johnny Carson began his career hosting a TV program called *Who Do You Trust?* Then he became a superstar late-night host,

Trump posing for a portrait at the Wollman Rink, for which he oversaw renovations as a real estate developer.

amassing a fortune. But with that came three bitter divorces and a number of public drinking embarrassments. As Donald Trump celebrates his success in 1985, Carson is receiving a Peabody Award for his contributions to America. But by all accounts, he is an isolated human being who trusts very few.

Same with Donald Trump.

Nevertheless, the builder wants Carson-like fame. Unlike his father and brother, who are content to enjoy their money privately, Donald is Mr. Ostentatious, and so is his wife. Gold fixtures dominate their triplex apartment high above the city of eight million people. Murals are painted on the ceilings. Donald's Atlantic City casino is over-the-top glitz, with Ivana Trump waving the dubious taste wand as the primary decorator of the garish facility.

"There has always been a display of wealth and always will be," Donald told *Playboy* magazine. "And let me tell you, a display is a good thing. It shows people that you can be successful. It can show you a way of life . . . It's very important that people aspire to be successful. The only way you can do it is to look at somebody who is."

One of the more fascinating things about Donald Trump is that he has never wavered in that philosophy—that operational greed is good. But behind the scenes he is not obsessed with jewels or gourmet food or fine wine. He uses his wealth as a marketing tool, a success brand.

And unlike some moneyed folks, Trump does not use affluence to demean. He has many loyal associates, such as former executive assistant Norma Foerderer and his secretary Rhona Graff. I have known these two women for many years, and they love Donald Trump.

As do his children.

But there is no question that Donald Trump did some dubious things in order to become famous. And history shows that he and others around him paid a price for that.

T T T

IN 1983, THE Nintendo video game console was released, beginning a mass market for electronic gizmos that eventually morphed into personal computers and smartphones. Today, famous people and their families suffer grievously due to the Twitter mob and the unbridled cruelty that social media facilitates. The machines, as I call them, are taking over the world and burning down traditional decorum.

Famous people, including presidents, can build walls around their homes and hire armed security protection. They can also avoid most face-to-face interaction with other human beings.

But they can't stop the false accusations, instant disparagement, and rank hatred that are launched with the flick of a thumb. If you are famous, you are a target. And sooner or later, the arrow will find you.

Throughout the rest of the 1980s, Donald Trump will expand his wealth and grow his fame across the land. All the while, his family is experiencing the Trump phenomenon in a variety of ways—some good, some bad.

Donald Trump's attention is squarely on increasing his brand, which, he believes, will lead to more power and greater wealth. His family are bystanders to that.

But a fall is coming, as it almost always does.

And Donald Trump will not be ready for it.

CHAPTER ELEVEN

TRUMP TOWER

MANHATTAN

FEBRUARY 2019

NOON

Thirty-six years after opening, Trump Tower is now an armed camp. Secret Service agents pat down visitors after they step through the security machines. Vehicles cannot loiter near the building, which is now almost impregnable. What was once a symbol of unbridled capitalism has been turned into a fortress.

President Trump's residence atop the high-rise is largely empty these days, as he resides in the White House with his wife, Melania, and their twelve-year-old son, Barron, named after the legendary hotel mogul Barron Hilton.

The Trump Organization, however, continues to operate out of the Tower, and deals are still being made. Presiding over the company is the president's eldest son, forty-one-year-old Donald Trump Jr. His siblings, Ivanka, thirty-seven, and Eric, thirty-five, are also part of the operation, although Ivanka is often in Washington advising her father on certain matters. Her husband, Jared Kushner, also works in the White House as an adviser.

But it is the outspoken Don Jr. who is his father's most vocal defender and, to me, the family historian. All three of the president's older children have a good rapport with him, but it is Don that is most like his father.

If you research the Trump children, you will find some incredibly nasty material. This is unusual, because the press usually lays off presidential kids unless they actively seek to do damage.

President George W. Bush's twin daughters are treated gently by the media, as is Chelsea Clinton. And those presidential children are and were politically active to some extent.

Until 1950, there was an unwritten rule in the press not to impugn the children of presidents. All that changed when *Washington Post* music critic Paul Hume attended a performance by Margaret Truman, who was singing professionally. Hume panned Miss Truman, Harry's daughter, saying she couldn't carry a tune.

After reading the article, President Truman fumed, and then wrote Hume a little note: "Some day I hope to meet you. When that happens you'll need a new nose, a lot of beefsteak for black eyes, and perhaps a supporter down below."

Truman wasn't referring to a human supporter.

Today, the press holds back nothing when it comes to Donald Trump and those around him. Cheap shots, negative speculation, and gross disrespect for the president are daily occurrences.

The media hatred for Mr. Trump rivals only what Abraham Lincoln experienced, but modern communication heightens the searing impact of the loathing campaign. It is yet another example of the deterioration of the country's fourth estate. Even if you don't approve of Donald Trump's policies and demeanor, you should support honest reporting. The man is not Satan. It is undeniable that some of his initiatives have helped the country—for example, the successful campaign against ISIS.

It is certainly true that some in the media embraced hatred while President Obama was in office, but not nearly to the extent we have today. Mr. Obama was often vilified on talk radio and on Fox News. If the criticism was about policy, where Mr. Obama certainly had some challenges, it was legitimate as long as facts were used in the analysis. But the negative personal stuff was disturbing, even though the vast majority of the press loved the president and his family.

The corrupting aspect of attack journalism is that it is almost always based on anonymous sourcing. The smears come from unknown people with hidden agendas. And it's easy to fabricate anonymous quotes. Very easy.

In general, the truth about presidents is difficult to find, especially in personal situations. Family interactions are mostly private, and memories are faulty. Many children see their parents differently even though they resided with them in the same house. Patti Davis scorched her father publicly. Her stepbrother, Michael Reagan, repudiated much of what she said.

As stated, the three oldest Trump children are united in their respect for their father even though their childhoods had unsettling moments. That is important to acknowledge if you want to know the truth about President Trump.

I know Donald Trump Jr. slightly. I never interviewed him before this book because I rarely speak with the children of presidents on the air. An exception is Ron Reagan Jr., who somehow morphed into an outspoken liberal. I also talked professionally with Michael Reagan, who became a conservative radio talk show host.

But if there is anyone on the planet who might describe Donald Trump the father with candor, it is his eldest son. He is a straightforward man.

And so, I took the elevator up to Don Jr.'s office in Trump Tower to interrogate him. I always use the word *interview* instead of *interrogate*, but Don Jr. and everyone else in proximity knew what this was. As they say, my reputation had preceded me.

T T T

IN THE MID-1980s and throughout the '90s, the Trump children were being raised in the Tower primarily by their mother and a bevy of trusted nannies.

Donald Trump was also present. Somewhat.

We began there:

TRUMP JR.: If we wanted to see him, we could see him. If we called, he could be in the middle of the most important meeting, he'd take the phone call. If we wanted to show up in his office, we could play trucks while he's dealing with the biggest guys in banking finance. We'd be making noise, and he was totally fine with it. He wasn't, "Let's go in the backyard for two hours and play catch." That wasn't his thing. He had some of what Fred had: "Come spend the day with me and we can go to the job site. You can watch me deal with things. You can watch me do deals in the office." But it wasn't a traditional [upbringing].

O'REILLY: So, no Little League games, no bowling?

TRUMP JR.: Very seldom. That was more common back then. Now, if I can't show up at one of my kids' things because of work, I'm like a leper. You're the only dad not there. In the eighties, it was different.

O'REILLY: So, he was working all the time.

TRUMP JR.: You want to keep him busy. A busy Donald is a happy Donald.

O'REILLY: Think back. You've got three kids at the dinner table. Did the family eat together?

TRUMP JR.: The kids did with our mom.

O'REILLY: How many nights [per week] would he be there?

TRUMP JR.: Probably two or three nights a week. My parents were very social. We'd eat at six o'clock, then they'd go out.

O'REILLY: Was it mostly adult conversation at the dinner table?

TRUMP JR.: We'd talk with him, but he'd also be talking with my mother about business. He was good with the kids. He would joke and he'd wrestle with us, but it was for five minutes.

O'REILLY: So, there was a lot of adult conversation, not so much what you kids were doing?

TRUMP JR.: Usually, yes.

O'REILLY: Politics at all?

TRUMP JR.: Not as often. Political conversation came later on.

O'REILLY: [Who was the] disciplinarian?

TRUMP JR.: My mother.

O'REILLY: Did he ever yell at you guys?

TRUMP JR.: He got me good once. He was often the instigator. Putting my brother and sister [on the floor] and letting them fight. He'd sit there and laugh, and my mother would have to come in with her Eastern European accent and stop it. He'd get us wound up, then call in my mother to clean up the mess.

O'REILLY: Ivanka, the daughter, was her relationship with her father different from yours?

TRUMP JR.: Yeah ... She's Daddy's little girl. I don't want to say favorite, but as a father, I understand. I love [my kids] equally, but there's a different level of protection [when you have a daughter].

T T T

O'REILLY: What did you do during the summers?

TRUMP JR.: First half, we'd travel with our mother. Second half, I'd work ... my first job was a dock attendant in Atlantic City. I was

The Trumps at Mar-a-Lago. From left, Ivana, Eric, Donald, Ivanka.

fourteen . . . You're out in the sun, making tips, you're in a marina, good-looking girls around.

Then [my father] says you've got to do something as it relates to real estate. So, he puts us in landscaping. I always say that Eric and I are the only sons of a billionaire that can drive a D10 Caterpillar, because we actually did it.

I remember going to him [and saying,] "We're making the same minimum wage we were making in the marina, but no tips. I'm working much harder and making less money. Why aren't you paying us more?" And it was a very Trumpian response: "Why would I pay you more than you're willing to work for?" That was a lesson. In life you're not going to get anything you don't ask for. If you want it, you better go get it.

TTT

Ivanka, Eric, and Donald in 1992.

THE MOST DIFFICULT childhood moments for Don Jr. and his siblings came after their parents broke up when he was twelve years old. We'll chronicle that in upcoming pages. It was tough on the kids, as Don will explain.

Overall, it is clear that the Trump children were not exactly reenacting *The Waltons*. They were chauffeured to elite Manhattan private schools and spent time in their other lavish homes in Greenwich, Connecticut, and later in Palm Beach. It was a privileged upbringing in every sense. There were happy days, but not *Happy Days*, a sitcom readily available to the kids on TV in Trump Tower. There was no Arnold's Drive-In; no Richie, no Potsie and certainly no Fonz. Donald Trump was not Mr. C; nor Ivana, Marion. The Trump kids experienced life in a far different way than most American children do.

That way was challenged beginning in 1989, when the Trump empire almost collapsed.

And when the family actually did.

CHAPTER TWELVE

MANHATTAN

APRIL 1990

MORNING

The prince of the city is under siege. An army of bankers and investors has Donald Trump surrounded, and unfriendly fire is everywhere. His balance sheet is insane, the Trump Organization has amassed debts totaling $3.4 billion. The real estate mogul, now forty-three, personally owes about $600 million—guarantees of borrowed money he now cannot repay.

In addition, Donald Trump is pursuing an extramarital affair with a woman named Marla Maples, a Georgia model. Just a few weeks ago, Marla was on the cover of *People* magazine with the blaring headline "Trump Princess."

The kingdom of Trump is on a cliff, and strong winds are blowing.

Throughout the 1980s, Trump put together deal after deal using borrowed bank money and revenue from junk bonds that sometimes paid 14 percent interest to those investors who purchased them. Donald ran wild with the cash, buying a football team, an airline, the legendary Plaza Hotel, and three Atlantic City casinos, among other things. He couldn't possibly micromanage all the projects, so he had to delegate. Obviously, that became a problem, one his father had warned him about.

Donald Trump became the quintessential real estate gambler who didn't know when to fold 'em because he didn't even know how the cards were being dealt in some key parts of his empire.

The casinos killed him. In October 1987, the stock market crashed, leading to a national recession. As Ronald Reagan was preparing to vacate the White House, the go-go '80s suddenly became somber, and many high rollers disappeared from the Trump Castle and the Trump Plaza in Atlantic City. The $1 billion Taj Mahal casino was just getting started and needed to gross approximately $1.3 million a day in order to simply break even. Trump carried enormous debt on all his gambling properties. Eventually, he could not make the interest payments to the banks and bond holders who had financed him.

Lawyers descended. Chase Manhattan, Bear Stearns, Citibank, and dozens of other creditors lined up demanding payment from the prince, or else.

But Donald Trump didn't buckle. He did what he always did: he made deals.

His 282-foot yacht went first. Then the Trump Shuttle, which had actually increased market share 20 percent from when Eastern Airlines owned it. The private jet was also sold. Yet billions were still owed by the Trump Organization.

Then Trump pulled off the biggest coup of his life until he won the presidential election of 2016: he convinced the banks to lend him even more money to pay off what he owed. It was beyond audacious.

The Trump pitch was a thing of ruthless simplicity, which I will paraphrase: "We have two choices. First, you can lend me more money so I can pay my debts and continue operating, eventually becoming profitable again. Or two, I can declare total bankruptcy and nobody will get anything."

Donald Trump got more money.

A bevy of financial organizations bailed him out, suspending interest payments on a third of his bank debt and giving him tens of millions of dollars to spend going forward. Trump gave up his interest in the Grand Hyatt Hotel and restructured his casino debt. The deals were a stunning save that few others could have pulled off.

In the process, thousands of junk bond holders lost their money as Trump declared limited bankruptcy on selected businesses six separate times. It was a giant mess that few totally understand even to this day.

But one thing was clear: Donald Trump remained a master negotiator. He kept control of Trump Tower, Mar-a-Lago, and portions of the New Jersey casinos where business was picking up. He used the bankruptcy laws to save himself, and it worked.

"Through cooperation rather than conflict, everybody has come out much better," Trump told the press.

There was some dissent following that comment, but not from most Trump employees—they were still working.

The time that Donald Trump bought with other people's money paid off fairly quickly. The 1990s saw the U.S economy come roaring back under the pro-business policies of President Bill Clinton. New York City real estate rose steadily in value, high-end apartments were rented for record amounts, business travel to the city picked up, and the slot machine people had some cash to burn. Slowly, the Trump Organization became profitable again.

But Donald Trump had changed. No longer was he the brazen gambler who sneered at risk. Cool on the outside but shaken on the inside, he decided that marketing was the key to enduring success. He would aggressively publicize his brand, and others would pay to be in business with him. For example, a hotel company would compensate Trump millions simply for putting his name on a building. Eventually, he would be paid for clothing bearing his name, cologne, sunblock, cuff links, and on and on. The Trump brand was everywhere.

And the more famous his name became, the more money he'd receive for essentially doing nothing. Donald would soon open Trump golf clubs with enormous membership fees. He turned his mansion Mar-a-Lago into a business. He got paid for all kinds of ventures while silent investors shouldered the risk.

Down the road, the Trump Organization would start buying

Aerial view of President Trump's Mar-a-Lago mansion in Florida.

properties outright again. But as he emerged from the grueling financial negotiations that took more than two years, Donald was looking to become more powerful through fame, not finance. He wanted to become a big star beyond the business world.

And he thought a young woman from rural Georgia just might help with that.

CHAPTER THIRTEEN

TRUMP TOWER
MANHATTAN
APRIL 30, 1990

Donald Trump is getting an enormous return on his investment in Marla Maples. The news coverage of their affair and the pending divorce action with Ivana is now a national phenomenon, with comparisons to the scandalous actions of Elizabeth Taylor and Richard Burton in the early 1960s. Trump and Maples have been an item for at least two years, but only recently has their relationship been made public. As one might expect, Ivana Trump is furious over the humiliation and the disruption to her life, not to mention their children's lives.

Maples is a model who came to New York City from rural Georgia in 1985, hoping to act in a television soap opera. Problem was she didn't have a specific job or the connections to get one. But now she is a huge star in the tabloid world. Her interview with Diane Sawyer of ABC News garnered record ratings for her program just eleven days ago.

The twenty-six-year-old blonde met Donald Trump under hazy

circumstances, the tabloids reporting a chance encounter on Madison Avenue. Few who know Donald Trump believe that scenario, but their introduction has never really been defined.

What is factual is that the two developed a friendship that is now impacting the entire Trump world. With Donald Trump hoping to expand his brand in order to attract outside investment to his company, the attention he and Marla are receiving is a major plus in his eyes, and he will make a variety of public statements affirming that belief.

In fact, the launch of the billion-dollar Taj Mahal casino in Atlantic City has generated tremendous publicity mainly because of Trump's divorce action. On April 4, he said this to the anchorman of the syndicated program *Inside Edition*, which was me:

"Unfortunately, the divorce created more of a hoopla for the building . . . It's not the greatest thing in the world, and I don't like capitalizing on a divorce because a divorce is a negative thing."

Marla Maples gets a kiss from Donald Trump at the stage door of the Palace Theater in New York following a performance of *The Will Rogers Follies*, in which Maples appeared, August 1992.

"What you had to explain to your children," I said, "must have been very difficult."

"It is difficult, but we keep the children insulated. We keep them away from television, and they're young enough that, frankly, it works out pretty well."

"But you love all this media stuff, don't you?"

"No," Donald Trump answered.

"But the press works to your advantage in the sense that you can use the press because you are famous and you are a marketable commodity."

Donald Trump paused for a second. "I don't think I use the press. I think what happens is my buildings use the press. This building [the Taj Mahal] is very unique."

T T T

THE BUSINESS OF tabloid journalism requires an outlook on life that is callous, to say the least. It is impossible to know the true feelings of any human being, yet that is the root of all tabloid reporting. Heroes and villains, good and bad—the more sordid the story, the better.

There are few journalistic rules. Anonymous sources, fine. Quotes taken as fact from people not on the scene, good. Denial of due process, all day long.

In the tabloid world, which today is most of the American media, verifiable information doesn't matter. As the newsroom cliché goes, don't let the facts get in the way of a good story.

Even though I first met Donald Trump during the Maples frenzy, I have no idea what really happened there. I also don't know anything about the Trump-Ivana marriage or what occurred in it. These are personal issues that historians are not qualified to judge. All I can do is report honestly about how things unfolded, and the documented consequences that followed.

With headline after headline about their affair dominating national news coverage, Donald Trump was becoming one of the most famous men in the world. No deal he ever made brought him close to this kind of attention. But he told me in Atlantic City that he was not happy with the news coverage of his personal life.

"You have a lot of very dishonest reporters, in my opinion. And I mean dishonest. I'm not talking about they are slightly off. I mean they are totally dishonest [because] they'll report things knowing that they are wrong.

"I'm more of a victim than a beneficiary [of the press], in all fairness . . . You cannot believe what you read. So, when you're out in Minnesota or Iowa, and you pick up some rag magazine or newspaper, and it says all sorts of things that have no basis in fact or truth, you just can't believe it. These are very dishonest people."

"So how do you think the public perceives you?" I asked.

"I think the people and I have a pretty good understanding and a pretty good relationship."

"What about ego?"

"Ego is an interesting thing. I have always been referred to as somebody with a big ego, but I've never met a successful person without a very large ego. And if you don't have a big ego, you're not going to be successful. It's as simple as that."

"Why couldn't you be humble and build the Taj Mahal?"

"Because it doesn't work with a different personality. If I were humble, you wouldn't have a building like this. You'd have a plain Jane building that nobody would come and see."

T T T

TODAY, DONALD TRUMP says nearly the same things about the press. Back in the spring of 1990, his assessment of the media coverage about him was accurate. In researching this book, we found much of what was reported to be fallacious or taken grossly out of context. Publications such as *Vanity Fair* and the *New Yorker* were generally snide and condescending toward Trump. On the other side, *People* magazine was, at times, fawning.

But behind the scenes, Donald Trump was actually orchestrating some of the press coverage about him. Quick documented story: in February 1990, the *New York Post* and the *Daily News* were brawling over the Trump-Maples situation, trying to outdo each other with lurid headlines and scoops.

The *Daily News* was more sympathetic toward Ivana Trump,

often hammering "The Donald," as Ivana called him. The *Post* was more supportive of the developer, and he appreciated that.

According to Jill Brooke, a TV writer for the *Post* and a reliable correspondent, Donald Trump himself engineered the biggest headline of his career by phoning the *Post*'s editor-in-chief, Jerry Nachman, and telling him that Maples was gossiping to friends that Trump was responsible for "the best sex she ever had."

Nachman actually put Donald Trump's call on the office speakerphone, where Ms. Brooke heard it.

On February 16, 1990, Miss Maples and her alleged compliment became the front-page headline in the *New York Post*, a newspaper founded by Alexander Hamilton, who had his own problems with the sensationalistic press.

After that revelation, the media insanity only accelerated, and so did Donald Trump's fame. But no one knew who had really engineered the headlines.

T T T

BUT THERE WAS a downside, a big one. The Trump children were all in Manhattan schools. You can imagine how awful the hysteria was for them. In fact, it changed the trajectory of their lives, especially for the oldest, Donald Jr.:

O'REILLY: **Once your father left the house and split up from your mom, you saw him less, right?**

TRUMP JR.: Yes, part of that was my choice. I was twelve, Eric was six. It hit me differently probably because it was so much more visible to me . . . so I went to boarding school in central Pennsylvania in eighth grade. Moved away from home at thirteen . . . and I was fine getting away from New York City.

O'REILLY: **When you were in Pennsylvania at school, how often would you be in contact with your dad?**

TRUMP JR.: Maybe once a week I'd call home to check in.

O'REILLY: **Did he come out?**

TRUMP JR.: He came out to drop me off when I went there the first time, and he came out at graduation.

O'REILLY: So, he saw the school twice.

TRUMP JR.: Saw the school twice in five years.

O'REILLY: And how about your mom?

TRUMP JR.: Same.

O'REILLY: So, you're doing your own thing?

TRUMP JR.: I'd see him vacations, Easter, Thanksgiving, you know . . . He's not a participation medal kind of guy, but if you're not doing great, he's going to call you out . . . Around sophomore year of high school he said [about my grades], "This is fine but this isn't going to get you anywhere in life. You've got to decide what you want to do. You can do more or you can do less. It's up to you."

O'REILLY: How did you respond?

TRUMP JR.: That's when I actually started working my ass off academically.

O'REILLY: So, he inspired you?

TRUMP JR.: He's not a teacher that puts you on his lap and says this is how you do something. He puts you in a situation to learn, and you rise to the occasion or you fail.

Donald Trump Jr. eventually went on to graduate from the University of Pennsylvania, and Wharton Business School, like his father. His sister and brother also attended boarding schools and good colleges. All three are working for their father today.

T T T

MEANWHILE, DONALD TRUMP was learning about the power of television, because with the Maples thing, he was all over it. However, as he became a household name in America, he also became somewhat addicted to the attention.

Adulation is a risky thing. Most human beings strongly seek acceptance, and some want constant flattery. But along with that can

Ivanka, Donald, Eric, and Donald Jr. at the press
conference for Trump Soho Hotel Launch, September 2007.

come confusion, alienation, and despair. In the beginning, being idol-
ized can bring satisfaction. But gradually, constant attention wears
human beings down. Add to that the reality that some will try to
exploit the famous person for venal gain, and you have a powerful
figurative drug, fame, that can bring grievous harm.

Elvis Presley is a vivid example. Supremely talented, Presley found
himself a national phenomenon in the mid-1950s. But fame overwhelmed the singer, and by age forty-two, he was dead, the victim
of a destructive lifestyle built around prescription drugs and dietary
excesses.

The list of fame victims is almost endless, and is not something to
be taken casually.

But Donald Trump wanted the attention that comes with mass adulation—and not only for business reasons. I saw it firsthand.

As the anchor of the syndicated TV program *Inside Edition* for six years, I had to cover Donald Trump and other "infotainment" situations. They did not interest me much, but if we wanted to stay on the air, the "Madonna" stories, as I called them, had to be in the lineup.

At the time, *Inside Edition* was a hybrid: half glitz, half news. I took the job because my contract allowed me to go all over the world to cover stories like the first Gulf War and the dismantling of the Berlin Wall. I never would have had that opportunity at another media agency.

David Frost, the British personality, was the first anchor of *Inside Edition*. But he was quickly dispatched back to London because the ratings were abysmal. I took his place, and things turned around. The program is still on the air.

Anyway, as part of my job, I covered Donald Trump, and he apparently thought I did a fair job. So, he invited me to go on a double date with him and Marla Maples and her friend from Georgia.

Trump had tickets to see Paula Abdul in New Jersey. With all due respect to Abdul, a talented performer, I wasn't exactly her audience. When Donald Trump called with the invitation, I said, "Can't we go to a hockey game?"

No, we can't.

So, I went on the expedition thinking maybe I would learn something.

I described the outing in my first nonfiction book, *The O'Reilly Factor*:

> We drove over in Trump's limo and were waved into a parking lot beneath the Brendan Byrne Arena. We popped out of the car and took an elevator up to a private box to watch the show.
>
> Slightly to my surprise, things were going okay. Trump and I chatted casually about the football season and his casinos. . . . The private box was luxurious. Everyone seemed to be having a good time . . .

There was an intermission after [the first act]. That's when things began to get interesting . . .

Trump suggested that we all take a walk around the arena. What? . . . So, Donald really wanted to walk around the arena?

Oh, yeah, he sure did!

I remarked to him that it was probably not a good idea to take such a stroll without massive security—like, to begin with, a battalion of full-metal jacket-armed, battle-tested U.S. Marines. Some rudeness might break out . . .

"No problem," Donald said. We would have Tony *and* Lou *with us.*

Okay, personal bodyguards Tony and Lou were certainly large and testy. But the odds against them were about 15,000 to 2—odds I did not like. . . .

You can picture it, I know. Within ten seconds, the hallway of the arena was in screaming, crowding chaos . . . the whole thing was nuts. Some people said nice things, some people were mean. We all got shoved. Most of the guys focused on Marla, who was sewn into a tourniquet-tight black outfit. They stared in a way that is usually seen only in prison. And then there were those who simply screamed the name Donald over and over. He loved it.

I felt as if I was in The Rocky Horror Picture Show. *I tried to blend into the crowd, keeping as far as possible from the celebrity couple. But our stroll wasn't enough for Donald Trump. He now wanted to watch the rest of the concert from the floor!*

So long, luxury box. Standing on the arena floor now surrounded by extra security guards, we watched Paula Abdul perform the rest of the concert. As she sang and danced, the crowd kept screaming: "Donald, Marla!"

T T T

ALONG WITH ACHIEVING massive name recognition, Donald Trump absorbed an important strategic lesson during the hectic year of 1990: the media could be manipulated, especially television. Astutely, he understood that his life had now taken a turn into show business, and it was like no business he knew.

Controlled most often by ruthless autocrats, the TV industry would be Donald's future because he could handle that world and use it to benefit himself in many ways.

It would take time for the TV thing to unfold, but when it did, Donald Trump was ready to parlay it into something that gave him extreme satisfaction.

Incredible power.

CHAPTER FOURTEEN

MANHASSET, NEW YORK

MARCH 2, 2019

NOON

Donald Trump's policy of scorched-earth rhetoric and complicated personal interactions, many based on monetary gain, means he will always have a ready supply of enemies. This week one of them was featured in three full days of congressional hearings. Michael Cohen, Mr. Trump's personal lawyer for about ten years, told the world that the president is a racist and a crook. Upon hearing that, the anti-Trump cadres raised a glass.

It seems that Cohen feels betrayed by his former client and wanted vengeance before he arrived at a federal penitentiary for three years. After pleading guilty to income tax evasion and a number of other things, Cohen evidently expected the president to pardon him. But Donald Trump says he had no intention of doing that, leading Cohen to turn on his former client.

During his diatribes against the president, Cohen said one thing that caught my attention above all: "He never expected to win the primary. He never expected to win the general election. The campaign, for him, was always a marketing opportunity."

Mr. Cohen is misleading anyone who might listen to him. Throughout the primary process in 2016, there was no clear-cut favorite on the Republican side. Donald Trump believed none of his competition had a stronger message than he did, and he successfully marginalized his opponents during the debates.

Trump also knew that his rally crowds were far larger than those running against him were drawing, and that TV news ratings spiked when he appeared.

So, Cohen's assertion about the primary outcome is nonsensical and apparently based solely on hatred toward Mr. Trump.

It is true that during his race against Hillary Clinton, Donald Trump had some doubts about a victorious outcome. Almost every poll had Mrs. Clinton ahead throughout the campaign. It is not hard to picture Trump saying something like "Well, if we lose, at least the brand is powerful." Donald Trump is a man who believes all setbacks can be turned into victories.

But Cohen's statement that Trump was not in it to win it is intellectually dishonest, and any astute political analyst would know it.

But few pundits repudiated Cohen's propaganda because it was negative toward Trump, and that's what the establishment media want. It doesn't matter whether accusations against the president are truthful or out of context. What matters is that every allegation receive as much publicity as possible, absurd or not.

The media loathing toward Donald Trump was a gradual movement. Before he became president, Trump's feuding with various people amused the press. For example, the three-term mayor of New York City, Ed Koch, intensely disliked the developer.

After Koch died in 2013, the *New York Times* reported that his personal papers featured writings like "Donald Trump is one of the least likable people I have met during the 12 years that I served as mayor. It is incomprehensible to me that for some people he has become a folk hero."

According to the *Times*, Koch was also fond of quoting a line from one of his assistants: "I wouldn't believe Donald Trump if his tongue were notarized."

For his part, Trump responded in kind, saying, "Koch achieved something quite miraculous. He's presided over an administration that is both pervasively corrupt and totally incompetent."

T T T

THROUGHOUT THE 1990S, the Trump Organization began expanding again, even as Trump himself became a tabloid favorite. In '92, he and Ivana divorced, causing front-page headlines about settlement money.

In 1993, Marla Maples became pregnant; she gave birth to Tiffany Trump in October. Two months later, Donald and Marla married in Manhattan. The ceremony was attended by O. J. Simpson, Rosie O'Donnell, Senator Alphonse D'Amato, and Don King, among others.

Beginning its tireless tradition of mocking and besmirching Trump, the *New York Times* wrote the wedding up this way: "Dr. Arthur Caliandro of the Marble Collegiate Church performed the ceremony in the Grand Ballroom, on an altar decked with white orchids and white birches. Dripping from the birches were cut-glass teardrops.

"Other than that, as the writer Julie Baumgold remarked after the ceremony, 'There wasn't a wet eye in the place.'

"The bride is taking her husband's name. The bridegroom is keeping his name, The Donald, a legacy from former wife, Ivana."

Cats all over the world should have sued.

T T T

NEWLY MARRIED WITH a baby daughter named Tiffany and three older children, Donald Trump begins charting both his financial and political future. It is 1994, and one of the most bizarre real estate deals in history is unfolding before his eyes.

Back in '91, a Japanese billionaire named Hideki Yokoi bought the Empire State Building, eventually turning it over to his daughter Kiiko Nakahara to oversee. The building had not been renovated since King Kong hung out there, and many leases were advantageous to the tenants.

For some reason, Nakahara brought Donald Trump in as a partner, hoping he could get some of the bad leases off the books. Incredibly, the wealthy woman gave the Trump Organization 50 percent equity in the building for its services.

But Trump wanted more—he wanted the city to change the name of the building to "Trump Empire State Building Tower Apartments."

King Kong threatened to come back, and the idea died.

The wedding of Marla Maples and Donald Trump, New York City, December 20, 1993.

Trump then sued many of the tenants, claiming they had turned the Empire State Building into a "high-rise slum."

After years of litigation, Donald Trump lost in court. But *all* was not lost. He waited, and when two American billionaires showed interest, he sold his Empire State Building stake for a reported $57 million. That was totally walk-away money—apparently, Trump had invested nothing in the building himself.

How do you say "the art of the deal" in Japanese?

Meanwhile, Donald Trump continued wheeling and dealing. He bought the Gulf and Western Building in Columbus Circle, renaming it the Trump International Hotel. He then sold the Plaza Hotel on Central Park, which had been a money drain.

In the late 1990s, he is a dervish of activity, buying a number of high-profile properties and a stake in the Miss Universe pageant. He also begins acquiring golf courses. For Donald Trump, life is pretty good—or so it seems.

T T T

THEN, IN 1999, big changes come into Trump's life: he divorces Marla Maples, decides almost out of nowhere to run for president, and his father dies.

Fred Trump is ninety-three when he passes away from Alzheimer's disease, which he had been living with for six years. In a long obituary, the *New York Times* calls him "one of the last of New York City's major postwar builders."

The newspaper goes on to list Fred Trump's considerable donations to charity, and ends with this: "Mr. Trump liked to be surrounded by familiar things and familiar people. He still employed Amy Luerssen, his secretary for 59 years. And he and his wife of 61 years still lived in the red-brick Colonial they built on a half-acre lot in the leafy, middle-class suburb of Jamaica Estates, in Queens."

Nowhere in the obit is there anything negative about Fred Trump or his son Donald. That would not likely be the case today.

In the weeks that follow, Fred's four living children divided a reported $20 million from the estate. Not that Donald Trump needs the money, but it easily handles his divorce settlement with Marla Maples.*

T T T

WITH THE REAL estate business once again brisk, and his personal wealth rising, Donald Trump has every reason to be content. But he's not. Marla is gone, and he has a new girlfriend, named Melania Knauss, a model from Slovenia. But Trump remains restless. So, on October 8, he goes on CNN and tells Larry King that he is forming an "exploratory committee" to pursue the presidency on the Reform Party ticket. Apparently, the wrestler Jesse Ventura has convinced Trump to do this.

For the next four months, Donald Trump campaigns across the country, telling voters that U.S. trade policies are stupid, that "universal health care" is good, and the national debt is bad.

From my perch as a prime-time anchor on the Fox News Channel, I did not see Donald Trump as a major political factor even after he said he'd like Oprah as his running mate. The 2000 presidential race would likely be between Vice President Al Gore and Governor George W. Bush of Texas. In the polls, Trump was averaging about 7 percent.

But the man had energy and seemed to enjoy campaigning. However, on February 14, Donald Trump dropped out of the race, a fitting Valentine's Day gesture to those who did not like him.

Back then, many believed what Michael Cohen told Congress: that Trump was using politics to benefit his business. Maybe true in 2000, but it is worth considering that Trump had been thinking about national politics for even more than ten years, as excerpts from his 1990 interview in *Playboy* prove.

Then age forty-four, Trump had obviously been contemplating the state of America and the world. He didn't like what he was seeing.

---

* That amount is equivalent to $30 million today. The Trump siblings would enjoy another windfall in 2004 when they sold Fred's real estate holdings for $177 million—$236 million today.

TRUMP: We Americans are laughed at around the world for losing a hundred and fifty billion dollars a year, for defending wealthy nations for nothing . . . Our allies are screwing us.

PLAYBOY: You have taken out full-page ads in several major newspapers that not only concern U.S. foreign trade but call for the death penalty, too. Why?

TRUMP: Because I hate seeing this country go to hell . . . In order to bring law and order back into our cities, we need the death penalty and authority given back to the police.

PLAYBOY: You believe in an eye for an eye?

TRUMP: When a man or woman cold-bloodedly murders, he or she should pay. It sets an example. Nobody can make the argument that the death penalty isn't a deterrent. Either it will be brought back swiftly or our society will rot away. It is rotting away.

PLAYBOY: You mean firm hand as in China?

TRUMP: When the students poured into Tiananmen Square, the Chinese government almost blew it. Then they were vicious, they were horrible, but they put it down with strength. That shows you the power of strength. Our country right now is perceived as weak, [we are] being spit on by the rest of the world.

PLAYBOY: Which political party do you think you'd be more comfortable with [if you ran for office]?

TRUMP: Well, if I ever ran for office, I'd do better as a Democrat than as a Republican—and that's not because I'd be more liberal, because I'm conservative. But the working guy would elect me. He likes me. When I walk down the street, those cabbies start yelling out their windows.

PLAYBOY: What's the first thing President Trump would do upon entering the White House?

TRUMP: A toughness of attitude would prevail. I'd throw a tax on every Mercedes-Benz rolling into this country and on all Japanese products, and we'd have wonderful allies again.

PLAYBOY: How would President Trump handle [the threat of nuclear war]?

TRUMP: He would believe very strongly in extreme military strength. He wouldn't trust anyone. He wouldn't trust the Russians; he wouldn't trust our allies; he'd have a huge arsenal, perfect it, understand it.

PLAYBOY: You categorically don't want to be president?

TRUMP: I don't want to be president. I'm one hundred percent sure. I'd change my mind only if I saw this country continue to go down the tubes.

T T T

AGAIN, THAT INTERVIEW is from twenty-nine years ago, and obviously little has changed in Donald Trump's political outlook. Over the years, he has registered to vote in all three parties, Democratic, Republican, and Independent.

For a time, he was close to Bill and Hillary Clinton. They even attended his wedding to Melania. In 2000, he supported George W. Bush but turned against the president over the invasion of Iraq.

Under the eight years of President Obama, Donald Trump seethed, believing Mr. Obama to be weak and ineffective.

It is interesting to note that Trump's populist and "strongman" approach to politics was formed while he was relatively young. There is no question that he has stayed true to his vision.

But without a political résumé, it was difficult for Trump to be taken seriously as a public policy force. I mean, who really cares what a bombastic billionaire thinks?

So, Donald Trump had to find a way to assemble a political profile. Using a strategy born of the Middle Ages, he had to become an apprentice.

CHAPTER FIFTEEN

———

TRUMP TOWER

MANHATTAN

NOVEMBER 2003

It takes a village to get Donald Trump ready for his close-up. Dozens of people who are now working on the soon-to-debut NBC program *The Apprentice* are waiting for "Mr. Trump" to appear on the set. As usual, he's late. As he sits in a private room getting what is called "hair and makeup," the show's creator, a former British Parachute Regiment commando named Mark Burnett, is going over the script with his star.

But Donald Trump has not read the entire screenplay because he doesn't do that. He will wing much of the dialogue, as he usually does, saying pretty much anything that pops into his head. If it doesn't work, they will edit it out of the final product. Donald, as always, is supremely confident that he, himself, can make the show entertaining. He can make it fabulous, a huge hit.

Right now, Donald is focused on aesthetics. His dyed blond hair is swept up in an elaborate style. The stylist has known Donald Trump for a long time; he trusts her to spray the mane so it will stay in place until Christmas, if necessary.

Trump's lead makeup artist is also a longtime confidant. The mogul favors a tan look, and likes flattery. The artist knows Trump is extremely disciplined in his grooming. His shave is always perfect, his clothes crisp. Donald Trump's appearance is important to the show, as it subliminally demonstrates that he is in command of himself and everyone around him.

Mark Burnett believes in Donald Trump and understands that unlike his other TV ventures, this one is unique. Burnett is not solely in charge as he usually is. His star will be available to him for only a relatively short time each week because Trump gets bored easily with repetition and the minutiae of the taping process. There will be a few "retakes," but not many. Burnett will get what he can on video and then rely on his genius in the editing room.

Putting together a mega-hit television program is an arduous task. I know; I've experienced it—twice. Most shows quickly fail for one simple reason: viewers don't watch.

It takes enormous energy and boldness to drive a news or reality program to success. Think back to those few who have been part of that. Barbara Walters and Katie Couric on *The Today Show*, Oprah, Mike Wallace on *60 Minutes*, Howard Cosell on *Monday Night Football*. There are very few individuals who break through and become icons on television. You must possess charisma and confidence; you have to be magnetic on the screen.

Without any formal TV training, Donald Trump accomplished television success, and it set him up for the presidency.

The Apprentice began in January 2004 and lasted until 2015, when the mogul was fired for a controversial remark about undocumented immigrants from Mexico. By that point, Trump was involved with politics and had tired of the TV grind. Been there, done that—for eleven years, a staggering amount of time for a TV program to run.

The venture was Mission Accomplished for Donald Trump. After the *Apprentice* success, almost every potential voter in the United

States knew who Trump was, a tremendous advantage if you are seeking national office.

Before we get into Trump's shrewd approach to *The Apprentice*, let's examine his public and private persona. Unlike most people, Donald Trump has few doubts about himself. He can do it. That's his strong belief. He can do it.

Even when he fails, as he did for a time running the Trump Organization, he is not dissuaded from his self-supporting attitude: whatever it is, he'll get out of it and prosper. Everything will be "terrific." The end result of his involvement will be "the greatest."

No doubts, no fear, no surrender.

And it's not an act. Donald Trump sees himself as the ultimate winner in life.

But if *you* don't see him that way, there may be a problem.

As Shakespeare incorporated into his works, every person has a tragic flaw. Or two. Maybe three.

For President Trump, it's insecurity, number one. If you are not with him, you are an enemy who must be challenged. This sometimes leads to chaotic behavior and verbal exaggeration. That's what happened in the John McCain "war hero" madness.

In the run-up to the 2016 Republican primaries, Senator McCain had little use for Donald Trump, and did not hide that. The late senator was a traditional legislator, and a brash outsider like Trump attacking the DC status quo offended him. However, McCain had something in common with Trump: he was not shy about giving his opinion.

So, when Donald Trump heard John McCain disparage him by criticizing Trump's assessment that Mexico was not sending quality people to America, he lashed back, marginalizing McCain's captivity in Vietnam: "He's a war hero because he was captured. I like people who weren't captured."

That statement was a poor decision by Trump, given that there is no question that as a POW, McCain suffered grievously in a North Vietnam prison. I spoke with Trump privately about the comment, as I was surprised by it. Trump had endorsed McCain in his 2008 presidential run against Barack Obama. In my private conversation, which will remain confidential because it was off the record, it became clear to me that Donald Trump had acted emotionally. I asked him to go on the record on my TV program, which he agreed to do.

In the meantime, the anti-Trump press, which was quickly growing in strength, killed him. Story after story appeared chronicling how Donald Trump despises Mexicans and the great American hero John McCain.

Reporter Sharyl Attkisson noticed the hysterical reaction from the press and wrote an article on her website criticizing the *Washington Post* for failing to report that Trump had acknowledged John McCain's heroism four times before making the "I like people who weren't captured" comment.

Attkisson's analysis was correct. The *Washington Post* omitted an important part of the story on purpose. The paper had wanted to hurt Donald Trump, as it almost always does. Yet the deceit was unnecessary, because Trump had hurt himself with the captivity statement.

On July 20, 2015, Donald Trump appeared on *The O'Reilly Factor.*

O'REILLY: When you were asked about McCain, you got into his war record, and I think you would admit here tonight that was a mistake because John McCain was a hero, and you know that.

TRUMP: But I haven't said anything different. In fact, Sharyl Attkisson analyzed what I said . . . and she said Trump did absolutely nothing wrong. He said the right things. In fact, he said "war hero" four times.

O'REILLY: But wait . . . The fact of the matter is we just played the clip [of Trump's remarks] where you said, "He was captured, and I like people who weren't captured." Now, you know that wasn't correct. He was on a bombing mission. He was shot down. He was tortured. He could have been released but said no because he wanted to stay with his captured comrades. Come on, Donald, you know that the way that came off wasn't correct.

TRUMP: Bill, no matter how you say it, what I said, including my remarks right afterward, right off the stage . . . and Sharyl Attkisson is highly respected, she said it was very unfair the way the media reported it.

O'REILLY: Maybe that was unfair, but you yourself—and I've known you for a long time and I want you to be honest—you do think John McCain is a hero. I know you do.

TRUMP: I do, and by the way, I said it. I actually said it four times.

T T T

OF COURSE, THE most efficient thing Donald Trump could have done there was simply to apologize for the "captured" remark. But that could not happen because it goes against Trump's personal philosophy, one that few people understand.

But his children do.

O'REILLY: Your father's not a guy who really admits mistakes.

TRUMP JR.: No, he doesn't.

O'REILLY: Have you ever heard him admit a mistake ... Has he ever said to you, "Don, I'm really sorry I made a mistake"?

TRUMP JR.: No. What he will do when he is wrong, and he knows it, he'll make small talk, and he's not a small talk kind of guy. And I'm like, "It's okay, you can say you're sorry." [And he'll say,] "What are you talking about?"

O'REILLY: Why doesn't he admit mistakes?

TRUMP JR.: I think he recognizes that in the world of mob mentality, you get no credit for being sorry. You get no forgiveness; you get no quarter.

O'REILLY: Do you think he sees it as weakness?

TRUMP JR.: I think there's an element of that, too. It's just another sign of weakness if you own it. [Better] to move on and say this is what I'm going to do [in the future]. I think the strategy has played out pretty well for him.

T T T

AND IT HAS. Many Americans have forgiven Donald Trump his trespasses because they believe his job performance is more important than his foibles. Trump has correctly assessed that his appeal lies in being brash, unrepentant, and successful. Everything else is background noise.

If you think about it, Trump's personal philosophy is shocking for a person in the public arena. But there is no question that his flamboyant presentation holds strong appeal for millions of people.

Somehow, Donald Trump figured out that his Pied Piper flute played a very different tune, one that might lead him to vast power. He just had to let the folks know what his viewpoint on life actually was. And being an entertainer on national television gave him that solid-gold opportunity.

T T T

THE BACKSTORY ON *The Apprentice* is fairly straightforward. In the early 2000s, Mark Burnett, who developed the hit program *Survivor* for CBS, was looking for another property. He pitched Donald Trump with a concept that various contestants would compete for a corporate job with nice money attached to the winner.

Trump would be the rich mogul who decides who gets kicked off the corporate "island" each week. It was *Survivor* with nice grooming, and it immediately appealed to the businessman Trump because he knew the following things:

- He was the sole star, and the plot lines would always feature him as a superhero in business: a strong, successful guy who rules his domain.
- His company would receive 50 percent of the profits with no investment on his part other than time. In fact, it appears that his overall compensation for *The Apprentice* clocked in at north of $200 million.
- *Survivor* had been *huge*, and Mark Burnett was hot in Hollywood.
- The Trump Tower would be the primary set (for a nice fee).
- His actual work time was short. He shows up, ad-libs most of the dialogue, and leaves.
- His other properties and overall brand are featured on the

program on a regular basis, giving him sensational marketing opportunities at no cost.

• He is seen worldwide as very powerful, the ultimate successful guy in America.

For Donald Trump, *The Apprentice* was the best deal he ever made, and the smart money knows it set him up for a presidential run.

Researching Trump's fourteen seasons on *The Apprentice* is pretty much a waste of time. Mark Burnett requires employees on all his shows to sign nondisclosure agreements—violate that, and you get sued. Of course, I could use anonymous sources, many of whom would trash Donald Trump. But that would be inappropriate because I couldn't possibly know why the anonymous source was denigrating Trump. There are also people who say good things about Mr. Trump's appearances on *The Apprentice*. Jeff Zucker, who presently runs CNN, was an NBC executive at the time, and he heaped lavish praise on Trump. Now Zucker is perhaps Trump's worst enemy, as his network has turned into a 24/7 Trump-bashing outfit.

As they say in Hollywood, it's complicated. So, let's just stick with the facts.

In 2004, Donald Trump and Mark Burnett appeared on a panel in Los Angeles to promote *The Apprentice*. The star said he initially had reservations about doing a reality show: "I don't want to have cameras all over my office, dealing with contractors, politicians, mobsters, and everyone else I have to deal with in my business. You know, mobsters don't like, as they're talking to me, having cameras all over the room. It would play well on television, but it wouldn't play well with them."

For his part, the astute Burnett recognized Donald Trump's appeal to so many people. He said this while sitting next to his star on that panel: "Donald will say whatever Donald wants to say. He takes no prisoners. If you're Donald's friend, he'll defend you all day long. If you're not, he's going to kill you. And that's very American. It's like the guys who built the West."

The Trump-Burnett team succeeded on a scale rarely seen in the entertainment industry. But more important, American history would be directly affected by their reality show—which really had only one reality in it: Donald Trump ruled.

T T T

IN 2019, THE uber-left *New Yorker* magazine ran a hit piece on Mark Burnett written by Patrick Radden Keefe. The guy tried hard in the story to brand Donald Trump a racist, and wrote a number of unflattering things about him. But the piece really amounted to nothing. At one point, the word-assassin unsheathed his knife this way: "Trump's natural idiom is vulgarity, and the targets of his ire—Colin Kaepernick, 'shithole countries,' any African-American who asks him a tough question—are clearly not chosen at random."

Clear to whom? Does anyone think Donald Trump would not have scorched a white football player who championed a movement to kneel during the national anthem and who wore socks depicting police officers as pigs?

Anyone?

Donald Trump and Mark Burnett, the creator of *Survivor*, in the control room of their new show, *The Apprentice*, Trump Tower, New York, September 2003.

And how about CNN's White House correspondent Jim Acosta, whom Trump hammers all the time? I believe he's not an African American.

The only reason I even mention the *New Yorker* attack is to document once again that what you read and hear about Donald Trump is largely fiction. The truth is much more nuanced. And here's the truth about *The Apprentice*: it was the single most important vehicle in Donald Trump's quest to be president of the United States.

The Apprentice convinced millions of people that the businessman was far more than a real estate mogul. Over a period of eleven years, the psychology of the show gave Trump the aura of authority, accomplishment, and vast influence.

Thus, in 2015, Donald Trump knew the table had been set. He believed that America was ready for a strongman in politics. He watched a lot of cable news and did not like what President Obama was doing. He would have fired Mr. Obama from *The Apprentice*.

So, well beyond revved up, citizen Trump decided to take his money, fame, and ambition into the world of presidential politics. As always, he had a plan of his own design. No consultants, no paid political action committees, no giant fund-raising apparatus—Trump was coming alone, and hell was coming with him.

But most important, America would never be the same.

PART II

CHAPTER SIXTEEN

WASHINGTON, DC
APRIL 16, 2015
7:30 P.M.

Donald Trump sits at a well-appointed table in the Grand Ballroom at the Hilton Hotel. He is attending the annual White House Correspondents' Association Dinner, a charity event that raises money for journalism scholarships. This is the nation's ultimate press social, and tonight President Barack Obama again is the keynote speaker. Comedian Cecily Strong from *Saturday Night Live* is the host.

Mr. Trump has been invited to the event by me, your humble correspondent, and is surrounded by Fox News people as well as Martha Stewart, Billie Jean King, actress Kelly Rutherford, and Brody Jenner, all of whom have seats at the table.

The dinner is a prestige item that blends show business with journalism—not that the two are separated anymore. Over the years, I have conversed with an incredible variety of people at the function, including the singer Katy Perry, the rapper Ludacris, Attorney General Eric Holder, the late Supreme Court justice Antonin Scalia, and a variety of senators and congresspeople.

But there is always tension inside the huge ballroom because of ongoing feuds and the personal loathing that thrives in the worlds of politics and media. It is not a good-natured event, although it pretends to be.

On this night, Donald Trump is subdued, not yet a publicly announced candidate for president. As usual, he is polite to those who approach him, posing for pictures and making small talk.

Also as usual, I ask him questions about certain famous people he knows. His answers are always pointed and sometimes very funny.

But there is nothing funny about the relationship between Donald Trump and President Obama. Four years ago, at this very dinner, in this very room, Mr. Obama savaged Trump in his speech from the dais. It was 2011, and the real estate mogul was thinking about bailing from *The Apprentice* and challenging the president in 2012. Perhaps with that in mind, Donald Trump had ramped up the phony birth certificate crusade, clearly teeing off Barack Obama.

Comedian Seth Meyers, who despises Donald Trump, hosted the 2011 dinner, which made a televised ambush a virtual certainty. As Donald Trump sat next to his wife, Melania, at a table purchased by the *Washington Post*, Meyers began introducing President Obama, who was adored in the room.

Upon taking the microphone, Mr. Obama did not waste any time.

TTT

"MY FELLOW AMERICANS, Mahalo. It is wonderful to be here at the White House Correspondents' dinner. As some of you heard, the state of Hawaii released my official long-form birth certificate.

"Hopefully, this puts all doubts to rest. But just in case there are any lingering questions, tonight I'm prepared to go a step further. Tonight, for the first time, I am releasing my official birth video."

At this point a clip from *The Lion King* appears on two large screens flanking the dais. The crowd laughs heartily, but not Donald Trump, who sits stone-faced.

President Obama continues: "Now, I warn you, no one has seen this footage in fifty years, not even me...."

"I want to make clear to the Fox News table—that was a joke. That was a children's cartoon. Call Disney if you don't believe me. They have the original long-form version."

As the cameras zero in on a stiff Donald and Melania Trump, the president reels off some other lines away from the birther stuff. But soon enough, he returns to his main theme.

"Donald Trump is here tonight! Now, I know he's taken some flak lately, but no one is happier, no one is prouder to put this birth certificate matter to rest than Donald. And that's because he can finally get back to focusing on the issues that matter. Like, did we fake the moon landing? What really happened in Roswell? And where are Biggie and Tupac?

"But all kidding aside, obviously we all know about your credentials and breadth of experience. For example, just recently in an episode of *Celebrity Apprentice*, at the steakhouse, the men's cooking team did not impress the judges from Omaha Steaks. And there was a lot of blame to go around. But you, Mr. Trump, recognized that the real problem was lack of leadership. And so, ultimately, you didn't blame Lil Jon or Meat Loaf. You fired Gary Busey! And these are the kind of decisions that would keep me up at night. Well handled, sir, well handled.

"Say what you want about Mr. Trump, he certainly would bring some change to the White House."

A picture of the White House then flashes on the screen along with the words: "Trump White House Resort and Casino."

Barack Obama's comedy bit was expertly delivered, and the message was clear: Donald Trump was a joke.

Looking back, I see that there is absolutely no way President Obama ever, in a million years, thought that the man he was mercilessly mocking at the Correspondents Dinner would someday be sitting where he sat: in the Oval Office.

Irony doesn't even begin to cover it.

In a harbinger of things to come, the liberal press went wild celebrating Obama's takedown of Trump. Never mind that it was an easy dunk because Mr. Obama commanded the microphone; the president's supporters were delirious with joy.

For his part, Donald Trump tried to stay classy, San Diego. He said this after the dinner: "The president was making jokes about me. I was having a great time. I was so honored, and honestly, he delivered them well."

T T T

FIVE YEARS LATER, the tone at the press dinner was a bit different. President Obama was on his way out of office, and few people, if any, knew how serious Donald Trump was about taking his place.

I must confess I had no idea that in just two months, Mr. Trump would announce his candidacy for the Republican nomination. I had invited him to the dinner because, historically, those things are long and boring. I knew Trump would entertain me in conversation because he always did.

Sitting a few feet away from us, the president and First Lady made small talk with those seated at the head table even as Donald Trump

President Barack Obama speaks as his "anger translator," played by Keegan-Michael Key, gestures during the annual White House Correspondents' Association Dinner at the Washington Hilton, April 25, 2015, in Washington, DC.

Donald and Melania at the White House Correspondents' Association Dinner, 2015.

made casual conversation at the Fox News gathering. Although both Donald and Barack would never admit it, they have a few major things in common.

First of all, the two men are off-the-charts ambitious and calculating when it comes to achieving their personal goals. Both use golf as a social tool. Each man is meticulous in personal appearance. Neither easily admits a mistake.

Presidents Obama and Trump both take slights very personally. They hold grudges. They are generally suspicious of people, and they are not effusive with affection, at least not in public.

I have enjoyed my personal time with both men and believe that I understand their life views. Finally, I know they do not respect each other.

Barack Obama firmly believes Donald Trump raised the birth certificate issue because of his skin color and his father's Islamic faith. But there is some pointed evidence that this is not true. There is no question that Trump sought to diminish Obama, but he does that to all his perceived enemies, no matter what color they are. And, as stated earlier, Trump's plan was to galvanize political support among Americans who disliked President Obama by demonizing him in a very personal way.

The birth certificate.

Here is backup for my assessment: If you study Donald Trump's public confrontations, they almost always devolve into personal insults: "Crooked Hillary," "Lyin' Ted (Cruz)," "Little Marco (Rubio)," that kind of thing.

Perhaps the best example of Donald Trump's slash-and-burn strategy occurred in December 2006, when Rosie O'Donnell, the cohost of *The View*, attacked Trump for berating a contestant in his Miss USA pageant. It seems Tara O'Connor, who won the competition, had some drug and alcohol skeletons that were brought to the public. Trump held a press conference saying O'Connor deserved a "second chance."

O'Donnell, who was once friends with Donald Trump, apparently didn't like that press conference and let Trump have it on national TV.

"And there he is, his hair looping, saying, 'Everyone deserves a second chance. I'm going to give her a second chance.' He's the moral authority? Left the first wife, had an affair. Left the second wife, had an affair. Had kids both times. But he's the moral authority for twenty-year-olds? Donald, sit and spin, my friend."

Almost immediately, Donald Trump threatened a lawsuit and blasted back.

"When Rosie talks about moral compass—what kind of moral compass does she have? I mean, just look at that face. Can you imagine her poor girlfriend having to kiss that every night? You can have her. I did something very nice for a very fine young lady. I gave her a second chance. Rosie O'Donnell didn't want me to give her a second chance. Of course, Rosie would like to spend a little time with her. That I can guarantee you."

Both Trump and O'Donnell are Caucasian, so race was not a factor here. But if Trump had spoken disparagingly of Whoopi Goldberg, it would have been. That I can guarantee you.

At this point, in 2006, I did not completely understand Donald

Trump's overall public demeanor. So, I invited him on my cable news program to discuss it in the context of Rosie O'Donnell.

O'REILLY: Listen to me for a minute. You are successful. You are smart. The Trump brand is the premier brand in America. There's no question about it. She goes on her program and smears and slimes you. She started it, not you.

TRUMP: She started it, I finished it.

O'REILLY: Well, you didn't finish it because it will go on. Why don't you just beat her intellectually? Why the personal stuff?

TRUMP: I've beaten her intellectually, Bill. She's easy to beat intellectually . . . look at her performance on *The View* today. She was a mess, she was nervous, she was fumbling, she was stumbling . . . Rosie was an absolute mess today, and you know why? Because she's concerned that I'm gonna sue her . . .

O'REILLY: But I'm saying to you that calling her Pig Face, getting into her sex life, these things—it doesn't make you look good.

TRUMP: Excuse me! She's allowed to make fun of my hair?

O'REILLY: That makes her look bad! Don't you understand that?

TRUMP: Excuse me, Bill. She's allowed to do that, but I shouldn't be doing it?

O'REILLY: . . . It makes her look terrible.

TRUMP: There are two types of people in this world: people that take it and people that don't take it. Rosie is a bully. Rosie was hit between the eyes . . .

O'REILLY: So, on the lawsuit, you can't win it and I'll tell you why, because you've got to prove damages, and you're not going to be able to prove that.

TRUMP: You know what, Bill. Don't be my lawyer . . .

O'REILLY: . . . Can I be your adviser? Don't do any more personal attacks . . . If you had just gone after her on the basis of what she said and just said, "Look, I'm not going to get in the gutter with Rosie O'Donnell," I think you would have won big here.

TRUMP: Except nobody would listen to that.

O'REILLY: **I would.**

TRUMP: . . . Nobody would listen to that. If I attack it on a purely intellectual level, which is essentially what I've done but using a little bit more venom. If I attack it on a purely intellectual basis, nobody would listen and the response would not have been nearly as effective.

There it is. You may want to read that last Trump answer again because it explains much about his thinking even while sitting in the White House. And he's not wrong. In America today, we the people are almost numb to controversy because there's one every ten seconds. Before almost anyone, Donald Trump understood that maulers win the debate, that harsh attacks get massive attention, that incendiary rhetoric rattles opponents.

That's what was behind the Trump birth certificate offensive. Trump wanted to establish himself as an anti-Obama person quickly. He wanted to tweak the president. It had nothing to do with skin color, in my opinion.

By the way, hurling insults is also how Donald Trump separated himself from the other sixteen people running for the Republican presidential nomination in 2015. Jeb Bush, at first the front-runner, was stunned by Trump's attacks on him and never recovered his verve.

Here's the truth: scorched-earth personal assaults work in the United States. They are unpleasant, uncharitable, and unseemly, but they work. We are a distracted people, but we'll focus when vitriol is flying.

Two further things on the Rosie O'Donnell incident. It would come back in a big way to haunt Donald Trump during the campaign.

And he never did file a lawsuit against the woman. Maybe he took my advice after all.

T T T

WHILE IT IS easy to comprehend exactly why Barack Obama does not approve of Donald Trump, the converse is harder to define. Before the birther business, President Obama did not have much to say about Trump. Why would he? Their paths were far apart.

So, it wasn't personal animus that drove Trump's disdain for Mr. Obama; it was politics, pure and simple. Donald Trump believes the former president is weak and, worst of all, a bad deal maker.

And in Trump world, there is nothing worse than a guy who gets the short end of a negotiation.

So, early in Barack Obama's first term, Donald Trump decided that if an untested senator could get elected president, Trump could accomplish that as well because he was smarter and tougher than Obama. All Trump had to do was marginalize the president and his party and then do the exact same thing to the Republicans who would run against him.

Rosie O'Donnell was the warm-up act. The main event would dwarf that.

Donald Trump's opinion of President Obama has been consistent: he believes the United States lost prestige all over the world and that Iran and China, in particular, took great advantage of Mr. Obama. He also thinks the economy was harmed by Barack Obama's income-redistribution policies. Finally, he knows he has nothing to lose by criticizing Obama because few who approve of him would ever support Trump.

However, an unwritten rule in history says that presidents should not attack other presidents. But there is certainly frost on the Obama-Trump pumpkin, that I can tell you. You can expect Barack Obama to do everything possible to see that President Trump is denied reelection in 2020.

T T T

AT THE WHITE House Correspondents' Association Dinner in 2015, President Obama once again had Donald Trump directly in his sights, as Trump sat just a few feet away. I remember feeling very alert as the president began his speech.

"There is one issue on every reporter's mind, and that is 2016. Already, we've seen some missteps.

"It turns out Jeb Bush identified himself as Hispanic back in 2009, which, you know, I understand. It's an innocent mistake. It reminds me of when I identified myself as American back in 1961.

"Ted Cruz said that denying the existence of climate change made him like Galileo. Now that's not really an apt comparison. Galileo believed the Earth revolves around the sun. Ted Cruz believes the Earth revolves around Ted Cruz.

"Meanwhile, Rick Santorum announced he would not attend the same-sex wedding of a friend or loved one. To which gays and lesbians across the country responded, 'That's not going to be a problem; don't sweat that one.'

"And Donald Trump is here. Still."

That was it about Trump. No further zingers. Just six words.

Mr. Obama then went on to say, "Anyway, it's amazing how time flies. Soon, the first presidential contest will take place, and I for one can't wait to see who the Koch brothers pick. It's exciting. Marco Rubio, Rand Paul, Ted Cruz, Jeb Bush, Scott Walker, who will finally get that red rose?"

No mention of Donald Trump as a possible contender for the White House. President Obama didn't seem to think it was possible. Nor did most of his adoring fans in the media.

But on that night in April 2015, Mr. Trump knew something that Barack Obama and the press did not know. He didn't need money to run for president. He didn't need Republican Party approval, either.

He had all he needed in the chair on which he was seated. He had guile and a game plan that would bring his message directly to the voters. He sensed many Americans were fed up with all the people inhabiting the vast ballroom of the Washington Hilton Hotel that evening—the "swamp" was dressed in tuxedos and gowns.

He also knew he was looked down upon in the room. Nobody had to tell him. But he believed he would soon wreak havoc upon the establishment that mocked and scorned him; that Barack Obama and his pals would soon learn the hard way that underestimating Donald Trump was not a good investment.

The reckoning was less than two months away.

CHAPTER SEVENTEEN

MANHASSET, NEW YORK

MARCH 17, 2019

8 P.M.

Before we chronicle Donald Trump's turbulent journey through the Republican primaries, including his confrontation with Megyn Kelly, it is important to understand the public speaking style he brought to his campaign—a style that motivated NBC to pay him tens of millions of dollars and then turn around in August 2015, when it was clear that Trump was finished with TV, and fire him for "derogatory" comments about Mexicans.

If you analyze what Mr. Trump says in public, you will see a clear pattern. He's a stream-of-consciousness kind of guy—that is, if a thought pops into his head, he says it. No filter. No concern about consequences. His verbal approach goes on steroids if Mr. Trump is speaking at a rally where the crowd is approving of what he is saying.

That kind of uninhibited presentation is usually associated with wealthy and powerful individuals who have less to lose than other people. However, in American politics, it is very unusual to hear provocative words about groups of people. Our politicians are almost always rehearsed, which is why few pay attention when they speak.

Here's a good example. Can you remember one thing that Hillary Clinton said in the 2016 campaign? Just one. Odds are you cannot, because I can't and I covered her. Mrs. Clinton took the usual liberal line, uttering vague generalities. As a result, her sound bites on TV and radio were sparse.

Donald Trump, on the other hand, was on the electronic media 24/7. And what he said was often so outrageous that the sound bite was played over and over. His dominance on TV and radio stemmed from the fact that he could say just about anything at any time—there was drama to his remarks.

Millions of Americans tuned into Trump's televised rallies to hear some bombast. And they always got it. Trump put on a verbal show unmatched in the history of presidential campaigns, that I can tell you.

In fact, Donald Trump made Andrew Jackson and Teddy Roosevelt look like Mister Rogers, rhetorically speaking.

Meanwhile, the TV networks didn't even bother broadcasting most Hillary speeches because few would have watched the dry proceedings.

But there was and is a major downside to shooting from the lip. Verbal mistakes and attacks on tape last forever. They can ambush you after decades of dormancy. Ask Tucker Carlson. The adage is "Everything you say can and will be used against you." Context and fairness have been effectively banished from media and partisan precincts. Social media, especially Twitter, has robbed the bank of accuracy. The loaded gun filled with out-of-context quotes is now pointed at every person in the political arena.

Donald Trump is a bold but undisciplined speaker. He talks too fast and, many times, does not finish his point, hopping to another thought in midsentence. His mind outraces his tongue.

That results in a joyful field day for his enemies, who can piece together sentence fragments from Trump to make him look villainous. This now happens almost every day.

Here are two very famous examples.

One of Mr. Trump's main political themes has been that the United States is damaged by a porous southern border. On the campaign trail he addressed this scores of times, sometimes overstating things, as he has a tendency to do.

It's kind of like the climate change people saying the world will soon collapse: hyperbole to get attention.

In his initial announcement of his candidacy on June 16, 2015, Donald Trump zeroed in on what he believes is a stark danger to public safety: violent foreign nationals who illegally enter the United States.

As the family of Kate Steinle found out after the thirty-two-year-old was killed in San Francisco by a Mexican who had been deported for crimes six times, this has become an acute problem in many parts of the country.

Candidate Trump promised to deal with the situation and used tough words to get his point across.

"When do we beat Mexico at the border? They're laughing at us, at our stupidity . . . The U.S. has become a dumping ground for everybody else's problems."

At this point, the crowd listening to Trump's speech cheers. This emboldens him as he continues: "It's true, and these are not the best and the finest. When Mexico sends its people, they're not sending their best. They're sending people who have lots of problems, and they're bringing those problems with them. They're bringing drugs. They're bringing crime. They're rapists. And some, I assume, are good people."

The "good people" line wasn't enough to mitigate the remarks. Donald Trump was immediately branded a racist for disparaging *all* Mexicans even though his words dealt with the crimes of some undocumented aliens, drug cartels, people smugglers, and corrupt Mexican officials. Those issues are real, but Trump lumped them all together in a generalized verbal stew and was immediately hammered by his enemies in the press.

Mr. Trump himself was surprised by the racist branding but did not back down. A few weeks later he objected to a Mexican American judge hearing one of his civil cases, as he felt the judge might be biased against him because of the June speech: not an illogical supposition. But it gave the anti-Trump forces even more ammunition, and the racist thing took hold in the media.

What Donald Trump does not seem to accept is that political correctness now dictates what can be said in America. If you generalize about a minority group in a negative way, you will be harshly punished. There is no explanation that will stop that. Corporations, in particular, will not tolerate any negativity toward minority people. Period.

Once racism was in play by the media, Donald Trump was on constant defense, a posture he does not like. Then came Charlottesville, Virginia.

TTT

ON SATURDAY, AUGUST 12, 2017, a group of white supremacists gathered to protest the proposed removal of a Robert E. Lee statue in the hometown of Thomas Jefferson and the University of Virginia. The diminishment of the Confederate general is an emotional topic in the South, and the exhibition that Saturday drew civilians engaged in the topic—as well as right-wing and left-wing extremists, some of whom had violent intentions.

The crowd numbered about two thousand. Some folks showed up simply to watch what might unfold, knowing that any demonstration featuring neo-Nazis could become explosive.

Others turned out to make their feelings known about the statue, both pro and con. They were not organized; they simply responded to a controversy in their area. Donald Trump is sympathetic to those who do not want historical statues replaced, believing that American history, both good and bad, should be on display.

Incredibly, despite the rally being so well publicized, the Charlottesville Police, along with the Virginia State Police, were poorly organized, and when violence began, they could not control the situation.

Horribly, one woman was fatally hit when a neo-Nazi purposely plowed his car into a crowd. Nineteen others were hurt in the fracas.

The White House, of course, was aware that the situation had quickly gotten out of control. President Trump's initial statement said this: "We condemn in the strongest possible terms this egregious display of hated, bigotry, and violence on *many sides*."

The use of the words "many sides" became a major problem because the media narrative was already established. The white supremacy movement had caused the violence. What was this "many sides" business? Yes, there were radical leftists on the scene looking for trouble, but so what? The Nazis were responsible.

Under severe media pressure, the president issued another statement to clarify: "Racism is evil. And those who cause violence in its name are criminals and thugs, including the KKK, neo-Nazis, white supremacists, and other hate groups that are repugnant to everything we hold dear as Americans."

Strong and specific words, but not enough for the Hate Trump media, which, again, was becoming increasingly invested in "the president is a racist" point of view.

Then Mr. Trump reignited the fuse. Answering some press questions, he ad-libbed this: "Excuse me, they didn't put themselves down as neo-Nazis. And you had some very bad people in that group. But you also had people that were very fine people on both sides. You had people in that group—excuse me, excuse me, I saw the same pictures you did—that were there to protest the taking down of [the Lee statue,] to them a very, very important statue and the renaming of a park from Robert E. Lee to another name."

Armageddon! "Fine people on both sides?" The media went wild. President Trump excusing racists, went the cry. *He's* a racist himself!

If you analyze the neo-Nazi part of the ad-lib, Mr. Trump was apparently trying to say that not all the pro-statue people were sympathetic to the fascists. Trump was attempting to make the point that not everyone present was a racist hater. But his ad-lib was garbled, not precise. And so, as with the Mexican immigrant remarks, he was figuratively hung by his tongue—as the racism brand surfaced again.

It is important to understand that the term *racist* has now been weaponized by the far left. It is thrown around to inflict harm. That is wrong. In a just society, the racist accusation should never be made unless there is evidence beyond a reasonable doubt. Many Americans who consume news are distracted and do not always understand the context of complicated statements. To some in the national media, there are no "fine people" in support of the Robert E. Lee statue. They are all racist if they hold that point of view. So, the president should have condemned them all, not endorsed their "fineness." But casual news consumers may not be aware of the overall Lee statue issue, thus confusion reigns.

And if anyone dared defend Mr. Trump, or even pointed out context, he or she risked being branded a racist as well.

To be fair, it is understandable why some black Americans and Mexican Americans might be suspicious of Donald Trump's mindset. He does not go out of his way to clarify statements that need more definition. In this explosive political time, words must be chosen carefully—or else.

I can state with certainty that Donald Trump did not believe he would be branded a racist when he sought the presidency. That was never in his mind. He actually believed the minority community would like him because he sought to improve the economy for all Americans.

To this day, Trump is perplexed by the racist label.

T T T

WHEN HE BEGAN his presidential campaign on that June afternoon, the media were paramount in Donald Trump's vision. In the past, Trump had manipulated the media better than anyone else ever had—and now he had a plan.

His initial read of the nation's press was simple, smart, and surgical. He knew he had to get his message out. And he also understood that would happen only if he were ultra-provocative.

So it is that Donald J. Trump embarked on a presidential campaign that would eventually stun the world. He was locked and loaded. No prisoners would be taken.

On paper, Trump's rhetorical shock-and-awe strategy looked effective—especially because most of his competitors were cautious.

But Donald Trump did not anticipate one important thing: there are no rules for the press anymore. And in the free-fire zone that developed, Donald Trump would become a major media moving target.

CHAPTER EIGHTEEN

NEW YORK CITY

JUNE 15, 2015

AFTERNOON

Donald Trump knows television. He watches TV news all the time and has been a genuine TV star himself. So, on the first day of his campaign for president, it is television that he seeks out.

Specifically, *The O'Reilly Factor*, on the Fox News Channel.

Trump is acutely aware that *The Factor* is the highest-rated cable news presentation in America, often reaching more than five million viewers for its two airings at 8 and 11 Eastern Time. He also believes that many *Factor* viewers will be receptive to his message. There is, however, one problem. The guy in the anchor chair is unpredictable. He could ask anything. He once called Congressman Barney Frank a liar on the air.

So, speaking before the taped interview begins, Trump jokingly tells Bill O'Reilly, your humble correspondent, to "take it easy on me."

To which I reply, "Why would I do that?"

Donald Trump is fascinated by success in all fields. His friend the late George Steinbrenner was like that, too. And Trump thinks about why people succeed; he actually studies achievement in the most competitive industries.

But what Donald Trump does not know that June afternoon is that the press is drastically changing. The rise of social media is devastating the newspaper industry because readers can now access information on their smartphones. Television and radio are losing younger audiences to video games and incessant texting. Broadcast outlets are becoming desperate for people to watch them, so new strategies are being employed.

One of those strategies will bring huge success to Donald Trump.

In order to cut through all the high-tech clutter and texting distraction, TV personalities now have to take chances and say outrageous things, at least sometimes, if they want to get noticed.

If you do that, you will get attention, and for a politician, that may lead to votes. If you don't do that, TV executives will largely ignore you because you don't pull in viewers, which are tabulated by daily ratings called "numbers."

Donald Trump's unspoken media strategy in his quest for the White House is to dominate television news and avoid the print press as much as possible. He knows that most of his Republican opponents are absolutely clueless about the media and that his likely Democratic opponent, if he secures the nomination, Hillary Clinton, generally despises TV news. Secretary Clinton feels comfortable only when she's controlling the situation and rarely does or says anything spontaneous.

Trump believes he is a commanding presence who generates good TV ratings. And he is absolutely correct about that.

But what Donald Trump does not anticipate leading up to his campaign kickoff is the intense media backlash that will soon develop. That will shock him.

However, during the first few months of the campaign, Trump will manipulate the TV news outlets in a way never before seen in America. Cable news will become one giant *Donald Trump Show*. And it all begins in a Trump Tower office looking out over Fifth Avenue.

T T T

FROM THE BEGINNING of his presidential quest, Donald Trump really had little to lose, and that's one of the main reasons he won. Unlike most politicians, Trump does not play scared. He lets it fly. Not particularly interested in verbal accuracy, Trump primarily wants reactions from his audience. If people don't accept him in the political role—hey, so what? His brand is everywhere. He can keep his day job.

As I prepared to interview candidate Trump, I did not think he had a chance to secure the Republican nomination. But I knew Donald Trump would make my daily life as a political commentator much easier, and was beyond pleased that he had given me the first interview. Trump was great copy, as they say in the newspaper world. Millions of folks would watch the interview and help my task, which was to stay atop the ratings. And there would be many more Trump stories to come.

As long as Donald Trump remained in the race, life would be good for TV news. Anything might be said, anything could happen. The one trouble spot was Trump's ego. As an interviewer, you have to control the candidate, or he will dominate the screen, reducing you to cabbage.

My style on television is confrontational. I brook no nonsense from anyone, especially hustling politicians. So, just before Donald Trump and I sat down to tape in mid-afternoon, I had already written the introduction that I would say later that evening on the air.

We would open the show with Trump speaking to an adoring crowd in his own building: "Ladies and gentlemen, I am officially running for president of the United States. And we are going to make America great again!"

Yay.

Then, from my anchor chair, I would deliver this: "Along with that announcement, the sixty-nine-year-old Trump released his net worth today—about nine billion dollars. He spoke for the better part of an hour, basically saying that current politicians are wimps who will never solve the intense problems America has. Trump says he can solve them . . ."

After that lead-in, we would begin the interview, which, again, had been taped a few hours earlier.

Speaking with powerful people on TV is like a prizefight. You have to measure your subject, jab a bit before the hard shot. I assumed Donald Trump had some rehearsed answers, but he rarely stays on script, especially if you rattle him. Other politicians—Jeb Bush is a good example—will never deviate from their preplanned words. So boring.

I began casually with Trump.

O'REILLY: **How are you going to defeat ISIS?**

TRUMP: **I would hit them so hard. I would find a general. I would find the Patton or the MacArthur. I would hit them so hard your head would spin.**

O'REILLY: **Are you telling me that you're going to send American ground troops into Syria [where ISIS was basing]?**

TRUMP: **I'm not telling you anything. And the reason I'm not . . . is because I don't want them to know the game plan.**

Clever answer to a provocative question—another ground war in the Middle East would rattle many Americans. Donald Trump parried the query well and never deviated from his answer—I'm not "tipping off the enemy."

But he was not tipping off the voters, either.

Then I turned to the Russian leader Putin, a source of angst for President Obama.

O'REILLY: **What do you do to Putin?**

TRUMP: **Putin has no respect for our president whatsoever. He's got a tremendous popularity in Russia. They love what he's doing, they love what he represents. So, we have a president who is absolutely—you look at them; the chemistry is so bad between those two people. I was over in Moscow two years ago, and I will tell you we can get along with those people and get along with them well. You can make deals with those people. Obama can't.**

O'REILLY: **So, you can make a deal with Putin to stop his expansionism?**

TRUMP: I would be willing to bet I would have a great relationship with Putin. It's about leadership.

O'REILLY: Based on what?

TRUMP: Based on a feel, okay? You know, deals are people.

O'REILLY: You sound like George W. Bush. He looked into Putin's soul and said he was a good guy. Come on.

TRUMP: Bush didn't have the IQ.

Again, Trump simply says he's going to make a deal with Putin. Period. End of discussion. He'll do it. That effectively kills follow-up questions, unless you want to ride a rhetorical merry-go-round.

Pretty brilliant when you think about it. No details on ISIS; he'll just get them. No specifics on Putin; he'll secure deals.

Let's go home.

But not yet. Sensing that he was getting overconfident, I pounced on Trump's promise that he would build a wall on the southern border and that Mexico would pay for it.

O'REILLY: I actually laughed when you said you're going to build this giant wall from San Diego to Brownsville and the Mexicans are going to pay for it. The Mexicans are not going to pay for the wall.

TRUMP: Let me tell you, the Mexicans are the new China. What they are doing to this country . . .

O'REILLY: [interrupting] They're not going to pay for the wall.

TRUMP: You have to let me handle that, okay?

O'REILLY: Well, how are you going to make them pay?

TRUMP: Because they are ripping us off so badly. Okay, I'll tell you.

O'REILLY: Tell me.

TRUMP: I'll start charging them for their products coming into this country. Mexico is living off the United States.

O'REILLY: So, you try to strangle them economically unless they pay for the wall.

TRUMP: They will pay, the wall will go up, and Mexico will start behaving.

THE UNITED STATES OF TRUMP

The interview was classic Trump: confident, dismissive of skepticism, combative all the time.

As president, Mr. Trump did handle ISIS well, but he has been haunted by Putin and Russia. Also, the wall remains elusive.

Wrapping up Donald Trump's first campaign interview, I asked about his political opponents.

O'REILLY: Final question, your Republican rivals. They're going to come after you.

TRUMP: It's okay.

O'REILLY: You don't really take criticism all that well. You lash back.

TRUMP: Yeah, I lash back. Why wouldn't I lash back?

O'REILLY: The president is supposed to have some kind of elevation, where you overlook some things. You're not real good at that.

TRUMP: I get things done better than anybody.

O'REILLY: Are you going to slash and burn through the Republican field?

TRUMP: Well, I don't have a lot of respect for many of them . . . Honestly, Bill, I won't be the nicest. I'm not going to slash them. I'm going to be honest. They don't have it.

O'REILLY: Are you going to look Jeb Bush in the eye and say, "You're this, you're that"?

TRUMP: Sure, I'm not a big fan of Jeb Bush. The last thing we need is another Bush, believe me.

O'REILLY: So, you're going to slash and burn.

TRUMP: This country—if we have another politician including Hillary, this country is going down.

T T T

THE RATINGS FOR that interview were enormous. Every network now wanted Trump as much as possible because he was taking viewers away from their electronic devices and bringing them back to the tube.

Trump understood that. He also knew it was all about him, just as he likes it, and just as he planned. In fact, the Trump mania became so pronounced that the very liberal CNN and MSNBC networks even started broadcasting his rallies.

No other Republican candidate got that kind of exposure, not even close.

As Trump brought in high ratings, which translated directly into advertising dollars, the other sixteen Republican hopefuls became media afterthoughts.

My program actually tried to get Jeb Bush on to reply to Donald Trump. But he was too busy the next day, and the day after that and the day after that . . .

It was incredible—the neophyte Trump was climbing in the polls, and some of his rivals were turning down national interviews. Meanwhile, Trump was making TV news great again as viewers poured in to watch him verbally annihilate someone or something.

The Donald was everywhere. It was like a nonstop Jerry Lewis telethon. Every day, Donald J. Trump was in your living room having his way with the national television media. He was ready to rumble and good to go.

That initial media blitz lasted almost eight long summer weeks, until the first Republican debate in Cleveland, Ohio.

Little did candidate Trump know what awaited him on that night, because there was no hint, and no way to prepare.

But suddenly a major campaign obstacle appeared. And her name was Megyn.

CHAPTER NINETEEN

CLEVELAND, OHIO

AUGUST 6, 2015

EARLY EVENING

The ambush is set. Ten men working to gain the Republican presidential nomination stand on a stage at the Quicken Loans Arena, anticipating debate questions from three Fox News journalists. The politicians are aware that basketball superstar LeBron James usually patrols this vast building, and they can only hope to score like he does.

It will not happen.

This is the first of twelve Republican debates—and the most anticipated, because one Donald J. Trump is standing tall in front of myriad television cameras. Since June, Trump has been pounding home his message that America is in serious trouble and that it's all because of career politicians.

Now those political people have a chance to verbally challenge Donald Trump, and twenty-four million Americans have tuned in to watch the cage match, the largest cable news audience in history.

Trump fears no one on the stage. He is certain he can out-talk all of them, and as he has stated, there is no other candidate that has impressed him.

In addition, there is a large pro-Trump crowd in the arena. He gets the loudest ovation when introduced this Thursday evening. That bolsters his confidence.

Jeb Bush, the former governor of Florida, is considered the Republican front-runner at this point. He did well managing his state for eight years, especially reworking the public school system and keeping taxes low. But the governor has two problems as he stands next to Trump on the debate stage: first, he is dull; and second, his brother's presidency was stigmatized by the Iraq invasion fiasco.

Donald Trump will hammer Jeb Bush on both those things.

Senators Ted Cruz, Marco Rubio, and Rand Paul do not have national profiles, so Trump does not see them as much of a threat. Cruz is ultraconservative, Rubio more moderate, and Paul a contrarian libertarian. Of the three, only Marco Rubio of Florida has breakout potential, because of his youth and ethnicity.

New Jersey governor Chris Christie is glib and aggressive, so Donald Trump knows he has to parry him quickly if it comes to that. Wisconsin governor Scott Walker is similar to Jeb Bush: not much charisma. Former Arkansas governor Mike Huckabee is smart, and so is pundit Ben Carson, but polling shows that neither of the two has a constituency, although Carson is beginning to move up.

Finally, Ohio governor John Kasich turned his state around economically and accomplished many positive things in Columbus. But he's wonkish and earnest, a hard sell in a nation dominated by emotional thinking and short attention spans.

So, Donald Trump is feeling strong on this humid August night. Unlike most of the other candidates, he has not pored over research papers or even rehearsed. He has his debate rap down, and it goes this way:

- President Obama is a disaster, a weak leader who does not stand up for America.
- Hillary Clinton is no different from Obama, except she's more corrupt.

- Jeb Bush is soft on illegal immigration, which is a grave threat to the nation.
- And all the others could never run a "great company" like Trump does or make great deals for Americans.

With those things ready to go, Trump is anxious to let it fly. He is a bit nervous but will not show a trace of it.

Directly facing the ten Republicans are Fox News moderators Bret Baier, Chris Wallace, and Megyn Kelly. They were chosen by their boss, Roger Ailes, for various reasons.

Baier is the face of Fox News Channel's hard news operation, anchoring a daily one-hour program that is efficient and honest. He is also "safe." That means he will not do or say anything that might raise some hell.

Chris Wallace, the son of the legendary CBS newsman Mike Wallace, has the pedigree and intelligence to make the debate a smooth flow. He is a prestige person at Fox News.

The third interrogator, Megyn Kelly, is the wild card. She is by far Fox News's most glamorous personality and an attorney to boot. She has worked her way up at Fox from Supreme Court correspondent, to morning co-anchor, to afternoon solo host, to prime-time anchor following my program at nine o'clock.

Many in the media loathe Fox News because of its conservative bias, but Megyn Kelly generally gets good press. In fact, a few years back, GQ magazine, very sympathetic to the left, would feature Kelly in a steamy pictorial—an unheard-of occurrence for a national newswoman. The incident caught Fox News brass by surprise, but nothing happened to Kelly publicly; by then, she had become a huge star.

Roger Ailes selected Megyn Kelly as one of the debate people because Fox needed a woman journalist on the panel, and he knew that Megyn had the ear of the Murdochs, who own Fox News. She was what they call in the entertainment business the "It girl." She had access to the very top of the corporation—a rarity for an employee.

Of course, all the high-profile anchors at Fox News wanted to work the debate. In twenty years, I was never selected, but I think my pitch to Ailes was somewhat unique. It went something like this:

"So, why don't you shock the world and let me ask the questions? Come on, you know 80 percent of what the candidates say is BS. I'll cut that down to 10 percent by calling them on it."

"No."

"Why not?"

"Because we'd like to host another debate sometime this century."

Roger Ailes was implying that my questioning would discourage candidates from showing up.

Could that possibly be true?

In truth, I understood. Ailes was not a politically correct guy, but he was a businessman. FNC ownership wanted Kelly, and they got her.

Actually, the two most qualified journalists at Fox to moderate the debate were Brit Hume and Charles Krauthammer. I would have turned it confrontational; they would have kept it informational.

Megyn Kelly chose my path.

The behind-the-scenes prep for any debate is intense. The moderators usually do much more homework than the candidates. With three people asking questions, there has to be a division of labor. All hands have to know what's on deck to avoid redundancy and confusion.

So, you have a battery of producers dividing up questions among the moderators and deciding to whom each question will be directed. At this point, things can get testy. When you have three ambitious journalists, everyone wants significant airtime and to ask questions of specific candidates. Baier, Wallace, and Kelly knew that all eyes would be on Trump—that was the zone where news would be made.

Fox News Channel debate prep had been a three-week process. From the beginning, there was tension between Kelly and the men. She knew she was a prime-time queen, and was in no mood to be a team player. Baier, Wallace, and the producers were tentative around Megyn, knowing how much power she had within the organization.

Shortly before the debate began, a decision was made to have each moderator quiz the candidates on their "vulnerabilities"—that is, their weak points.

Kelly wanted Trump.

Kelly got Trump.

That decision was not political in any way. The consensus about Kelly was that she did not care much about ideology. She was not a political party person. Her focus was primarily on herself.

And, by extension, on Donald Trump.

T T T

THE DEBATE OPENED with a few questions of little consequence, the candidates and moderators feeling each other out.

Then, in what would become one of the most famous political debate moments of all time, Megyn Kelly suddenly morphed from a journalist into a prosecutor. Her voice firm, her eyes locked on candidate Trump, she commanded the room.

KELLY: Mr. Trump, one of the things people love about you is that you speak your mind and you don't use a politician's filter. However, that is not without its downsides, in particular, when it comes to women. You've called women you don't like "fat pigs," "dogs," "slobs," and "disgusting animals." Your Twitter account—

TRUMP: Only Rosie O'Donnell.

KELLY: No, it wasn't. For the record, it was well beyond Rosie O'Donnell.

TRUMP: (sarcastically) Yes, I'm sure it was.

KELLY: Your Twitter account has several disparaging comments about women's looks. You once told a contestant on *Celebrity Apprentice* it would be a pretty picture to see her on her knees. Does that sound to you like the temperament of a man we should elect as president? And how will you answer the charge from Hillary Clinton, who is likely to be the Democratic nominee, that you are part of the war on women?

TRUMP: I think the big problem this country has is being politically correct. I've been challenged by so many people, and I don't frankly have time for total political correctness. And to be honest with you, this country doesn't have time, either. The country is in big trouble. We don't win anymore. We lose to China. We lose to

Mexico, both in trade and at the border. We lose to everybody. And frankly, what I say—and oftentimes it's fun, it's kidding; we have a good time. What I say is what I say, and honestly, Megyn, if you don't like it, I'm sorry. I've been very nice to you, although I could probably maybe not be, based on the way you've treated me. But I wouldn't do that.

▼▼▼

THE REST OF the debate unfolded with no candidate standing out. However, Donald Trump spoke the most, clocking in at ten minutes, thirty-two seconds. Jeb Bush was next, at eight minutes, thirty seconds. The other eight candidates barely had enough time to introduce themselves. It was clear that the Fox News crew believed Trump and Bush were the front-runners, with Cruz and Rubio second tier.

Megyn Kelly whispers to Chris Wallace, her fellow Fox News moderator, during the first Republican presidential primary debate, at the Quicken Loans Arena in Cleveland, August 6, 2015. Looking on from the stage are candidates Donald Trump and Jeb Bush, the former governor of Florida.

That first showdown in Cleveland was the most discussed of the twelve debates, and by far the most dramatic with the Trump-woman component.

T T T

IF YOU WATCH the video of the Kelly-Trump interaction, a few things emerge. Kelly's tone is accusatory, not inquisitive. She had a perfect right to pose that kind of provocative question to a politician, but there was an advocacy to her query, and the words "war on women" are instructive.

What war on women? That has not been established as fact—it's an opinion. So, Kelly linking Donald Trump to a subjective point of view he might not agree with could be considered unfair and biased against him.

Megyn Kelly's question was obviously deeply researched and painstakingly written out. It was clearly not designed to have Trump explain anything. Rather, the question was the classic "gotcha" query, a journalistic hand grenade that could not be challenged because Mr. Trump had, indeed, used pejorative language toward some women. But under what circumstances? The potential voter could not possibly know.

In her multifaceted question, Kelly did not provide any context for her litany of verbal accusations against Trump; nor did she frame her words in any other way but as condemnation.

It might be argued that Kelly wanted to be perceived as holding a brutish man responsible for verbally assaulting a number of unidentified females, rather than trying to elicit an important response from a presidential candidate. Her tone starkly implied that women were "victims" of candidate Trump and that she, in virtue, was calling him on it.

Subsequently, Megyn Kelly advanced that "protector of women" theme on many occasions against many men, in effect, becoming a one-person media judge and jury.

Because of Kelly's challenge and her insinuation that Donald Trump was irresponsible toward women, the candidate faced the issue throughout the campaign. His enemies, often militant anti-Trump

lawyers, besieged him with accusations, which the press then gleefully exploited.

Even when it was proved that some women were paid to accuse
Donald Trump of wrongdoing, the theme continued; Trump was dis-
respectful to women, and no female should ever vote for him.

It is worth noting that a few weeks later, Mr. Trump would actually
increase the gender pressure on himself by making fun of candidate
Carly Fiorina's face. Months after that, a video was made public in
which Donald Trump was caught describing his awful conduct toward
women. Later, we will chronicle that story in these pages.

On this debate night, Megyn Kelly's question could, of course,
have been much shorter and delivered in a far more objective way.

For example: "Mr. Trump, in the past you have publicly insulted
some women by mocking their appearances. Do you regret doing
that, especially because you are now seeking the highest of office in
the land?"

Very tough question but not nearly as provocative as the one
Megyn Kelly put forth. Also, depending on how Trump answered,
follow-up questions could have more clearly exposed his attitude
toward civil discourse when discussing women.

For his part, Donald Trump stayed cool on the debate stage, but
he was angered. He attempted to deflect the question as a trifle compared to the big problems facing the country. But then he got personal, his annoyance toward Kelly becoming obvious.

As a high-profile anchor at Fox News, I instantly knew that the
media would be asking me about the debate controversy, as it was
the story emerging from the telecast.

Although I thought Megyn's tone was harsh and calculated to
bring attention to herself, in my opinion, the woman question was
a legitimate one. However, nuance would never be reported by the
press, which basically wanted to create trouble for Fox News and
Donald Trump. Anything I opined would be used in a harmful way,
no matter how well thought-out it was.

So, I decided to say nothing, a rarity for me, until I told candidate Trump on the air that Kelly's question was within journalistic bounds. Apparently, Megyn took offense that I did not use my

program to immediately support her, and she was not shy about stating that on many occasions.

Speaking for FNC, Roger Ailes publicly stood by Megyn Kelly, but the backstory is fascinating and did have a direct effect on the presidential campaign.

The day after the debate, Kelly was lionized by the liberal media but condemned by many conservatives. Overnight, she became a polarizing figure. Trump supporters loudly criticized Megyn, and a good number of those folks watch Fox News. So, even as Megyn was being worshiped in the anti-Trump precincts, there was trouble in Fox News City.

Later, the *New York Times* and others would speculate, using Kelly's 2016 book *Settle for More* as a source, that there had been "collusion" before the debate between Megyn Kelly and Fox News management on the Trump question. That is false.

On debate night, Roger Ailes and his wife, Beth, were watching the telecast in their Cresskill, New Jersey, home. According to Mrs. Ailes, as Megyn Kelly began reciting the list of offenses she assigned to Trump, the Fox News chairman bolted upright and said, "What the f*** is that? I can't believe she's doing that!"

Ailes spent much of the night and all of the next day fielding calls about the situation. One of those calls was from Donald Trump.

The Fox News boss also made some calls himself—one of them was to debate producer Bill Sammon. Ailes was furious over the Kelly question because it was making his life a living hell.

T T T

THERE HAS BEEN so much false stuff written about Fox News that it actually rivals the inaccuracies stated about Donald Trump. Agenda-driven writers rarely tell the truth, and it is important that Americans understand that.

Maverick journalist Hunter S. Thompson did state the truth about journalism more than forty years ago: "There are a lot of ways to practice the art of journalism, and one of them is to use your art like a hammer to destroy the right people . . . who usually deserve to be crippled because they are wrong."

Thompson's statement sums up the attitude of "advocacy" news agencies. They were small and rare when he was reporting in the 1970s and '80s; now they are common. Corporations well understand that millions of Americans want their political and social opinions reinforced in the media. So, many folks choose to consume news from ideological operations, and there are vast amounts of money to be made from those slanted presentations.

If an information outlet clearly defines its point of view, there should not be a beef. The consumer then knows what he or she is getting. But when a newspaper like the *New York Times* markets itself as an unbiased news provider, the entire industry is severely damaged. Nonliberals will not get a fair hearing in the *Times.* Or at CNN. Or at MSNBC. Or at the *Washington Post*—and there are plenty of others. In fact, all those agencies have used their power to "get" certain individuals, Donald Trump being one of them.

When he began his quest for the presidency, Trump naïvely thought he could win over some media people to his cause. Fox News was among that group.

But Roger Ailes, having a close relationship with the Bush family, initially favored Jeb Bush. Ailes, however, rarely imposed his belief system on his employees, understanding that is dangerous for any news executive to do.

In my twenty-plus years at FNC, neither Ailes nor anyone else even suggested a political point of view to me.

It was known within the organization that Roger Ailes did not believe President Obama's policies had been successful, but while tough on Mr. Obama at times, FNC did not push any of the Republican candidates, allowing the GOP chips to fall where they might.

TTT

THE DAY AFTER the Kelly-Trump shootout, Friday, August 7, 2015, Roger Ailes was driving with his teenage son to Gettysburg, Pennsylvania, for a tour of the Civil War battlefield.

Ailes had spent the morning trying to figure out how to handle the Kelly controversy. First, he believed that no one in Fox News management knew in advance that Megyn was going to drop a verbal bomb on Donald Trump. Then the question becomes: Did Bret Baier, Chris Wallace, and their producers know in advance and not tell management?

Within Fox News headquarters, the word was that Kelly's question was discussed among the moderators, but no one called Roger Ailes about it. Apparently, there was also some discussion about the ramifications of Kelly confronting candidate Trump, but everyone knew that Megyn Kelly was not subject to the same rules that governed most FNC employees. So, in effect, she was on her own if she tossed the Molotov cocktail.

As chairman of Fox News, Ailes knew he had to support Megyn Kelly, or the press, hostile to FNC in general, would crush the organization. A news agency simply cannot side with a political candidate over a handpicked debate moderator because it would lose all credibility.

So, when candidate Trump's call came in to Roger Ailes as he sat in the backseat of a car with his son, the conversation was strained. Ailes had known Donald Trump for years, and the two men went at it. Trump's position was that Megyn Kelly had purposely embarrassed him, and that Ailes should scold her publicly.

Ailes replied that this was not possible but that he would speak with her in private. Donald Trump said that that was not acceptable and that he would no longer deal with FNC.

That scenario was related to me by Roger himself, who was agitated by the entire situation. I told him that Trump needed Fox News and that he would eventually cool down.

I was half right, as we will see.

After the first debate, few political analysts really knew how the American public would react, including me. We had to wait for polling to indicate how much, if any, damage had been done to Donald Trump by Megyn Kelly.

We didn't have to wait long.

CHAPTER TWENTY

NEW YORK CITY

AUGUST 18, 2015

EARLY EVENING

Donald Trump is back. Eleven days after threatening to declare war on Fox News over the Megyn Kelly incident, the candidate sits in his Trump Tower office feeling very confident before his interview with me on the Fox News Channel.

That's because a number of post-debate polls have rolled in showing Mr. Trump with a commanding lead among likely Republican voters, even after the Kelly question and some controversial comments by the candidate afterward.

The consensus polling has Trump at 24 percent, Jeb Bush at just 13 percent, and Ben Carson rising to 9 percent.

It looks like the Kelly thing actually *helped* candidate Trump in the polls.

It is clear Governor Bush is in trouble, even though there is no single reason that his campaign has not caught on. Bush has plenty of money, but, inexplicably, he avoids TV programs like mine, where he could get free airtime and mix it up a little.

But he's Dr. No, almost every time we call.

In contrast, Donald Trump is everywhere. The guy would do *Chiller Theatre* if he thought he could get a few votes. And there are plenty of invitations because, as stated, Trump brings in viewers.

But my analysis zeros in on another reason the TV moguls are courting Donald Trump. The feeling among many in the Manhattan media precincts is that Hillary Clinton is a lock for the Democratic nomination. The topic is discussed openly in the saloons off Sixth Avenue, where many press people slake their thirst.

The prevailing wisdom is that Bernie Sanders has a following but that Mrs. Clinton has the liberal donor class, and the fix is in. The so-called "superdelegates," who are allowed to vote any way they want at the convention, will go big for the former secretary of state.

And that is exactly what will happen.

But the fix extends far beyond party politics. Some media decision makers, such as CNN chief Jeff Zucker, a former friend of Donald Trump, enjoy cake, eating it, and digesting the sweet while shaping the presidential race. Zucker knows Trump is great for his network's ratings, but he also believes Hillary Clinton will annihilate Trump in the general election, a satisfying outcome for the very liberal Zucker and other media poohbahs who see it the same way.

So, "let's get Trump on" becomes the mantra of the TV news industry. "We win both ways because he'll never beat Hillary, while Marco Rubio just might."

While preparing for the interview with Trump this evening, I have to decide whether to ask him about Megyn Kelly. A few days after the first debate, the candidate called me at home and vented about Kelly. He wanted my opinion, but all I said was that the question had been legit. I did not criticize Kelly because I don't do the behind-the-back stuff. I did tell Mr. Trump that I would have asked the question differently but did not define it further. Luckily, Trump was so fixated on chastising Megyn that he didn't ask.

In addition, Fox News was still hearing from angry viewers, and Roger Ailes wanted the situation to recede. I understood that if I shot it out on the air with Trump over Megyn Kelly, something the candidate would relish, it would blow the entire thing up again.

Roger had been good to me, so I decided to avoid the Megyn subject entirely, even though no one suggested that I do so. Looking back, I think I made the right decision.

Kelly aside, it was clear to me that Donald Trump was gaining support by hammering two selected groups: illegal aliens, especially those convicted of crimes; and violent Muslims.

I already had Trump on the record about radical Islam when he briefly explored running for president in 2010.

O'REILLY: Do you believe, overall, there is a Muslim problem in the world?

TRUMP: There is a Muslim problem, absolutely. You just have to turn on your television set.

O'REILLY: And you think it encompasses all Muslims?

TRUMP: No, and that's the sad part about life, because you have fabulous Muslims. I know many Muslims, and they're fabulous people . . . Unfortunately, at this moment in time, there is a Muslim problem in the world. And you know it, and I know it, but some people don't like saying it because they think it's not politically correct.

O'REILLY: Why doesn't the Muslim community throughout the world speak out more forcefully against the jihadists?

TRUMP: Well, there's something that brings a level of hostility that I've never seen in any religion. You can say what you want about the Koran, there's something there. There's a tremendous hatred of us.

Donald Trump has never wavered from that belief, one that his core supporters have applauded time and time again.

Likewise with regard to the millions of foreign nationals who have entered the United States illegally over the years. Candidate Trump is calling for a tough policy to be imposed on that front.

So that's where we began on a mid-August night in 2015.

O'REILLY: The *[Wall Street] Journal* says you're killing the Republican Party over immigration. And you say?

TRUMP: We have to bring our country back, Bill. We're in big trouble. We're losing so much. We have at least eleven million illegals in the country. Not only the jobs are taken, but everything else. And you know about the crime wave because I think no one has covered the crime wave better than you . . . We've spent 113 billion dollars on illegal immigrants. We have to do something about it, and we have to start by building a wall. A big beautiful wall. A big beautiful, powerful wall. It can have a gate; it can have a door; we'll let people in legally. But we have to stop what's happening to our country because we're losing our country!

T T T

THERE IT IS—"WE'RE losing our country."

Although I did not know it when Trump used that phrase on my program, there, clearly stated, was his key to the White House kingdom. "They are taking away our country!"

Of course, "they" are the cowardly politicians, disapproving journalists, and the politically correct, bleeding heart Hillary backers.

Us. Them. Who are you with?

No other Republican candidate had a theme that came close.

Let's see. Would the crowd respond to a new Medicaid proposal or a strong threat against jihad?

Would voters rally to Jeb Bush's educational theories, or to Trump denying "bad" people entry to the United States?

While the supercilious media looked down on Trump's populist words, the folks heard them loud and clear. Here was a candidate who spoke straight and was sick of politics as usual—just as they were. What did President Obama do for them in eight years other than force a confusing new health care system down their collective throats? Where was the opportunity for working people? Why was it always politically correct groups that received support?

Wages were stagnant, new jobs scant, foreign nationals all over the place, and ISIS was beheading people on video.

And Megyn Kelly was worried about Donald Trump calling far-left radical Rosie O'Donnell a pig? Come on.

A tidal wave was beginning that August night. I felt it while looking into the camera asking candidate Trump questions. The folks were responding to blunt talk and specific ideas that sounded good: a wall on the border, payback to radical Muslims, getting tough with China.

Most important, tens of millions of Americans sincerely believed they were, indeed, losing their country, and at last there had appeared a presidential candidate who agreed with them. This wasn't John McCain or Mitt Romney, establishment politicians who allowed an articulate Barack Obama to roll over them. Donald Trump would never stand for that, his supporters thought. After all, he went after Obama hard with the birth certificate!

From my vantage point, Dr. Jekyll–Trump had found a magic formula and was just beginning to figure out how to turn himself into a political Mr. Hyde.

And if you and Robert Louis Stevenson were paying attention, it was clear that transformation was developing quickly.

T T T

PERHAPS THE FIRST appearance of Mr. Hyde–Trump on the campaign trail came the day after the Kelly-Trump confrontation, on Friday, August 7. Speaking on CNN, a still teed-off candidate Trump related how he observed Megyn Kelly as she was asking the "woman" question during the debate.

"You could see she had blood coming out of her eyes, blood coming out of . . . wherever," Donald Trump told an interviewer.

The outcry was immediate. Trump's rivals scorched him, and other Republicans said he was now an unacceptable candidate. Liberal democrats, of course, were beyond crazed.

Although Trump quickly issued a statement saying that the word *wherever* had meant her "nose," not anything to do with the menstrual cycle, women's groups went wild with condemnation.

If Donald Trump had been a corporate employee, he likely would have been fired immediately. The hue and cry was deafening.

But Mr. Trump was not an employee. He answered to no one—not even to fund-raisers, as he was financing much of his campaign with his own money. The last person Donald Trump had ever deferred to was his father, Fred. And that was a long time ago.

However, candidate Trump did have to consider the court of public opinion, and he did not know how the debate and the bitter comment about Megyn Kelly afterward was going to play out.

The polls clearly answered that question: Trump remained well ahead in the Republican field.

That was a turning point for candidate Trump. He began to understand that his in-your-face presentation was actually inoculating him against bad press and pressure groups. The more outrageous his rhetoric, the firmer his supporters stood by him. Modern politics had never seen anything like this. It was almost as if Don Rickles were running for president.

Assessing his unique situation, Donald Trump decided that he would never apologize for anything. That would show weakness. In fact, going forward in the campaign, Trump would step up the insults. They received massive attention and, apparently, buoyed his strongman image.

So, he let them fly.

T T T

IT IS NO accident that Andrew Jackson is one of Donald Trump's favorite presidents. If someone insulted the southerner, Jackson might actually shoot them. Our seventh president actually participated in a number of duels, killing at least one man and getting shot in the chest himself. Jackson carried that piece of lead in his body until he died.

Andrew Jackson believed that if someone insulted him, that person should pay a price. Donald Trump adheres to that point of view as well.

So, candidate Trump injected invective into the race for president. Here are a few examples:

After falling behind Ben Carson in a poll taken in Iowa, Trump insulted the state when he tweeted: "Too much Monsanto in the Corn Creates Issues in the Brain?"

He branded Senator Rubio "Sweaty Marco."

He branded Senator Cruz "Lyin' Ted."

He branded Senator Elizabeth Warren "Pocahontas."

Trump tweeted this about Jeb Bush: "[He] has to like the Mexican illegals because of his wife" (who is Latina).

He tweeted that Charles Krauthammer was "one of the worst and most boring pundits on television."

He said MSNBC personality Mika Brzezinski was "bleeding badly from a face-lift."

Well, I guess all the invective is better than shooting people—like Jackson did.

The historically interesting thing here is that the insults are part of a strategy: Never be boring. Always go on offensive. It really doesn't matter what you say as long as it gets attention.

During World War II, the adage was "Loose lips sink ships."

In Trump's war of attrition to win the presidency, that adage was changed to a quote from *The Untouchables*: "He pulls a knife, you pull a gun . . ."

That's the Trump way.

Trump supporters, at least many of them, were amused by his campaign antics. What would he say next? In a country where social media assaults the senses every second of every day, Donald Trump's verbal aggression became part of the attraction for some voters.

In addition to the mocking came verbal exaggeration, which the Trump critics uniformly said were "lies."

As stated, candidate Trump mostly does not use precise language. In order to make points, he often exaggerates. A vivid example of this is when he said he saw thousands of Muslims celebrating after the 9/11 attack.

There were reports in New Jersey that some anti-American activity took place in the aftermath of the terrorist attacks, but nothing large-scale. Didn't matter to candidate Trump: bad Muslims were on display, and what difference does it make if it's twelve or twelve thousand?

Trump yells, "You're fired," after speaking to several GOP
women's groups at the Treasure Island Hotel & Casino,
April 28, 2011, in Las Vegas, Nevada.

Bad is bad.

What the anti-Trump media never understood is the insults, hyperbole, and bombastic presentation isn't chump change; it's Trump-
change—meaning, it's insignificant. Millions of Americans believe
they are lied to every day by the media—and don't even get them
started on career politicians.

Donald Trump's "lies" are overlooked because the greater good is
served by the man slapping down folks who deserve to be slapped:
terrorists, criminals, fake news people, violent foreigners who sneak
into America.

Barack Obama, Hillary Clinton, Jeb Bush, and most other politicians were never going to call out the bad people. Trump would, so
who cares if he embellishes or insults?

He'll "Make America Great Again" by taking a licking while he
keeps on ticking. He's not afraid, and he never backs down.

Andrew Jackson had nothing on Trump. Old Hickory would have been wearing a MAGA hat as he drew his pistol in those nineteenth-century duels. America in 2015 had become soft and polarized. It needed a verbal gunslinger to clean up Dodge.

Donald Trump understood this, viscerally. And he had the stomach for the attacks that he knew awaited him.

By August 2015, Trump also understood the nomination was his to lose. He saw that his supporters did not give a rip what the *New York Times* thought or what was said by snooty commentators on CNN.

Trump had outfoxed the TV media and survived the first onslaught of attacks. The political apprentice was beating the career guys while barely breaking a sweat.

For those of us covering the presidential campaign honestly, the old rules had been obliterated. We were now all on Trump time.

Even Hillary Clinton.

CHAPTER TWENTY-ONE

LAS VEGAS, NEVADA

OCTOBER 13, 2015

LATE AFTERNOON

Hillary Clinton is not worried. As she stands on the Democratic presidential debate stage at the Wynn hotel ballroom, she knows she will not be denied again. This time there is no young, charismatic guy up against her. In fact, President Obama, who defeated Hillary Clinton for the nomination in 2008, actually wants his former secretary of state to be the next president. Mr. Obama believes Mrs. Clinton would carry on his policies and add to his legacy.

So, very quietly, President Obama has suggested to his vice president, Joe Biden, that he stay out of the race. Eight days from now, Mr. Biden will accede to the president's wishes and announce that he is not running. It is a decision he will regret.

Barack Obama likes Joe Biden but knows he is not nearly as disciplined as Hillary Clinton. As vice president, Biden actually opposed the Navy SEAL raid that killed Osama bin Laden in Pakistan. Biden has other decision-making deficits and is prone to verbal gaffes. The much-derided Sarah Palin held her own with Biden in a 2008 debate, not a good sign.

Both Barack Obama and Hillary Clinton see a very weak field on the Republican presidential side and are delighted that a one-man wrecking ball named Donald Trump is creating chaos in the GOP ranks. The president does not really know Trump, but Hillary does, having taken his substantial campaign donations and socialized with him as a senator from New York.

As Hillary Clinton looks at her Democratic competition immediately before the CNN-sponsored debate begins, she sees no threat, as the field is thin.

Bernie Sanders is a cranky old socialist who has accomplished little as a senator from Vermont.

Martin O'Malley is a far-left former governor from Maryland; Jim Webb is a senator from Virginia; and Lincoln Chafee is a politician from Rhode Island.

Webb and Chafee will drop out of the race this month. O'Malley will hang in until February, but in reality, this is mostly the JV, as President Obama might say.

Only Bernie Sanders will eventually cause Mrs. Clinton some grief.

Hillary Clinton has studied hard for this debate, as she always does. She is a driven woman who feels she has been treated unfairly for most of her adult life. It has been one controversy after another, very similar to what Donald Trump has experienced. But while Mr. Trump lashes out publicly against his tormentors, Mrs. Clinton internalizes, and seethes.

However, Trump and Clinton have one very important trait in common: they do not trust many people. In fact, Hillary has just two close confidantes: Cheryl Mills and Huma Abedin, who is married to the problematic former congressman Anthony Weiner.

According to her pollster and adviser Joel Benenson, Hillary's latest controversy, using her private email server for State Department business, is not a major concern of most Democratic voters. While the conservative media is pounding Hillary into pizza dough, *her* potential voters don't much care that she may have violated national security laws for unexplained reasons.

On that subject, just a few minutes from now, her rival Bernie Sanders will say: "The American people are sick and tired of hearing about your damn emails. Enough of the emails! Let's talk about the real issues facing America!"

That statement got applause and a smile from Hillary Clinton, who basically had just one jazzy line the entire evening.

"I'm a progressive who likes to get things done. And I know how to find common ground and I know how to stand my ground."

That description separates Mrs. Clinton from her husband, Bill Clinton, who, as a two-term president, governed center-right. Hillary has become more liberal than Bill and now believes his campaign presence only helps her in the South and Far West. If he stumps for her in the big media markets, some jaded press person will remind folks of the bad old Lewinsky days.

Hillary has put together a campaign staff that mirrors the one Barack Obama used with success. She still has hatchet man John Podesta around but relies more on younger people like Robby Mook and Jen Palmieri for day-to-day tactics.

Mrs. Clinton is a gifted fund-raiser, but she is not good at relating to everyday people. So, hers will be largely a media campaign—not the retail politics that Bernie Sanders will embrace. However, even though the American press has drifted far into left-leaning waters, Hillary does not trust the media. It has brutalized her and Bill Clinton in the past. So, no spontaneous press interactions for her. She will be tightly scripted throughout the campaign.

This evening, though, Hillary Clinton is confident that CNN will not surprise her as Megyn Kelly did Donald Trump. Anderson Cooper will not relitigate Whitewater, or Travelgate, or Lewinsky. CNN makes money broadcasting primarily to liberal Americans, so a safety net for Democrats is firmly in place.

Anyway, Anderson likes her.

What's not to like?

TTT

MY INTERACTIONS WITH Hillary Clinton have been few but respectful. In the fall of 2008, I interviewed her in South Bend, Indiana, during the primary season. Candidate Clinton was forty-five minutes late for the chat, and I used the time to talk with her Secret Service advance detail. They didn't much like her, the consensus being she was imperious.

Those conversations were off the record, so I did not use them in my reportage. I asked the same questions when I interviewed then-senator Barack Obama in York, Pennsylvania. There, the Secret Service guys generally considered the candidate a good guy.

My TV conversation with Hillary Clinton was standard issue except for one moment. While discussing the war in Afghanistan, I asked her how she would defeat the Taliban. She did not have a strategy. So, I followed up, asking her where the Taliban command and control was.

She fired back: "Tell me."

"Quetta, Pakistan," I said.

That exchange stayed with me because you don't often see Hillary Clinton miss a quiz question. She knows her stuff, but what she doesn't know, while standing in the Wynn hotel in front of an adoring CNN crowd, is that the political world is changing.

In 2016, it will no longer be about policy; it will be about emotion.

And Hillary Clinton does not show emotion.

Donald Trump never believed Senator Sanders would defeat Hillary Clinton. Based upon my private conversations with him, I think it's likely he didn't even watch the debate in Vegas or substantial portions of the other five Democratic debates to come.

Why would he waste time on that? Sanders was a "Communist," and Hillary was "Obama Lite." Neither could possibly make America great again. In fact, both would ruin America, he often told those around him. Obama was bad; Clinton and Sanders were worse!

Trump believed he could beat Hillary if everything broke his way. She had a controversial past, was deeply disliked by traditional conservatives, and now had the FBI looking at her private correspondence.

For Donald Trump, it was all good. Obama beat her, and Trump saw himself as much smarter than the president. After two Republican debates, Trump was dominating his party. Things were working out even better than he planned. The TV networks were all over him, and his big issues (border security, a better economy, and getting tough on Muslim terror) had taken root. He knew the Democrats were soft on those things and were so politically correct that they could never stir up emotion like he could.

As for candidate Hillary, she dreaded plowing through the fields of Iowa and the diners of New Hampshire. But she and her female confidantes fervently believe the time has come for the first woman president. She has paid her dues and has also paid a huge price in personal pain.

No billionaire with a checkered past will defeat her. She has the liberal press, Hollywood, a bevy of Wall Street bankers, and, most important, a well-liked president, at least among Democrats, supporting her.

Whom does Trump have? The cops?

As Anderson Cooper begins the debate questioning, Hillary Clinton is prepared to answer and prepared to serve.

In less than thirteen months, she will be president-elect; it is her time.

Finally.

CHAPTER TWENTY-TWO

NEW YORK CITY

OCTOBER 31, 2015

MORNING

It is Halloween, but Donald Trump is not frightened. Rather, he's bored. Three days ago, he endured another debate, the third episode of his new reality show called *When Will It All End?* This chat-fest was at the University of Colorado at Boulder. According to the snap polls, phone surveys taken immediately after the debate, Ted Cruz won the contest, but candidate Trump held his own.

Twelve days before the Boulder spectacle, Donald Trump demonstrated his increasing muscle with the media. Trump believed the first two debates were too long; he got bored standing on stage with nine other men. So, he told CNBC, the debate sponsor, that he would not show up in Colorado unless the program clocked in at two hours, and that included opening and closing statements by the participants.

The second debate put on by CNN ran more than three hours, which was totally unacceptable to Trump. So, it was his way or the highway. Ben Carson joined him in the demand.

CNBC, understanding that Trump was the viewer draw, caved: two hours it would be.

At this point in the campaign, Donald Trump has learned much. Yesterday, an NBC News poll told the world that Trump and Ben Carson were tied among Republican voters, with 26 percent each. No one else was close: Ted Cruz had 10 percent, Marco Rubio 9, and Jeb Bush 5.

The Bush number is disastrous. The campaign is now in its fourth month, with multiple debates in the books, and the governor has little support anywhere. His message is muddled, he looks uncomfortable on television, and his loathing for Donald Trump is obvious but not providing him with anything positive.

Trump sees Bush as a boring politician with little to offer. He knows the governor is done.

Donald Trump divides the world into winners and losers. His Republican competition all fall into the latter category. Trump believes he has the nomination already secured, even if Ben Carson is polling well. There is no question that candidate Trump has been the star of the debate show, and he has drawn far more people to his campaign rallies than any other candidate.

Dr. Ben Carson is a kind man who has led an impressive life. Born into poverty in Detroit, he attended Yale and went on to medical school at the University of Michigan. Carson then rose to become the director of pediatric neurosurgery at the famous Johns Hopkins Hospital in Maryland. In 2008, he was awarded the Presidential Medal of Freedom, the nation's highest civilian honor.

Ben Carson's personal accomplishments dwarf those of any presidential candidate running in 2015.

But—and there's always a "but" in politics—Carson is soft-spoken, knows little about foreign policy, and has a fuzzy message. He believes religion is a societal stabilizer and laments the decline of American culture, but specificity often eludes him.

There are no catchy slogans, no villains, and not much energy attached to the doctor's campaign.

Carson polls very well among Evangelicals and very conservative voters, but he lacks the firepower personality that Donald Trump possesses. Up against standard politicians, Carson has held his own, but the contrast with the rambunctious Trump has hurt him.

In addition, Trump is beating Carson in the poll question that really matters: Whom do you trust with the economy? NBC has Donald Trump at 41 percent among all the GOP candidates, Carson at just 11 percent.

Candidate Trump knows Dr. Benjamin Solomon Carson cannot beat him in the primaries because he does not have breakout potential. The person who challenges Hillary Clinton needs a vengeance agenda, which the doctor lacks. Many Republican voters will not be satisfied with a simple victory over Mrs. Clinton. They want her punished in the process.

As he reads the NBC poll, Donald Trump is happy because it has effectively eliminated most of his competition.

Time will take care of Ben Carson.

T T T

EVEN AS HE was traveling around the country campaigning, Donald Trump was still running his business; building hotels, residences, and golf courses. He never stopped working or politicking. He slept just four hours a night, often ate fast food, and rarely exercised. Golf was his only diversion.

Mr. Trump is the classic adrenaline junkie, which explains much of his conduct. When he gets bored, which is often, he does something to create excitement, action. Since Trump does not drink, use narcotics, smoke, or meditate, he stimulates his environment by embracing confrontational behavior. He'll create feuds, tweet challenges, say outrageous things in public. Then, when a reaction comes, as it always does, Trump counterpunches, hoping to "win" whatever challenge he's facing. It's a game. He's a fabulously wealthy man. If he loses, so what? And Donald Trump has the capacity to forget his losses quickly.

He is also a man of steel. He can absorb personal attacks with more resilience than anyone I've ever covered or known in my life.

President Trump on his golf course at the Trump Turnberry resort in South Ayrshire, where he and his wife, Melania, spent the weekend as part of their visit to the UK, July 15, 2018.

His enemies pound him without letup or mercy. Trump answers back and goes about his business.

But he never forgets.

With the holiday season and the end of 2015 approaching, Donald Trump likes his odds to get the Republican nomination. His message is simple and strong. Thousands cheer when he shows up in their neighborhoods, and the media still relentlessly pursue him. Every day, he is the center of attention, and instant gratification (a must for him) is almost always available.

The first vote in Iowa is just three months away. Before that, four more tedious debates are scheduled—a situation Trump now detests. Been there, done it, too many people onstage. Don't they know the competition is over? Don't they realize that only one candidate can Make America Great Again?

So, to keep his adrenaline pumped, Donald Trump is formulating a plan on this, the Eve of All Hallows.

It is an audacious plan.

The kind Donald Trump likes very much.

CHAPTER TWENTY-THREE

LOS ANGELES

JANUARY 27, 2016

MID-AFTERNOON

Fox News is being battered. A still-angry Donald Trump has announced that he will not show up for FNC's debate tomorrow night in Des Moines, Iowa. The sixth Republican debate is scheduled three days before the first actual presidential vote, the Iowa Caucus.

Candidate Trump does not expect to win Iowa, as caucus voters are generally extremely right or left. In fact, Ted Cruz and Hillary Clinton will win the 2016 contest.

For months, Roger Ailes, the Fox News boss, has been seeking détente with Donald Trump. But the candidate remains aggrieved over the Megyn Kelly question in August and does not want her moderating the Fox News debate in Iowa.

Ailes knows he cannot accede to Trump's request, and a stalemate has developed. Now the situation has gone public, as Trump is saying he won't show up, and just today, Fox News has fired back in a press release.

"We're not sure how Iowans are going to feel about [Trump]

walking away from them at the last minute, but it should be clear to the American public by now that this is rooted in one thing—Megyn Kelly, whom he has viciously attacked since August and now has spent four days demanding she be removed from the debate stage. Capitulating to politicians' ultimatums about a debate moderator violates all journalistic standards, as do threats, including the one leveled by Trump's campaign manager Corey Lewandowski toward Megyn Kelly.

"In a call on Saturday with a Fox News executive, Lewandowski stated that Megyn had a 'rough couple of days after that last debate' and he 'would hate to have her go through that again' . . . We can't give in to terrorization toward any of our employees.

"Trump is still welcome at Thursday's debate and will be treated fairly, just as he has been during his 132 appearances on Fox News and Fox Business, but he can't dictate the moderators or the questions."

The statement is classic Roger Ailes, who almost always stands by his personnel, and is insulted that Donald Trump does not understand that a news organization will lose all credibility if it allows politicians to dictate anything.

For his part, Trump does not care what the reasoning is; Fox has been unfair to him, and its statement puts the organization into the enemy camp.

Privately, Ailes does not want this fight because he knows a good portion of FNC's audience favors Trump. He suggests to Megyn Kelly that she refrain from publicly commenting on Trump, which she basically does. More than anything, Roger wants the controversy to die, but it will not.

I made it a policy not to involve myself with corporate politics, but I did discuss the problem with Roger Ailes, at his request. Based on my long acquaintanceship with Trump, Ailes asked me to speak with the candidate privately, putting forth that the debate was important to America and that he should attend.

So, I did.

I got nowhere.

Donald Trump strongly believed that Megyn Kelly grilled him

much harder than the other candidates and that she was using him to get famous.

There was little that I could say to dissuade him from his viewpoint. Megyn Kelly was adamant that she had done her job well, so there was no give on either side.

Realizing the private chat was going nowhere, I asked Donald Trump to confirm his appearance on the *Factor*. We were based in LA that week, but satellites are wonderful things. After some cajoling on my part, Trump agreed. That was very gutsy on his part, and smart. He knew he would reach millions of Fox News viewers. What he didn't know was how I would frame the issue—I could hammer him. I had before, during other interviews.

But that's Trump: he's a risk taker.

However, he rarely overlooks perceived slights, and the Kelly thing was very personal with him. He believed, and was correct, that Megyn Kelly sought to hurt him in the August debate.

I am not a person who gives up easily, so I still felt I had a chance to persuade Donald Trump to show up for the Iowa debate. If I could make a strong case on TV with him sitting there, he might change his mind, right?

Here's how it went down. We begin with my introduction. Again, I was in Los Angeles; Mr. Trump in Florida:

O'REILLY: So, I appreciate your coming on. Most politicians would have dodged this interview. But I have to tell you something. I don't think not showing up for the debate tomorrow night is good for America. Voters are still assessing you. They need to see you in high-profile situations. Or am I wrong?

TRUMP: Well, I think you're wrong because, frankly . . . I was not treated well by Fox. They came out with this ridiculous PR statement. It was, like, drawn up by a child. And it was a taunt. And I said, "How much of this do you take?" I have zero respect for Megyn Kelly. I don't think she's very good at what she does. I think she's overrated, and she's the moderator. I thought her question last time was ridiculous, and everybody said I won the debate. In fact, everybody said I won all six debates. So, I don't mind debating, I actually like debating.

O'REILLY: By walking away from it, you lose an opportunity to persuade people that you are a strong leader. That's my opinion.

TRUMP: Well, I understand your opinion, Bill . . . but Fox is going to make a lot of money on the debate . . . I just don't like being used, and when they issued that [statement,] it looked like it was done by children.

O'REILLY: Got it, but if you're elected president, you're going to get a lot more than that.

TRUMP: Frankly, you're a lot tougher than Megyn Kelly, in my opinion.

O'REILLY: Look, it doesn't matter. I'm trying to convince you that your [strategy] is wrong because it's better for the folks to see you in a debate format . . .

TRUMP: Everybody said I won that [Kelly] debate and I gave a great answer. Believe it or not, Rosie O'Donnell was very good for me in that debate. The only time Rosie's ever been good to me.

O'REILLY: You're making my point. You gained in that . . .

TRUMP: This also has to do with the attitude of Fox, Bill.

O'REILLY: I'm the flagship on Fox; we've treated you fairly.

TRUMP: Can I just say one thing? We've had six debates . . . We're going to go on forever with these debates. At some point, you've got to do other things.

O'REILLY: If I had been the moderator in August, I would have asked you about those [women] comments. I wouldn't have asked it the same way, but once you say something about Carly Fiorina, you open the door to it.

TRUMP: Excuse me, Bill. You would not have asked the question that way. I love pressure, that's why I'm doing your show tonight.

O'REILLY: Kelly's question was within journalistic bounds, okay?

TRUMP: I disagree.

TTT

THERE ARE A number of important takeaways from that Q-and-A. First, Donald Trump was sincerely angry with Fox News, and that would last a few more weeks.

Second, he thought debates in general no longer helped him. He was leading in the polls, so why give his competition more exposure? He had said all he wanted to say in that forum.

Finally, his assertion that the Rosie O'Donnell "pig" thing had helped him was most likely true. The very far left and strident O'Donnell is loathed by many conservatives. Insulting her did not hurt Trump with his growing base, and neither did his attacks on Megyn Kelly.

The simple truth is that partisan voters do not want their preferred candidate to look bad, and when someone does that, anger toward that someone flies.

Fox News and Megyn Kelly were besieged by furious Trump supporters who, to this day, believe their candidate was unfairly set up. Emotion ruled, and without a doubt, Donald Trump capitalized on that emotion.

I failed in my attempt to persuade Mr. Trump to debate in Iowa, and subsequently, the TV audience for that forum was half what it was for the FNC debate in August. So, Donald Trump won again.

By this time, it looked as if nothing could stop him from securing the Republican nomination for president. His base was becoming more devoted and had bought into his confrontational style. The press was beginning to turn on Trump but still believed that Hillary Clinton would smash him in the general election, so the Hate Trump movement had not broken out yet. The chieftains at the liberal newspapers and TV networks were fine with criticizing Trump, but they stopped short of trying to destroy him. They believed Hillary would soon take care of that.

Trump himself was enjoying his rallies and the mass adulation he received. The regular folks wanted a new political paradigm, one that put America and working people first; one that scorned political correctness and called out those who practiced it.

Donald Trump was all about that. While the media obsessed over his misstatements and tough talk on illegal immigration and terrorism, the average Trump supporter did not care about his exaggerations or PC offenses. They actually liked them.

To Donald Trump supporters, he was an avenger, a powerful person who would stop liberal madness and restore "greatness" to America. Trump was the anti-Obama, and the Trump train was speeding to the success station with the folks all aboard.

Next stop, New Hampshire. Then on to Super Tuesday. Who woulda ever thunk it?

CHAPTER TWENTY-FOUR

FOX NEWS STUDIO

WASHINGTON, DC

MARCH 2, 2016

EARLY EVENING

Charles Krauthammer is not happy. The genius Fox News commentator knows Donald Trump is now unstoppable, that he will be the Republican candidate for president, and Charles doesn't like it.

It is the day after the Super Tuesday primary vote that Trump won big, taking seven states while Ted Cruz won three and Marco Rubio one.

The Grand Old Party turnout was massive: 8.5 million votes compared to 4.7 million in 2012—that's up 81 percent from when Mitt Romney was the Republican headliner. The vast majority of Super Tuesday votes went to Donald Trump.

That pretty much seals the deal after Trump won the New Hampshire primary on February 9. The tally in that vote was Trump, 35 percent; John Kasich, 16 percent; Ted Cruz, 12 percent; and Jeb Bush with 11 percent.

On the other side, Bernie Sanders smashed Hillary Clinton in

New Hampshire 60 percent to 38. Donald Trump and his campaign are taking strong notice of that.

The South Carolina primary was held on February 20, and Trump won again. Jeb Bush quit the race, and the other Republican aspirants were tottering. It takes big money to run a presidential campaign, and GOP donations to Trump's competition are drying up. It is essentially over.

As he reads the Super Tuesday exit polling research, Charles Krauthammer well understands the situation. Republican voters, his party, are fed up with cowardly politicians who couldn't even stop Barack Obama. They want a "strongman" outsider to batter Hillary Clinton, a person much maligned and detested by many conservative Americans.

Despite his spirited campaign, few GOP voters believe the socialist Bernie Sanders can beat Hillary for the nomination.

Krauthammer also disapproves of Mrs. Clinton but viscerally dislikes Donald Trump. In July 2015, he called Mr. Trump a "rodeo clown." So, Charles is caught between two political rocks, and it is indeed a hard place. He is FNC's top political analyst and an intellectually honest man. So, he pounds both Trump and Clinton, drawing the public ire of Mr. Trump, and disdain from more than a few Fox News viewers.

Unlike many so-called TV news analysts, Krauthammer is not a company person. He says what he believes, not what he's told to say. And what he believes is that both Clinton and Trump are bad for the country.

For years, Charles Krauthammer was a weekly guest on the *Factor*, and we always had lively debates. I was not close to him personally, but we established an honest rapport. Charles felt that Donald Trump was not qualified to run the country and was boorish to boot. Trump's brash personal presentation and flamboyant lifestyle offended Krauthammer, who believed in the federal system and, most of all, in traditional decorum. Charles did not want the drastic change that a Trump presidency would bring.

Paralyzed from the neck down after a pool accident while attending Harvard Medical School, Krauthammer could cut through the fog and bring wisdom to almost any policy issue. He was brilliant, a word I seldom use.*

But I thought his personal revulsion for Trump clouded his vision. It also didn't help that the candidate publicly disparaged Charles. I mean, nobody in authority did that.

By the way, Mr. Trump once told me, after I said something he didn't like, that I needed a psychiatrist. I laughed and told him it wouldn't do any good. Trump was Trump: insults fell from his mouth like water from the falls of Niagara. I didn't take it personally.

But Charles Krauthammer did, even though he kind of provoked Trump with the clown remark.

Despite his following among conservatives, Krauthammer's anti-Trump posture had little effect on Republican voters, who were now solidly behind Trump. Apparently, they didn't much care what anyone said about their guy; their support was firm.

Donald Trump at a campaign event in Las Vegas, Nevada, February 22, 2016.

---

* Sadly, Charles Krauthammer passed away due to complications from cancer on June 21, 2018. He is missed.

The exit polling from eleven states on Super Tuesday was clear about that. Both Krauthammer and I absorbed the following:

- 90 percent of Republican voters were angry or dissatisfied with the federal government.
- Just 57 percent of Democrats felt that way.
- 50 percent of GOP voters wanted an "outsider" as president.
- Only 14 percent of Democrats did.
- Donald Trump's support was across the board among rich and poor, old and young.

So it is that Donald Trump, with no political experience, is poised to become the Republican nominee for president of the United States. That stark reality, which few thought would ever occur, is sinking in across the land.

But within his own party, there is a rebellion brewing against Trump. And tomorrow it will break wide open.

CHAPTER TWENTY-FIVE

DETROIT, MICHIGAN

MARCH 3, 2016

EVENING

As dusk descends, the Secret Service is awaiting the arrival of candidate Donald Trump at a private air terminal a few miles outside Motor City. Along with the federal agents are a number of Fox News personnel, including me, your humble correspondent.

I had arranged a short meeting with Mr. Trump before his motorcade made its way to the historic Fox Theatre in downtown Detroit for the eleventh Republican debate. (The theater is not attached to the Fox Corporation.) My intent with that meeting was to lock down the first interview with Trump after this evening's debate on live TV. Whoever secured the first Q-and-A on the debate stage immediately after the formal debate ended would have a nice scoop, as they say in the journalistic world. I was confident I would get the interview because it was an FNC event, again starring Kelly, Baier, and Wallace.

Donald Trump had finally put aside his grievances with Megyn

Kelly, largely because the controversy of last August had subsided and there was nothing to gain by boycotting another Fox News debate.

As usual, Trump's motorcade waited by the Jetway steps as the candidate and his entourage, which included his wife, Melania, emerged. The group then climbed into the cars for the drive over to the terminal, where Trump and I were set to chat.

But a funny thing happened on the way to the forum. The Trump caravan sped on by, leaving a bunch of Secret Service guys and O'Reilly standing there looking at tarmac.

After a few rather testy phone calls to Trump surrogates, a picture emerged. The candidate was in a foul mood, and Mitt Romney had caused it. Trump was not speaking to anyone before the debate.

Earlier in the day, the man who lost to President Obama in 2012 had given a speech at the University of Utah, his adopted home state. Romney blistered Donald Trump for twenty minutes, an attack that was now burning up social media.

Trump fired back at Romney in Maine, where he was holding a rally. But the media damage was done.

Mitt Romney is not usually a confrontational man; he's generally genial and cautious with his words. In 2012, Trump endorsed Romney and donated to his campaign, something Trump pointed out to his Maine supporters earlier in the day.

"He was begging for my endorsement. I could have said, 'Mitt, get on your knees.' And he would have dropped to his knees!"

That was just the beginning. Trump was simply warming up to what would be a long tirade. The question was: Why would Mitt Romney go after Donald Trump? It seemed to be out of context and character.

Having covered the Romney-Obama race, a few things were clear. The former governor of Massachusetts failed to connect with working Americans on the campaign trail. Even though the economy was sluggish under President Obama, Romney did not seem to be agitated that many Americans were struggling. Also, he declined to challenge

Barack Obama aggressively in the debates; nor did he give Americans a compelling reason to vote for him.

Mitt Romney was a wealthy, establishment guy with beautiful homes in San Diego, New Hampshire, and Utah. He was a patrician who worked well within the Republican Party and actually did a good job as governor of Massachusetts, a very liberal state.

Massachusetts voters have a long tradition of electing uber-leftists like Elizabeth Warren and Barney Frank, but they want the head person in the statehouse to keep taxes under control, and that's why Romney won.

In 2012, millions of conservative and working Americans were blaming Barack Obama for what they believed was an intentional "weakening" of America and their economic circumstances. Mitt Romney failed to harness that disenchantment, to say the least.

Thus, President Obama beat him fairly easily, by 5 million popular votes. The electoral count was 332 to 206. Romney lost Florida and Virginia, two states he had to have.

Of course, Democrats and the press were overjoyed.

Just before his air raid hours ago in Utah, Mitt Romney dined with his 2012 running mate, congressional Speaker of the House Paul Ryan. Therefore, the Republican establishment had to know what Romney was about to do.

Shortly after Romney's attack on Trump, Senator John McCain, whom Obama defeated in 2008, essentially endorsed the governor's trashing of the Republican candidate. So, what the deuce was going on?

After Trump's huge victory on Super Tuesday, it was clear he would have enough delegates to win the nomination. But that's not what the GOP chieftains wanted. Like Charles Krauthammer, many establishment Republicans saw Donald Trump as a vulgarian who would get crushed by Hillary Clinton in the general election. So, they apparently decided to sanction a bold move in order to tie up the convention and replace Donald Trump as the nominee. That was the hope.

Mitt Romney was designated to deliver the message. And he did, with relish.

"Here's what I know. Donald Trump is a phony, a fraud. His promises are as worthless as a degree from Trump University. He's playing members of the American public for suckers. He gets a free ride to the White House, and all we get is a lousy hat!"

Romney went on and on, his remarks a blessing to the Democrats and to the media, which had recently decided to cover Trump more as a national menace than a presidential candidate. Many press executives were pleased that he would be the Republican nominee, but now they would begin to disassemble him so that Hillary would not have to break a sweat.

Mitt Romney's scathing sound bites gave the leftist press cover. Now it wasn't just the "liberal media" going after Trump; *it was his own party!* So, the reportage got more vicious, the analysis more dishonest. An anti-Trump groupthink developed in the national media that is still in place to this day.

For the press, it was an *Invasion of the Body Snatchers* scenario. Everyone was the same.

On the political front, it is hard to fathom what the Republican power brokers were thinking. Yes, Mitt Romney was a private citizen who could say what he wanted, but it is impossible to believe that the Republican National Committee was unaware of Romney's intent. The poohbahs knew. But what was the reasoning?

Donald Trump had wiped out the field, drawing enormous numbers of voters to the primaries. He was a political phenomenon in much the same way that Senator Barack Obama was in 2008. What did the RNC think? That Ronald Reagan would rise from the grave? Whom did the Republican establishment expect to replace Trump at the convention? Mitt Romney? Daffy Duck?

Politically, the Romney speech was a disaster for the GOP. Again, it gave the press free rein to viciously attack Trump, it began the "Never Trump" movement within the GOP, and it angered Trump supporters, many of whom saw Mitt Romney as a traitorous wimp and the GOP leadership as spineless idiots.

But most important, Romney's play deeply hurt Donald Trump, who would never again fully trust his own party. In addition, Trump would come to despise his predecessors Romney and McCain, as well as the entire Bush family.

This would hurt him down the line.

T T T

THE LAST MEN standing assemble on the debate stage in Detroit wishing the spectacle were over. Donald Trump, Marco Rubio, Ted Cruz, and John Kasich are all that remain from the original seventeen Republican candidates.

Ten times over the past seven months, these men have confronted one another in debate format, and they have had enough. They are tired. They've said what they have to say.

But the Republican Party lined up twelve debates—and so, the show must go on, even though Donald Trump is now a lock for the nomination.

"We all knew early that the blowtorch Trump was using in his campaign would knock out the real issues," Governor Mike Huckabee, a candidate who dropped out in February, told me in the spring of 2019.

"Donald's strategy of dominating media coverage worked. Republican voters wanted to blow up the system, and Trump promised that. The rest of us could not get known because the press was not interested in us. It was all about Donald and whatever attacks he was launching."

Mike Huckabee went on to endorse Trump and retains no hard feelings. To him, Donald Trump's brilliant strategy worked, and that was that.

The Detroit debate amounted to nothing. At the start, Donald Trump set the low bar by actually saying to Megyn Kelly, "You're looking well."

I was hoping Megyn would reply, "No thanks to you," but she didn't.

Bored with the lengthy and laborious process, the candidates all knew that the Republican campaign had devolved into personal insults, primarily between Rubio and Trump. Here's a sample:

- Trump: I have never seen a human being sweat like this man sweats . . . It looks like he just jumped into a swimming pool with his clothes on. [Trump splashes water on the stage] It's Rubio.
- Rubio: [Trump] was having a meltdown. First, he had this little makeup thing, applying makeup around his mustache because he had one of those sweat mustaches.
- Trump: Little Marco Rubio is just another Washington, DC, politician—that is, all talk and no action.
- Rubio: He's always calling me Little Marco and I'll admit he's taller than me. He's like six two, which is why I don't understand why his hands are the size of someone five two. Have you seen his hands? And you know what they say about men with small hands? You can't trust them!

A few days later, Donald Trump brought up the "hands" thing at a rally, telling the audience that some other parts of his body were not small. Or something.

It is impossible to know what the great debaters Stephen Douglas and Abraham Lincoln might have thought about all this, but history does record that Abe never called the diminutive Douglas "Little Stevie." At least not in public.

The Detroit debate seemed to go on longer than a Greek Orthodox Mass on Easter Sunday. The only memorable thing was when all three other candidates said they would endorse Donald Trump if he were the nominee.

I think I saw Marco Rubio perspire a little when he said that.

T T T

As THE SHOW wrapped up, I was looming offstage to snare Trump. He was not going to avoid me again; nor was another reporter going to get between us.

My camera guy and I quickly approached the candidate, and the director switched from the moderators, who had just signed off, to me. I love live TV.

I didn't even say hello to Donald Trump; I just started the interview. Here are the highlights:

O'REILLY: Romney hit you hard today. Are you surprised?

TRUMP: He is a failed candidate.

O'REILLY: Were you surprised?

TRUMP: . . . He did a horrible job. He wants to become relevant again. He really let us down. Four years ago, I supported him. I helped him a lot. He really, really let us down. He knows I feel [that way] . . . but I think my retort was far stronger than his, and if you look on Twitter and at what's happening, I think he made a fool out of himself, if you want to know the truth.

O'REILLY: Why do you think he did it?

TRUMP: Because I think he's a jealous guy, and I think he'd like to run but he didn't have the guts to run this time, and he probably should have. I don't think he would have done very well, and I told him he was a choker. I mean, he's a choke artist, and that's what happened with his last . . .

O'REILLY: Do you think he's angling to go into the convention if you don't have enough delegates?

TRUMP: He might be—and that's why he didn't support anybody—but he doesn't have it. He would be beaten so badly by Hillary, your head will spin, so he doesn't have it.

O'REILLY: . . . What about your personality engenders these people to come after you?

TRUMP: I tell it like it is. I tell the truth. Our country needs that.

O'REILLY: But Romney feels that you're a danger to the country.

TRUMP: I don't think he feels that at all.

O'REILLY: You think he's a phony?

TRUMP: I would say he's a phony, yeah. I mean, he doesn't feel that way at all.

O'REILLY: . . . So, just jealousy on his part?

TRUMP: I don't know what it is . . . but I think he made a fool out of himself. He shouldn't have done it.

O'REILLY: . . . You need to get, on our calculations, about thirty million people who are not supporting you now to support you to defeat Hillary Clinton.

TRUMP: I think I'm going to defeat Hillary. We're going to win Michigan, we might win New York . . . I'm going to win Pennsylvania. I'm going to win Ohio. I'm going to win a lot of states. I'm going to win Florida; Florida is my second home.

TTT

AFTER A LITTLE more back-and-forth, I released Donald Trump to the hordes of reporters lined up to get sound bites.

Eight months after that Detroit night, the candidate did not win New York, but he was dead on about the other states he'd mentioned. At this point, the press and the Democrats were still somewhat underestimating Donald Trump, but not me. I believe my eyes. Trump had captured imaginations, and millions of Americans were willing to take a chance on him.

His competition knew it. I spoke to all three of the other candidates that night, and although they would not admit it on the air, they all knew Trump would win the nomination. His appeal to disenchanted

"Make America Great Again" hats at a Trump rally at the Las Vegas Convention Center, Las Vegas, Nevada, September 20, 2018.

Americans was just too strong. It wasn't about ideology or issues or money.

None of that mattered in March 2019.

No, it was all about attitude. And no one had attitude like candidate Donald Trump.

No one.

CHAPTER TWENTY-SIX

NEW YORK CITY

MAY 4, 2016

LATE AFTERNOON

The dominoes fell quickly. On March 15, the Ides, Senator Marco Rubio dropped out of the race, but not before saying, "Donald Trump will not make America great; he'll make America orange."

The senator was apparently miffed that Trump had said Rubio had "the biggest ears I've ever seen."

Then Ted Cruz and John Kasich left the contest, on May 3 and 4, respectively.

The Cruz departure was especially bitter. Angry over the fact that Trump had linked his father, Rafael Cruz, to Lee Harvey Oswald, the man who murdered President Kennedy, Senator Cruz held a press conference where he brutally attacked Donald Trump. Here's a brief sample: "Whatever lie he's telling, in that minute he believes it. The man is utterly amoral. Donald is a bully . . . Bullies don't come from strength, they come from weakness."

Nevertheless, shortly after Cruz packed it in, Donald Trump said this: "I want to congratulate Ted. I know how tough it is. I had some moments where it was not looking so good, and it's not a great feeling, so I know how Ted feels. And Heidi, and their whole beautiful family."

As the winner, Trump had turned magnanimous. He had created chaos and upended traditional campaigning, but now was the time to be conciliatory. Donald Trump fully realized he needed to win Texas, Florida, and Ohio in order to become president. That meant he'd have to court Cruz, Rubio, and Kasich.

Mr. Trump appeared on my program the evening of May 4 to talk about it:

O'REILLY: So, I'm a bit confused. Once it was "Lyin' Ted." Now he's a smart, tough guy. What happened?

TRUMP: Well, I want to be gracious, and he was a good competitor. He was a very strong competitor, and it worked out . . . We had a tremendous victory . . . He competed really hard and tough. I respect that.

O'REILLY: He really gave it to you yesterday.

TRUMP: I know. He said some things and made up some things . . . but I understand it. It's not easy.

O'REILLY: So, you won the battle and you're releasing the prisoners. Would you consider Ted Cruz in your administration?

TRUMP: Well, he's certainly a capable guy. So, it's something we can think about. It's a little too soon to think about it too much.

O'REILLY: Kasich dropped out today. Did you talk to John?

TRUMP: I have not. I have a good relationship with him . . . He's somebody that I've gotten along with during the debates. During intermission, I would always seem to be talking with John.

O'REILLY: Marco Rubio is [now] saying good things about you. We thought he might be out in the sun too much; it's hot in Miami. You've got to win Florida. Would you consider Rubio for vice president?

TRUMP: I don't want to talk too much about that, Bill. I am

considering a number of people . . . and I would certainly consider
him . . . Marco and I have gotten along very well.

O'REILLY: Would the campaign slogan be "Big Don and Little
Marco" . . . ?

TRUMP: I think it would be "Vote to Make America Great Again."
Maybe we'll go that way.

O'REILLY: If history is any indicator, the Clinton campaign will
go after you through surrogates. "Move On," those [kinds of]
sleazy websites are going to tear you up. How are you going to
respond . . . ?

TRUMP: I'll be able to figure it out with Hillary. It depends on
where she's coming from. But if she wants to go low road, I'm
fine with that. And if she wants to go high road, which is what I'd
prefer, I would be fine with that.

O'REILLY: You're fine with the low road? Most people don't want
to go on the low road.

TRUMP: No, I can handle the low road if I have to do it. I mean,
we've had some low roads over the last few months.

▼▼▼

THAT Q-AND-A WAS instructive on a number of fronts. First, Donald Trump's campaign against Hillary Clinton would feature many
detours onto the low road, with the "Crooked Hillary" and "Lock
her up" stuff—that was mostly in response to Clinton-generated allegations of misconduct against Trump.

Second, once he emerged victorious, Donald Trump was quick to
forgive his competition. The past is not important to Trump; winning
in the future is. He can forge positive relationships with people who
have damaged him, if he ultimately prevails.

But there are some people, like Jeb Bush, John McCain, and
Megyn Kelly, who were not forgiven, and vice versa.

Finally, I have interviewed and spoken with Donald Trump
scores of times. He sometimes exaggerates and often overstates, but
he's never said a calculated untruth to me. The media theme that

"Trump lies" is based mainly on spontaneous statements that roll off his tongue when he's not concentrating, which is much of the time.

The important thing to absorb if you really want to understand Donald Trump and how he achieved power is that he is a disrupter—a man with a plan—and that plan is almost always to embrace mayhem as a vehicle to getting what he wants.

That's what that Rafael Cruz–Oswald thing was all about. Say anything to disrupt your competition, in this case Ted Cruz. Distract him, wear him down emotionally. Donald Trump plays the hardest of ball while in the political and business arenas. Once he gets what he wants, victory, he'll label the vanquished "great" or whatever. Other presidents, like Franklin Roosevelt and Lyndon Johnson, were disrupters as well. They just kept quiet about it; they had others inject the chaos.

Trump is incapable of being quiet. His strategy is smash mouth and hand to hand.

Those tactics, including the loaded-speech technique, have worked for him, and he crafts his behavior by believing that the end justifies the means, an old cliché but one that is alive and well in contemporary America. Rationalization has become a national pastime. No American can escape it.

As with most human beings, Donald Trump will sometimes consciously mislead for convenience or to protect himself. But as you saw with the "low road" comments, if you ask him a straight question, you'll usually get a straight answer.

Trump is not a precise orator and he absolutely enjoys embellishment. So, Americans can decide about the "lie" accusation as well as the morality of his competitive tactics, which are on vivid display. One thing is certain, Trump does not disguise who he is or what he does.

And in November 2016, Americans did decide—by electing Donald J. Trump president.

But before that monumental occurrence, many strange days would unfold.

The Doors had nothing on Donald Trump, who was now ready to state his case at the Republican National Convention in Cleveland.

But on the way there, the national media had a surprise for the candidate. An unpleasant surprise.

CHAPTER TWENTY-SEVEN

MANHASSET, NEW YORK

APRIL 4, 2019

7:45 P.M.

In the future, historians may not fully understand how the news coverage of candidate Trump actually helped him become president. And as I type these words about two and a half years after Trump's election, it is important to understand exactly what was taking place in the spring of 2016.

As Donald Trump does a victory lap across the country, celebrating his long, hard-fought Republican primary win, the nation's media chieftains are not happy. On May 26, as Trump passes the 1,237 pledged delegates he needs to secure the nomination, there is little joy in the nation's newsrooms because candidate Trump is the antithesis of Barack Obama, whom the press basically adored.

From the beginning of the campaign, the newspaper industry has loathed Donald Trump, generally cheap-shotting him whenever possible. In fact, in the run-up to the presidential vote, more than 240 editorial boards will endorse Hillary Clinton. Just 20 dailies and six weekly periodicals will suggest that their readers support candidate Trump.

Some of that lopsided Hillary boosterism is because of Trump's personal style. It is clear he has little affection for newspapers, preferring the action of TV news. He certainly doesn't court editors, who very much enjoy having their wisdom appreciated.

The American newspaper industry is dying and not nearly as relevant as it once was. Weekly magazines such as *Time* and *Newsweek* are also on the financial rocks, along with political magazines such as the *Weekly Standard*, which will fold in December 2018. Donald Trump likes being on the covers of magazines but rarely takes a peek inside them.

Television is another story.

In the beginning of the campaign, as we stated, TV news executives basically loved Trump because he brought in viewers and supplied endless narratives. But as it became clear that he was becoming a political force, attitudes began to change. What most Americans don't realize is that 90 percent of the national news flow on television is controlled by just six corporations. And those corporations all have entertainment subdivisions that are extremely liberal. Thus, the CEOs of the media companies are usually sympathetic to the left because they have to deal with Hollywood, which is, you guessed it, liberal to the core. A conservative executive would not be well received in the salons of Beverly Hills.*

Broadcast executives usually hire personnel who think the way they do. According to data published by the firm political.law, less than 10 percent of working journalists in the United States today are registered Republicans.

So, what to do? Making money still trumps (pun intended) ideology in TV news, but not by much. Disney, Comcast, CBS, Fox, Time-Warner, and Tribune all want as much profit as they can squeeze. However, the movie and TV show people generally hate Donald Trump and loudly express that revulsion. Some Fox entertainment employees even threatened to quit their jobs to protest the Fox News

---

* In May 2019, executives from the Disney and Comcast corporations threatened to boycott the state of Georgia because it passed a strong anti-abortion law. Conservative CEOs never would have done that.

Channel, perceived to be the only network favorable to Donald Trump. There was fear and loathing all over the place in the media, solely caused by candidate Trump, who, to the horror of the left, had actually criticized Mexicans and Muslims.

I've borrowed the fear-and-loathing description from the late Hunter S. Thompson, whom I quoted earlier. Here's another gem from him, printed in the *San Francisco Examiner* in 1985: "The TV business is uglier than most things. It is normally perceived as some kind of cruel money trench through the heart of the journalism industry, a big plastic hallway where thieves and pimps run free and good men die like dogs, for no good reason."

It didn't take long for the TV moguls to figure out how to exploit Donald Trump in a different way. The two left-wing cable news outfits, CNN and MSNBC, launched an unprecedented Hate Trump campaign across the board, believing that their liberal viewers would watch such a thing religiously.

For example, Donald Trump was once treated nicely by the *Morning Joe* program on MSNBC, but relatively quickly, that show turned into a daily Bash Trump fiesta. All the other MSNBC programs followed.

Candidate Trump actually thought CNN chief Jeff Zucker was his friend because Zucker once oversaw *The Apprentice* on NBC. Candidate Trump was wrong. Zucker unleashed his liberal staff to destroy Trump. They took to the task enthusiastically.

The Fox News Channel was the lone dissenter as the network nightly newscasts, once guardians of hard news, continued to take their anti-Trump cues from the *New York Times*, headquarters for the "Resistance." The network morning programs, staffed mostly by liberal folks, followed their evening cousins.

FNC continued to present Donald Trump in a mostly favorable way. My program grilled him but did not denigrate the candidate. In fact, we treated all the candidates the same, with the exception of Governor Bush, who would not cooperate with us. That was strange, as I have a decent relationship with the governor. But I had to point out his dodge.

In addition, I treated Hillary Clinton and Bernie Sanders equally.

I was skeptical but not unfair to either. I also challenged candidate Trump because my job is to scrutinize all those in power or seeking it. Therefore, I had some doubts.

Could Trump actually govern with the establishment firmly opposed to him?

Did Hillary Clinton have any policy ideas apart from what President Obama had championed?

And come on, Bernie Sanders, your policies would crash the economy and eventually bankrupt the nation.

Fox News management under Roger Ailes generally played by the rules. News coverage was delivered in a straightforward way, prime-time opinion was the Wild West. That formula had lifted FNC to the top of the cable news industry. The left despised Fox News, and dark Internet organizations tried hard to harm its on-air talent, sometimes succeeding.

Thus, it wasn't difficult for me to recognize the coordinated "get Trump" tactics because I had been attacked that way myself.

On the other side, the Trump campaign was often annoyed with me because I would not put its surrogates on my broadcast. As I told them, if I wanted zombies, I'd watch *The Walking Dead*.

Same thing with all the campaigns: no surrogates. But the candidates themselves were welcome.

Donald Trump took advantage of that; Hillary Clinton and Bernie Sanders did not.

T T T

IT DIDN'T TAKE long for the Hate Trump strategy to pay off for NBC News in particular. For nineteen consecutive years, MSNBC was a ratings disaster. But by loathing Trump every hour on the hour, the network increased viewership as Democrats tuned in to hear the scandal du jour.

CNN was not as successful on the Hate Trump front. Yes, it tried, but it was no match for the NBC bloodbath. Simply put, Wolf Blitzer could not sneer as well as Lawrence O'Donnell.

Fox News did fine with campaign reporting and analysis. *The O'Reilly Factor* dominated the cable news ratings. I like to think it was our tough, clear political coverage coupled with my charm and charisma.

You may see it differently.

Donald Trump was somewhat surprised that the press was turning on him. He had always been able to negotiate good deals with the media. But the country was changing, and largely because of Trump's flamboyance, hammering him had become very profitable.

The outfit political.law summed it up succinctly: "The liberal media perpetuate political bias so forcefully and unrelentingly, it's gone from subtle background noise to the entirety of their narrative. Is it any wonder Americans have record-high distrust for the mainstream media?"

And, as we will see, that distrust actually saved Donald Trump from defeat at the hands of Hillary Clinton, whom the press really didn't have much use for, generally speaking. But she was far more acceptable than Trump.

So it is that as June 2016 approached and the Hate Trump strategy kicked in, the media had the best of both worlds: big-money ads were being sold, and Donald Trump was being marginalized in the process.

What could go wrong? The election in five months would not even be close. Hill will chill, Trump will go down.

Wait and see.

CHAPTER TWENTY-EIGHT

CLEVELAND, OHIO

JULY 21, 2016

EVENING

It is the biggest night of Donald Trump's life. He has pulled off an amazing accomplishment, capturing the Republican nomination for president with no political machine or experience. Along the way, he received more primary votes than any GOP candidate in history, 14 million.

Now, as Donald Trump joins the Republican National Convention, the nation awaits his victory speech. As usual, there is no extensive entourage advising Trump. He has some writers, and advisors like Paul Manafort and Sean Spicer, but he basically continues to rely on himself for just about everything.

His daughter Ivanka will introduce him tonight. She and her husband, Jared Kushner, have the candidate's trust, along with the Trump sons Don Jr. and Eric. But that's about it for the inner circle.

Trump barely knows his choice for vice president, Mike Pence, the governor of Indiana. Pence spoke last night at the Quicken Loans Arena to a friendly but not frenzied crowd.

Unlike Sarah Palin eight years ago, Pence was selected because of his low-key, Christian profile. The flamboyant and secular Trump needs the Evangelical vote that rejected Mitt Romney in 2012. Thus, the buttoned-down Governor Pence received the nod. In 2008, John McCain hoped Governor Palin would supply dash to the Republican campaign. But now, with Donald Trump leading the ticket, dash is not a problem.

Behind the scenes, there was confusion over the VP selection because Trump could not make up his mind. At first, he favored the outspoken governor of New Jersey, Chris Christie. But while twinning the volatile Christie with the volatile Trump might have worked in a remake of *The Wild Bunch*, it was not a road map to the White House.

Paul Manafort was the influencer here, pointing out how the stability and conservatism of Pence would provide balance. Trump finally acceded.

Although the arena crowd is jazzed as Reince Priebus, chairman of the Republican National Committee, finishes up his remarks, there has been some serious negativity here in Cleveland.

The Bush family didn't show up for the convention; nor did Mitt Romney and John McCain. Even home state governor John Kasich blew off the convention proceedings, a serious display of disrespect.

Senator Ted Cruz did attend and, yesterday, gave a speech that did not endorse Donald Trump: "Vote your conscience, vote for candidates up and down the ticket whom you trust to defend our freedom and to be faithful to the Constitution."

Cruz was heavily booed.

It is clear to all that many in the Republican establishment will not support Donald Trump for president. However, after two brutal losses to Barack Obama, the GOP mainstays have lost clout and affection. Traditional and conservative Americans are frustrated with nonconfrontational leadership. So, it doesn't matter a whit that the Bushes are not in Cleveland.

The avenger would be there, and that's all that mattered.

In addition to the GOP stalwarts, six major companies that sponsored the GOP convention in 2012 have disappeared: Wells Fargo,

UPS, Motorola, JPMorgan Chase, Ford, and Walgreens Boots Alliance have all decided not to participate in the Trump coronation.

This is a signal that the "racist" attacks on Trump are working. Generally speaking, American companies are cowardly and could not care less about what is true. If there is controversy in the marketplace, even one contrived by political zealots, they run.

This un-American posture would soon greatly expand during the Trump era and become a genuine threat to freedom of speech and due process.

Outside the convention hall, taking full advantage of the first amendment, the usual left-wing suspects are venting. Carl Bernstein, of Watergate fame, called Trump a "neofascist" as part of CNN's objective and fair election coverage.

Donald Trump isn't going to let any of that affect his demeanor on this night. Here he is, in the middle of the action, winning, the center of worldwide attention. Trump knows he has reached the pinnacle, almost.

In a few minutes, thousands of militant supporters will cheer his every word, applause filling the massive arena. LeBron James, Michael Jordan, even Joe Willie Namath never came close.

It is a stunning achievement for the second son of Fred Trump who once yearned to conquer Manhattan.

Now he is one achievement away from being the most powerful man in the world.

T T T

POLITICAL CONVENTIONS ARE essentially choreographed propaganda displays that can wear the strongest person out after four days. Certainly, I was spent. Outside of the Ted Cruz drama, the Republicans behaved like Republicans: mostly polite and predictable. But political rhetoric is usually tedious, and Cleveland was no exception. As a commentator on TV, I could do little to liven things up.

As he readied himself for his prime-time speech, which would begin at 10:15 Eastern, Donald Trump might have heard the song "Here Comes the Sun" played as his daughter Ivanka took the stage

Donald Trump takes the stage to introduce his wife, Melania Trump, during the first night of the 2016 Republican National Convention in Cleveland, Ohio.

to introduce him. It was a nice touch, as Trump's eldest daughter is generally considered a sunny presence.

But shortly afterward, the estate of the late Beatle George Harrison, who wrote the song, lodged an objection. The statement issued said the use of the tune by the Trump campaign was "offensive and against the wishes of the George Harrison estate."

Given that American democracy is on display at both presidential conventions, that seems kind of petty.

In fact, it was kind of petty.

T T T

IT IS SHOWTIME, the main event. As thirty-two million Americans watch, Donald Trump kisses his daughter and approaches the microphone, an object he profoundly loves.

For the next seventy-five minutes, candidate Trump would ruminate, bloviate, holler, and promise. The National Public Radio correspondent described Trump's speech this way:

Trump repeated a similar litany that re-created Nixon's dark canvass. Then he blamed it all on Clinton, adding that he was sure President Obama was deeply sorry he had appointed her Secretary of State.

It probably does not matter that the president will say very much the opposite about her next week when Clinton is nominated by the Democrats in Philadelphia. In a world depicted in a Trump speech, fantastic assertions are far from an aberration.

For example, Trump repeatedly promised to solve the nation's and the world's thorniest problems quickly . . .

ISIS would be defeated . . . trade deals would be ripped up and renegotiated, and billions would flow into America to create jobs . . .

T T T

THAT REPORT SIMPLY reinforced the fact that NPR is not a fan of Mr. Trump, but its reporter, Ron Elving, deserves some attention even though sarcasm dominated his speech coverage. Let's look at some of Elving's "fantastic assertions."

As I write these words, President Trump has been in office just over two years. In that time, ISIS has been largely defeated, applications for unemployment insurance are at a sixty-nine-year low, NAFTA and other trade deals have been renegotiated, and billions in corporate money have flowed back to the United States because of the Trump tax revision.

Facts can be annoying things. What say you, NPR?

That is not a partisan question. The fact is that NPR's analysis of the Trump speech turned out to be shallow. So, should NPR acknowledge that?

After candidate Trump's speech, many media outlets laced him as NPR did. The *Washington Post*, a charter member of the Hate Trump Club, called Trump's words "relentlessly gloomy."

Other detractors dubbed the speech "Mourning in America," a pivot off Ronald Reagan's hopeful ad that proclaimed "Morning in America."

But Donald Trump does not care about any of that. He saw the folks, he heard the thunderous applause. Against heavy odds, his marketing campaign and fearless style were working. Now just one person stands in his way.

But that woman is just as determined as candidate Trump to win the presidency, and she has an army of supporters, including the powerful American media.

Once upon a time, even Donald Trump supported Hillary Clinton and, donated money to her senatorial campaign. But that was then.

As he boards his private jet to fly from Ohio to New York City, Donald Trump understands that he has to make new calculations. He must find a way to rattle his Democratic opponent, demoralize her as he has his GOP rivals.

But Hillary Clinton has been through hell and doesn't fear Trump. In fact, she thinks he's an amateur who can't possibly defeat her.

Donald Trump certainly isn't the slick Barack Obama who took away her minority support and made campaigning look easy while she struggled to relate to the folks. No, this is a real estate hustler with bad hair and a cheesy TV résumé; a casino operator who should be back in Atlantic City, where he belongs.

Triumph awaits Hillary Clinton. Everyone knows that.

Well, not quite everyone.

CHAPTER TWENTY-NINE

PHILADELPHIA, PENNSYLVANIA
JULY 28, 2016
EVENING

Life is always complicated for Hillary Clinton. It's as if there's a thundercloud everywhere she goes. It is never easy, never calm. Turbulence is attached to her like a skin mole.

Mrs. Clinton's résumé is beyond impressive: First Lady for eight years, senator from New York, secretary of state under President Obama. But in every situation, there has been unrelenting controversy. The only person in public life who comes close to Mrs. Clinton in the chaos category is a man named Donald Trump.

So, how did Hillary Diane Rodham, a brilliant but sheltered girl from Illinois, arrive at this point in life? Raised in a traditional family, she was once a "Goldwater Girl," working for the far-right Arizona senator Barry Goldwater as he sought to defeat President Lyndon Johnson for the presidency in 1964. But then things quickly changed: Hillary packed up to attend the all-female Wellesley College, outside Boston, during the Vietnam War years. From there, it was on to Yale Law School, liberal politics, feminism, and a fellow traveler named Bill.

On this humid summer night, Hillary Clinton readies herself for her convention speech in Philadelphia. The month of July has been hellish for her. In particular, there has been more intense controversy about the "email scandal," which has battered her throughout the primary campaign against socialist senator Bernie Sanders, a man she should easily have crushed.

But that did not happen, as Sanders defeated her badly in the first primary vote, New Hampshire, and then went on to win twenty-one other state primaries and caucuses, compiling 43.1 percent of the total votes cast. Once again, Hillary Clinton was forced to defend herself within her own party as the ghost of Barack Obama appeared to be standing beside Bernie Sanders.

The email thing again raised concerns about Mrs. Clinton's honesty, an ongoing problem for her. Federal officials discovered that she had been using her personal server to conduct State Department business, some of it classified. But why would she do that?

Hillary Clinton could not put forth a cogent explanation—and presto! Yet another Clinton scandal enveloped the country.

In her debates with Bernie Sanders, candidate Clinton refused to explain or even discuss the email deal in detail. And the crusty Sanders, as we saw, allowed her to avoid the issue.

That was strange. The Republicans were kicking one another all over the place, but Bernie Sanders seemed tentative around Hillary Clinton. I have no answer other than the possibility that Sanders knew he was going to eventually lose: the superdelegates were in Clinton's pocket, and he wanted to remain in good standing within the party.

The New Yorker put it this way: "Sanders saw Clinton as a clueless, corrupt, temporizing, muckraking member of the neoliberal elite; she saw him as unserious about the details of policy, reckless, self-righteous, swept up in his own sense of ideological purity and 'not a Democrat.'"

Whatever they thought of each other, Sanders has hurt Clinton with younger Democratic voters. But the feds have hurt her more.

After press reports about Hillary's emails, the FBI was tasked with investigating Mrs. Clinton's alleged security breach, and on July 5, Director Comey held a rare press conference defining the problem:

Although we did not find clear evidence that Secretary Clinton or her colleagues intended to violate laws governing the handling of classified information, there is evidence that they were extremely careless in their handing of very sensitive, highly classified information.

Although there is evidence of potential violations of the statutes regarding the handling of classified information, our judgment is that no reasonable prosecutor would bring such a case.

Construction on the gallows instantly stopped.

One major problem, however.

Director Comey is not a prosecutor; he's a cop. Attorney General Loretta Lynch should have been the one holding that press conference on behalf of the Justice Department. But since she had met strangely and privately with Bill Clinton in Arizona, Ms. Lynch was tainted.*

The clarification by Comey was highly unusual, and he acknowledged that he had ventured into a legal gray area. However, he justified it by saying, "In this case, given the importance of the matter, I think unusual transparency is in order."

Backstage at the Philly sports arena, Hillary Clinton well understands that she has not just dodged a bullet; she has avoided a drone strike, barely. Faced with potential federal charges, she put forth publicly the only explanation she had: that she used the private server as a matter of "convenience."

Her detractors immediately rejected the Church Lady rationalization, verbally bludgeoning her and the FBI. Talk radio and Fox News ran full-time with the story for weeks.

But like Donald Trump in Cleveland, Hillary Clinton believes her supporters will stay with her no matter what. And the happy crowd now on the floor of the Wells Fargo Center reinforces that belief— despite another disaster two days before the convention began.

On July 23, an internet activist group called WikiLeaks posted

---

* That meeting was discovered by a local Arizona reporter.

twenty thousand emails hacked from Democrat National Committee officials. Some of the correspondence showed that the DNC chair, Florida congresswoman Debbie Wasserman Schultz, was working against Bernie Sanders when she should have been keeping neutral.

Schultz, a rabid partisan and Hillary supporter, was forced to resign just a few hours before the convention was set to begin, an unheard-of occurrence and one that totally obliterated the announcement that Virginia senator Tim Kaine would be the VP nominee.

Thus, WikiLeaks had an immediate impact on the presidential race. The shadowy organization began in Iceland ten years ago, run by an Australian named Julian Assange who, apparently, despises Hillary Clinton. In a private email, Assange stated, "We believe it would be much better for GOP to win . . . She [Clinton] is a bright, well connected, sadistic sociopath."

Assange took a strong interest in Middle Eastern politics and objected to Mrs. Clinton's behavior as secretary of state—at least, that was his reported rationale for attacking the DNC.

Still unknown to Hillary Clinton is the source of the hack. A few weeks from now, President Obama will be told by U.S. intelligence officials that Russians were involved in providing the stolen emails to WikiLeaks.

The president will not share that revelation with Hillary Clinton. We don't know why.

Yet, even with all the July chaos swirling around, Mrs. Clinton has not lost focus. She remains disciplined and driven. She will not be denied the presidency again.

T T T

IT FALLS TO thirty-six-year-old Chelsea Clinton to introduce her mother, whose speech will close the Democratic National Convention. Like Ivanka Trump with her father, Chelsea is one of the few people in the world whom Hillary truly trusts. The mother of two young children, Chelsea is the calm Clinton, a woman of charity and thoughtfulness.

Hillary's speechwriters have crafted a sixty-minute presentation for the candidate that emphasizes two themes: first, that Americans should come together for the "greater good"; and second, that Donald Trump is the devil, and the "greater good" is to smite him. Hard.

Chelsea's setup is to portray her mother as Joan of Arc: "I'm voting for a fighter who never gives up, and who believes we can always do better when we come together and work together. I hope my children will someday be as proud of me as I am of my mom. I am so grateful to be her daughter."

The introduction complete, Hillary Clinton takes the stage resplendent in a white pantsuit. Her TV audience will number around twenty-seven million, significant but smaller than that for the Trump speech.

Time magazine columnist Joe Klein, a pro-Democrat observer, wrote this about the speech:

> *The smartest thing about Hillary Clinton's acceptance speech Thursday night was that she didn't try to compete with the oratorical athletes who spoke before her during one of the most stirring weeks of speech-making I've ever witnessed. She couldn't summon the passion of Michelle Obama and Joe Biden, so she didn't try. She couldn't summon the conversational brilliance of her husband or Barack Obama, either. She stayed within herself, solid, but showing flashes of her wicked humor at times.*

I was in Philadelphia the same time Joe Klein was, and I have to say I did not "feel it" the way Klein did. Like the Republican Convention, the speeches were mostly predictable, and the "conversational brilliance" escaped me entirely.

But then again, I am a simple man.

Mr. Klein did signal his agenda in the column by writing "we're not going to get flashy speeches from Hillary Clinton. . . . We saw what we're going to get [in Philadelphia]—and considering the unthinkable alternative, that should suffice."

But, of course, it did not suffice. And as Hillary Clinton left the arena stage, basking in the applause of her supporters and most in the media, there was doubt in some precincts—although not on the part of the political partisans or most in the national press, who were certain they had just seen the first woman president speaking this evening.

No, the doubt was harbored where the votes actually come from: the folks.

TTT

As STATED EARLIER in these pages, it is journalistic fraud to try to psychoanalyze politicians or anyone else as part of news coverage (or even when writing a book). But in America, we see that disgraceful exercise on TV all the time. Trump is this, Hillary is that. You fill in the blanks.

I do not know Mrs. Clinton. I've been in her presence exactly twice.

I do know Donald Trump, though. We are not close friends, but we have an honest rapport.

So, in order to write about Donald Trump and the 2016 presidential campaign in a fair and perceptive way, I had to find some insightful material on Hillary. I did cover the campaign on a daily basis, but my observations on television were mostly about policy and tactics, and were not personal. And in the end, personal decided the Clinton-Trump race.

In 2000, Hillary Clinton was elected senator in New York State. Hoping to derail Mrs. Clinton before the vote, Peggy Noonan, a former speechwriter for Ronald Reagan, wrote a book entitled *The Case Against Hillary Clinton*.

The title, of course, defines Ms. Noonan's view of her subject.

Subsequently, Peggy Noonan would become a columnist for the *Wall Street Journal*, where she now routinely criticizes Donald Trump, and has even done some witch-hunting in support of the gender prosecutors.

Ms. Noonan was brought up in Massapequa Park, on Long Island. In her book, she fantasizes about a conversation with one of her childhood friends, a real person, who is now married with three daughters, living a working-class life. Ms. Noonan is trying to convince her former schoolmate not to send Hillary Clinton to the Senate.

God, remember the Hillarys? The Hillarys would only be nice to us, would only look at us in the hall and say hello when they were running for senior council president. And then only because every vote counts. So, she'd actually talk to people like us, and I wish I could say we told her to drop dead but we didn't, did we? We were a little honored, because we knew what she knew: She was a superior person.

You wanted a decent life, she wanted power. You made a marriage, she made a deal. You became a citizen, she became an operator; you became someone who contributes, she became someone who connives to tell contributors what to do and how to do it. She portrays herself as a victim, but she's a victimizer. . . .

She has neither your class nor your courage. If you want a woman to represent your point of view, then you can find one in New York, which has plenty. Don't fall for the one who only wants to use this place as a stirrup to climb onto a horse called the presidency.

She doesn't know your concerns, and she doesn't share them, either. She is not like you. She was never like you.

T T T

HARSH. "NOT LIKE you," "never like you."

Written about sixteen years before Hillary Clinton's triumphant night in Philadelphia, leading to the final push for the White House.

It's almost haunting.

CHAPTER THIRTY

NEW YORK CITY

AUGUST 22, 2016

MIDDAY

"Donald Trump is a racist." That's the theme in the national news again today, after candidate Trump reiterated that, if elected president, he will "round up" the "bad" undocumented aliens and ship them out of the country "so fast your head will spin."

Well, as I am looking at research in my office on Sixth Avenue, my head *is* rotating somewhat. The press knows that in seventy-eight days, Donald Trump may be elected president, and that must not happen.

So, the national media narrative is this: Trump hates blacks, Hispanics, and Muslims.

Blacks because of the Obama birth certificate thing.

Hispanics because the candidate staunchly opposes illegal immigration from Mexico.

And Muslims because Donald Trump is calling for a freeze on immigration and refugee acceptance from "terror-prone regions."

Having spoken in detail with Donald Trump about all these issues, here's what he really believes when you strip away his overstatements designed to fire up voters.

The "birther" thing was a political tactic to curry favor with anti-Obama voters. Trump could not have cared less about the facts surrounding the president's birth. He simply signed on to a foolish conspiracy theory in order to get attention. It was divisive politics, not skin color.

Illegal immigration bothers President Trump on a number of levels. He is a "law and order" guy and sees the failure to control the southern border as weakness in apathetic politicians. He believes immigration anarchy harms the country.

On the Muslim issue, Donald Trump is not sympathetic to that religion's culture. He is deeply offended that the Muslim world has not risen up en masse against jihad. As a New Yorker, he took 9/11 very personally and does not believe it benefits the nation to accept many Muslim immigrants. It's not about ethnicity for Mr. Trump; it's about the soft reaction to terrorism in the Islamic world.

Donald Trump's belief system on illegal immigration and Islamic terrorism is in sync with that of at least half the country. And because most politicians stay silent on ethnic issues for fear of being branded racist, Donald Trump quickly built support with his blunt talk on these issues.

On the other side, many Americans who oppose Trump aren't really interested in the "why" of his presentation. They detest him and believe he's dangerous.

The liberal media (where virtue signaling rules) is part of that crew and is pouncing on Trump every time he puts a negative comment out against any minority or women. Suggesting racist and misogynistic motives is a cheap tactic but one that is now firmly embedded in the American media culture. If you criticize minorities or women, even with validation, you are demonized, boycotted, not worthy of a fair hearing.

The truth about Donald Trump is this: his bias is almost always transactional, not personal. If he opposes something, ethnicity does not matter. Likewise on the positive front. His acceptance of a situation is based on whether it is a positive for him, not based on any ethnic profile.

Still don't believe that? Barack Obama and Hillary Clinton are of different skin colors. Who got it worse from Trump?

By the way, FDR and Dwight Eisenhower were both transactional human beings and governed the country that way. So, Donald Trump is not unique. Only his tactics are.

T T T

BACK TO THE dishonest press. Rather than examine issues that affect Americans directly, the media's campaign coverage of Donald Trump has devolved into smearing him and/or widely publicizing all allegations against him.

In most presidential contests, that kind of constant pressure on a candidate would destroy a campaign. Not this year. I labeled that tactic the "scandal du jour," and it exists to this day.

T T T

COMING OFF THE Republican National Convention, the Trump campaign is disorganized and trying to figure out how to counteract the hostile press coverage. As for the candidate, he believes that big rallies generate enthusiasm and positive local press for him. Thus, during the campaign, Donald Trump will do an astounding 323 campaign appearances—186 in the primaries and 137 in the run-up to the election. It is estimated that 1.4 million people attended a Trump campaign rally.

By contrast, Hillary Clinton will hold an impressive 278 events and also spend an incredible $253 million on TV ads, as opposed to Trump's $93 million.

But candidate Trump will do far more free television appearances than Mrs. Clinton, who avoids forums where she might be challenged. Trump does not do that, talking even to media outlets that are openly hostile to him.

On this day, he appears on *The O'Reilly Factor*, a fair venue:

O'REILLY: So, your campaign has new leadership. Both Corey Lewandowski and Paul Manafort have left. . . . What's going on?

TRUMP: Well, I wanted to keep Paul as a chairman . . . but I ultimately decided I want to run the campaign the way I want to run the campaign . . .

O'REILLY: The debate is going to be everything. You know that, right? . . .

TRUMP: Well, I think it's going to be very important. I don't know if it's make-or-break . . .

O'REILLY: Are you going to keep calling her "Crooked Hillary" during the debate . . . ?

TRUMP: Well, I'm not going to say what I'm going to be doing . . . We'll see what happens.

O'REILLY: . . . The tone right now is you're going to be the guy you were in the Republican [debates]—boom! Take no prisoners. Or are you going to be a little bit more measured?

TRUMP: . . . I may be the way I was and I may be a much different person. I can't tell you. . . . But it will be an interesting hour and a half.

O'REILLY: It will. I can't wait.

TRUMP: It'll probably get a pretty big audience. Almost as big as *The O'Reilly Factor.*

The first debate, just shy of a month from now, will be seen by more than eighty-two million people in the United States alone. That's about twenty episodes of *The Factor.*

T T T

SO IT IS that Donald Trump is running his campaign with no one person carrying out his orders. He gets advice from people like Steve Bannon, Newt Gingrich, Rudy Giuliani, Jeff Sessions, and Chris Christie. Still, even though he has no experience putting together a political organization, it is Trump's show.

Hillary Clinton will have twice as many field offices as Trump,

From left, Tiffany Trump, Donald Trump Jr., Kai Madison Trump, Melania Trump, Donald Trump, Donald Trump III, Ivanka Trump, and Eric Trump at a live town hall event on NBC's *Today Show*, April 21, 2016.

will raise twice as much money ($502 million), and will surround herself with political people of vast experience.

It will not matter.

For the next few weeks, both candidates will set up strategies for the end run. However, both will be challenged in ways they could never have foreseen. Events will unfold quickly and with an intensity rarely seen in American politics.

Shocking October surprises are on the way.

CHAPTER THIRTY-ONE

NEW YORK CITY

SEPTEMBER 10, 2016

LATE AFTERNOON

It is my sixty-seventh birthday, but instead of cutting into a calorie-laden cake, I am reading a transcript of Hillary Clinton's remarks from last night at a Manhattan fund-raiser. The "gala" was sponsored by an LGBT group, and Mrs. Clinton went to town on Donald Trump and his supporters.

Candidate Trump would never have been invited to address that crowd, and therein lies the divide between the two campaigns. Hillary is driving a theme that she will champion various groups. That's called "identity politics."

Mr. Trump, on the other hand, is focused on one very large group: traditional working Americans who are fed up with "politics as usual."

Speaking before folks who adore her, Hillary Clinton uncharacteristically got caught up in the emotion of the room, something that happens to candidate Trump quite often. Emotion is risky in politics, as Hillary Clinton will find out after her speech, which began confrontational and built.

Thank you all [for the opening ovation]. You know I've been saying at events like this lately, I am all that stands between you and the Apocalypse . . . I think we know what we're up against. We do, don't we?

Donald Trump has pledged to appoint Supreme Court justices who will overturn marriage equality . . . and there's so much more that I find deplorable in his campaign: the way he cozies up to white supremacists, makes racist attacks, calls women pigs, mocks people with disabilities—you can't make this up. He wants to round up and deport sixteen million people, calls our military a disaster. And every day he says something else which I find so personally offensive, but also dangerous.

Strong but, so far, standard political attack speech. The American people have heard it all before. Candidate Trump gives that kind of talk all the time.

But then everything changes as the speech veers into a dark place:

I know there are only sixty days left to make our case. Don't get complacent and don't see the latest outrageous, offensive, inappropriate comment and think, "Well, he's done this time."

We are living in a volatile political environment. You know, just to be grossly generalistic, you could put half of Trump's supporters into what I call the basket of deplorables. Right?

The crowd goes wild, in sports parlance. This emboldens candidate Clinton who is now unleashed.

The racist, sexist, homophobic, xenophobic, Islamophobic— you name it. And unfortunately, there are people like that. And he has lifted them up.

T T T

HILLARY CLINTON'S PRIMARY campaign theme up to this point has been "America is stronger if we all work together." In an instant, that has been changed to "millions of Americans are disgusting human beings."

Former secretary of state Hillary Clinton speaks during the LGBT for Hillary Gala at the Cipriani Club on September 9, 2016, in New York City.

It is one thing to demonize a political opponent; it is quite another to attack individual voters who may see things differently from you.

Hillary Clinton's words were even more stunning because she is not a well-loved candidate. Her primary task is to persuade unaligned voters that she will represent the entire country if elected president.

That concept is now in ashes.

It would be hard to envision Bill Clinton delivering the speech his wife has just given. A genius at political communication, the former president would instinctively know that calling voters you don't know "deplorable" and implying that they are haters is, well, deplorable.

And what good does the name-calling do candidate Clinton? Did she win one vote with that pejorative? President Clinton obviously did not go over Hillary's speech before she gave it.

For candidate Trump, the Hillary speech is a gift that keeps on giving. Not only does it ensure that his base will *never* defect to the Clinton camp no matter what he does, but it also inoculates him against smears, because no matter what she says about Donald Trump, in the minds of Trump supporters, Hillary is worse.

"She attacked *me*."

So it is that the presidential campaign of 2016 has gotten real personal, real fast. It is now the Deplorables vs. the Clintonistas.

In a few days, the candidates will enter the debate ring, with both camps wanting blood. It will be the impulsive Donald Trump against the "mean girl" Hillary Clinton.

The nation is ready to rumble.

CHAPTER THIRTY-TWO

UNIONDALE, NEW YORK
SEPTEMBER 26, 2016
EVENING

Debate day at Hofstra University on Long Island did not start out well for Hillary Clinton. The *Washington Post*, quickly moving toward a Hate Trump posture, posted this headline: "Voters Strongly Reject Hillary Clinton's Basket of Deplorables Approach."

The newsprint banner was based on a new *Post* poll showing that 65 percent of respondents thought it was unfair to describe "a large portion of Trump's supporters as prejudiced against women and minorities."

Not to be outdone, Donald Trump had tweeted: "My team of deplorables will be managing my Twitter account for the evening's debate. Tune in!"

In reply, Hillary's people had tweeted the aforementioned *Apprentice* joke that President Obama had aimed at Trump: "You didn't blame Lil Jon or Meat Loaf. You fired Gary Busey. These are the kinds of decisions that would keep me up at night."

And so, indignity running unabated, the stage was set for the first presidential debate of 2016.

NBC News had the forum. *Nightly News* anchor Lester Holt was the inquisitor. I was outside the Hofstra auditorium doing a live lead-to-debate show that was a huge pain. A crowd of people stood behind the platform from where we were broadcasting, and in their exuberance, some were yelling things. I felt like I was at a Mets game.

While preparing for the *Factor* that night, I had called folks in both campaigns. I am not using anonymous sources in this book, because that would be a disservice to you, the reader. Anonymous sources *always* have an unstated agenda, which is often not known by the reporter. So, if a source is not identified, there is a good chance you are getting propaganda, not facts.

Many reporters don't care.

Never let the facts stand in the way of a good story.

From what I could ascertain from my reporting on debate day, candidate Clinton had studied and memorized stuff for days, a situation she later confirmed.

Candidate Trump put in a few hours the day before and did memorize an answer to the "women" question that he knew was coming, and also the Obama birth certificate deal.

Onstage, the candidates shook hands but clearly loathed each other. Mrs. Clinton was wearing a red pantsuit; Mr. Trump was in a traditional dark suit with a blue tie.

The moderator, Lester Holt, was inclined to let the candidates hammer each other, which was good. Debate questions, with a few exceptions like Megyn Kelly's, are rather dull—the excitement, if any, comes from hostile interactions.

Even with the debate taking place in front of a record TV audience, the highlights are scant.

Mrs. Clinton did run down the "women as pigs, dogs, and slobs" checklist.

Mr. Trump answered by saying, "I was going to say something extremely rough to Hillary, to her family, and I said to myself, 'I can't do it.'"

That would change down the road.

Clinton opined that Trump was buddies with Putin and invited him to "hack into Americans."

Trump said he would have a "great relationship" with just about everybody. He also said it might not be Russia doing the hacking; it might be "somebody sitting on their bed that weighs four hundred pounds."

My favorite Trump retort was on the Obama birther thing: "I was the one that got him to produce the birth certificate . . . and we think we did a good job."

Whereupon Hillary Clinton said that Trump's entire campaign was founded on "a racist lie."

And so it went.

The only concrete thing that debate viewers might have taken away from the spectacle was about governance. It was clear from his answers that Donald Trump would make presidential decisions based on his gut; Hillary Clinton, on party consensus. She would lead almost exactly the same way Barack Obama was leading.

The press, of course, instantly declared Hillary Clinton the debate winner; the polls a few days later would show Americans felt that way, too.

Why? Because they heard the press declare Hillary the winner. Thus, the circle of life continues, as the Lion King well knows.

But Donald Trump, who has a great relationship with lions, saw the debate differently.

And he would soon state that on *The O'Reilly Factor*.

CHAPTER THIRTY-THREE

NEW YORK CITY

SEPTEMBER 28, 2016

LATE AFTERNOON

In six weeks, the United States of America will elect a new president, and most polls have Hillary Clinton leading Donald Trump. The Clinton campaign is confident, but the candidate is weary from more than a year of being on the road.

Running for president is a brutal undertaking, one that could destroy a normal, sensitive human being. In addition to the travel and event performances, the attacks on the candidates are relentless and often dishonest. Decorum and civility are not part of any party platform. You've heard the expression "dog eat dog?" Forget that. Now the dog dismembers you, tries to destroy every fiber of your being, and then eats you.

In the past, presidential candidates had to deal with only a few national media people, many of whom could be co-opted with favors and flattery.

As chronicled in my book *Killing Kennedy*, JFK's political machine enjoyed very favorable press coverage. In fact, the *Newsweek* writer who would become editor of the powerful *Washington Post*, Ben Bradlee, was a sailing buddy of the young president. In Kennedy's case, the press actually covered up his indiscretions.

President Franklin Roosevelt also derived benefit from a favorable media, as did Dwight Eisenhower.

Beginning with the Vietnam protest years, then extending into the Watergate debacle, the American media became more negative toward the presidency. TV reporters such as Dan Rather and Sam Donaldson specialized in aggressive coverage and were rewarded in the marketplace.

Then came social media and "black-op" political action groups, which used cyberspace as a war machine. To this day, these smear operations are backed by millions of dollars donated by ideological zealots.

The result is that most presidential candidates are torn to pieces online, and that viciousness is regularly enabled by the establishment media. President Bush the Younger was battered on a daily basis during the Iraq War, so much so that he rarely even looked at news coverage. His advisers tracked things.

For the past fourteen months, both Hillary Clinton and Donald Trump have been savagely attacked in print and in the electronic media. But Trump got it worse than any political candidate. Ever.

In a number of private conversations with me, candidate Trump would rail against what he saw as bias against him. I basically put forth what he already knew: that his populist message threatened the politically correct social landscape. Also, that his failure to absorb press punishment silently, as many politicians do, guaranteed that the negative coverage would continue. Once you hit back against the press, they come after you harder. Media chieftains often take delight in breaking human beings. It's a power thing.

Sometimes Mr. Trump would actually complain to me about *me*. One time, I even raised my voice to him in my own defense. Basically, he believed some of my coverage of him was "negative."

Fine. That was true. It was. But I provide honest analysis always.

For example, if candidate Trump says Mexico is going to pay for the border wall and I don't believe that will happen, I'm going to say it.

If I believe that denigrating John McCain's captivity in Vietnam is wrong, that will be opined.

But here's the thing about Donald Trump: once a candid discussion happens, he doesn't harbor grievances. He moves ahead. He generally respects people who are straightforward.

And here's the other thing about Mr. Trump: he can absorb more punishment than any person I have ever known, with the exception of Senator McCain.

Ironic, isn't it?

Two days after the first debate, which the left-wing press had awarded to Hillary Clinton, candidate Trump entered the No Spin Zone.

T T T

O'REILLY: **Is there something that Hillary Clinton said during the ninety minutes [of the debate] that has stuck in your mind?**

TRUMP: **I think there is . . . I saw when she's talking and talking about what she's going to do and how she's going to do it—I realized she's been doing this for twenty-six to thirty years, and nothing ever gets done. Even when she went to the United States Senate from New York, she said she was gonna bring back jobs to New York, and it was a disaster. Upstate New York is a total disaster. And I started to say, "Wait a minute, Hillary, you've been there twenty-six years, and you haven't done it. Why all of a sudden are you gonna do it? You're not going to do it."**

That statement is pure Trump. Hillary Clinton was a senator for eight years, not twenty-six. But the candidate was referring to her entire public service résumé, First Lady, etc. The media calls Trump's hyperbole "lies." But here's the truth: Donald Trump doesn't really care about verbal precision; he wants to present his message in a vivid way. And he does.

The Factor interview continued with a challenge:

O'REILLY: When she was a senator from New York, you were friendly to her. She and her husband went to your wedding. You weren't real critical of Hillary Clinton at the time. Did you think she was doing a good job back then?

TRUMP: Bill, I was a businessman, I was all over the world. I was doing great and, frankly, got along with all politicians. I didn't go around criticizing them, because when you're a businessman you have to get along with politicians.

O'REILLY: Now I'm going to ask you to grade Lester Holt, the debate moderator. A is best, F is worst. You say . . . ?

TRUMP: When I first did it, I thought he was fine. But when I reviewed it . . . I realized he was much tougher on me than he was on Hillary. The first half of the show was great, but then he hits me with the birther question, and of course, he likes to correct things where I happen to be right.

O'REILLY: All right, give me a grade.

TRUMP: C.

O'REILLY: He interrupted you forty-one times; interrupted Hillary seven times. That's more than I interrupt you, by the way.

TRUMP: He's worse than you.

O'REILLY: Really? That's bad!

For the record, I worked with Lester Holt at WCBS-TV in New York City. He's an honest guy.

During the rest of that interview, it was crime, sanctuary cities, and Colin Kaepernick, the emotional issues that Donald Trump was successfully harvesting across the country.

After the broadcast that night, I thought about Trump, Clinton, and the campaign in general. If the press coverage were honest, they'd have to report that Trump was doing extraordinarily well for a first-time political candidate. But the coverage was not honest, so that assessment was not widely heard outside conservative precincts.

However, unbeknownst to mostly everyone, everything about the campaign was about to change—for the worse.

Lurking about was Donald Trump's past and a subversive group named WikiLeaks—and the two were about to collide.

And the sound of that collision would be heard around the world.

CHAPTER THIRTY-FOUR

NEW YORK CITY

OCTOBER 7, 2016

4:08 P.M.

Donald Trump's past has just caught up with him. The year was 2005, and a cocky Mr. Trump was doing a guest appearance on the afternoon soap opera *Days of Our Lives*. As part of the process, Trump was being interviewed by an NBC-owned show called *Access Hollywood*. The co-anchor of the syndicated program, Billy Bush, was talking with Trump before the formal TV shoot began.

Both men were wearing microphones but may not have known the mics were "hot"—that is, they were recording every single word the men were saying.

For whatever reason, Donald Trump and Billy Bush began discussing women in sexual terms. Again, the banter was being picked up and stored in an NBC camera.

And there it stayed until now, eleven years later, after Donald Trump has won the Republican nomination for president.

There are conflicting reports about who dug up the old video and why. What has been established is that NBC executives were made aware of the explosive content but were hesitant to make it public, mostly for legal reasons.

Then someone leaked it to the *Washington Post*, which was not at all reluctant to expose Donald Trump. The paper posted the tape on its website, and all hell broke just a few minutes after 4 p.m.

Wikipedia describes the situation this way: "*The Washington Post* published a video and accompanying article . . . [showing] Donald Trump and television host Billy Bush having an extremely lewd conversation about women in 2005 . . .

"In the video, Trump described his attempt to seduce a married woman and indicated he might start kissing a woman that he and Bush were about to meet. He added, 'I don't even wait. And when you're a star, they let you do it. You can do anything.'"

The article then goes on to quote an explicit slang term that Donald Trump used in his description of his aggressive interactions with women.

T T T

WITH THE SECOND presidential debate just two days away, disaster doesn't even come close to describing what has now descended on the Trump campaign.

Damage control? Impossible. Every responsible politician and commentator in the country has to condemn Trump's words. No one can possibly defend the man. It is Gary Hart times a thousand.* Even Indiana governor Mike Pence, Trump's running mate, has severely criticized the behavior.

Inside the Trump campaign there is anger, especially after Republican National Committee chairman Reince Priebus calls to discuss Trump quitting the race. The candidate seeks opinions from Steve Bannon, Stephen Miller, and his three grown children. All urge Donald Trump to proceed and "go down fighting."

Trump immediately puts together a plan. He obviously has experience in the scandal area. Various strategies are discussed with inner circle people, but it is the candidate who will make the decisions.

---

* Democrat Gary Hart was forced to withdraw from the presidential campaign in 1988 after he was found to be having an extramarital affair.

But how can Donald Trump continue in the race when many in his own party are calling for him to quit?

One name answers that question: Hillary Clinton.

If any other high-profile candidate were running against Trump, the *Access Hollywood* thing would most likely have ended his candidacy. But Hillary gives Trump cover.

After some thought on wording, candidate Trump issues a short video statement: "I've never said I'm a perfect person, nor pretended to be someone that I'm not. I've said and done things I regret, and the words released today on this more-than-a-decade-old video are one of them. Anyone who knows me knows these words don't reflect who I am. I said it, I was wrong, and I apologize . . . We'll discuss this more in the coming days. See you at the debate."

In addition to the contrition, Trump and his advisers put forth that his crude words were less serious than the misbehavior of President Clinton and the enabling of his wife Hillary, who, as Trump described it, "bullied, attacked, shamed and intimidated his [Bill Clinton's] victims."

Donald Trump also asserted that "this was locker room banter, a private conversation that took place many years ago. Bill Clinton has said far worse to me on the golf course—not even close."

It is the best the Trump campaign can do: a quick apology and a fallback attack on Bill and Hillary's conduct in the White House and beyond.

Sensing she has Trump on the ropes, Mrs. Clinton quickly replies on Twitter: "This is horrific. We cannot allow this man to become president."

But the American public vividly remembers Hillary Clinton standing by her man while he was under siege in the White House over the Lewinsky affair. The voters also easily recall the "it's only about sex" mantra many Democrats endorsed during the impeachment of Bill Clinton.

So, much to the chagrin of the national media, the Trump tape is likely not a knockout punch. In America, voters are now much different than in the past; indeed, they are almost jaded.

Politicians are routinely smeared so badly on social media and in the press that it's like rhetorical Novocain. We the people almost expect depictions of bad behavior on the part of the powerful and famous. Also, as a society, we have widely accepted the "but he or she is worse" rationalization. And millions of Americans truly believe that Hillary Rodham Clinton is far worse than Donald Trump, no matter what his indiscretions.

Finally, the largely phony "virtue signaling" from other politicians and the press just annoys much of the electorate, which understands rank hypocrisy when it sees it. The truth is that every human being is a "sinner," it's just a matter of how bad the actions are. These days, many "sins" are forgiven by the nonideological public.

Sniping away smugly on cable news panels while condemning Donald Trump (or, for that matter, Hillary Clinton) does not usually sway voters who approve of the candidate. In some cases, press attacks solidify support because the candidate might be perceived to be the victim of media unfairness and overkill.

That's how Bill Clinton eventually survived in the court of public opinion—and while impeached, escaped eviction.

And that's also how Donald Trump will survive this day. But, behind closed doors in the Trump Tower campaign headquarters, some demoralization had set in—the consensus being that all the hard work the staff has put in might be destroyed by stupid behavior.

There is just one month to go before the vote. Two more debates, millions of dollars in TV ads yet to come.

But first, another shocking story on the same day Donald Trump's knees buckle—this one a direct hit on his competition.

T T T

THE "HOT MIC" in Seoul, South Korea, was aimed directly at the president of the United States, Barack Obama, and then president of Russia, Dmitry Medvedev. It was March 27, 2012, and the two men were having a private conversation about future missile defense negotiations that was being picked up by an open microphone.

"This is my last election," Mr. Obama told Mr. Medvedev. "After the election I have more flexibility."

The Russian replied, "I understand. I will transmit the information to Vladimir."

That would be Putin.

Another hot mic, another embarrassment as Obama's words certainly empowered Russia and the villainous Putin.

Fast-forward to 2016, when every American diplomat knows that the Russians are aggressively looking to compromise the U.S. government. And as we saw in July, Russian operatives successfully hacked into the email correspondence of the Democratic National Committee, resulting in its leader, Debbie Wasserman Schultz, having to resign.

This morning, October 7, another email dump. Working with Russian hackers, the subversive group WikiLeaks dropped twenty thousand Democratic missives, including some from Hillary Clinton's campaign boss, John Podesta.

This time the U.S. national intelligence apparatus issues a rare statement, saying that the Russians were attempting to interfere in the American election process.

According to later analysis by the cybersecurity firm Dell Secure-Works, a group of Russian intelligence–linked hackers called "Fancy Bear" faked out Mr. Podesta by sending him a phony Google security alert that contained a misleading link. Apparently, this con is called "spear phishing."

When Podesta answered the email, the hackers were able to get his Gmail credentials.

Democrats are furious with the hack and release; their Republican opposition, not so much. The face of WikiLeaks, the aforementioned Julian Assange, is becoming famous for all the wrong reasons.

Her anger rising, Hillary Clinton issues a statement about Assange: "I think he is part anarchist, part exhibitionist, part opportunist, who is either actually on the payroll of the Kremlin or in some way supporting their propaganda objectives . . ."

As the story built, reaction to the DNC hack eventually led to the infamous "Russian collusion" investigation into the Trump campaign, which severely damaged governance in America for almost two years.

So, the Russian intruders won big.

As for the DNC and Podesta emails themselves, they did not

amount to much, although WikiLeaks would drip them out to the public throughout the election cycle.

Essentially, the stolen emails showed that Hillary Clinton curried favor with wealthy Wall Street firms and received big money from them for speaking engagements.

Also, left-wing writer Thomas Frank editorialized that the leaks showed Podesta and the Democrat machine cozying up to the "elite" money people.

Claude Rains might have been *shocked*, but few others were.*

The email dump, however, could not compete with the Trump-women controversy, which dominated news coverage for weeks.

But the hackers did succeed in hurting Hillary Clinton by proving she was deeply involved with securing lucrative paydays from Wall Street at the same time she was trying to convince voters she'd protect them from exploitative capitalism.

Thus, Mrs. Clinton once again finds herself with an honesty deficit, with her party and liberal zealots saying one thing and Hillary doing the exact opposite.

At the same time, Donald Trump finds himself with a woman problem, which will expand and be used to attack his character. For American voters, the presidential race has now become another chaotic reality show in which the next episode could bring just about anything.

What few will understand after the explicit Trump tape and the illegal hack are made public is that one of the candidates has deep experience in the reality show world.

And that experience will be on vivid display in St. Louis, the site of the second debate.

It is forty-eight hours away.

---

* The actor telling Humphrey Bogart in *Casablanca* that he was shocked gambling was allowed in Rick's Café.

CHAPTER THIRTY-FIVE

ST. LOUIS, MISSOURI

OCTOBER 9, 2016

9 P.M.

The second debate is getting nasty. Both candidates have dropped all pretense. There's no handshake upon their taking the stage, and the personal attacks are flying in the auditorium at Washington University.

Donald Trump, fighting for his political life, is determined to show his supporters that he is still strong and in command after the *Access Hollywood* disaster of forty-eight hours ago.

Candidate Trump has decided to go on the offense: he will show no weakness tonight, no uncertainty. It is Trump's Battle of the Bulge, a brazen counteroffensive against enemy forces who believe he is finished.

The event in St. Louis begins with Donald Trump holding a press conference before the actual debate. Sitting with him are three women who, in the past, have accused Bill Clinton of sexual misconduct: Paula Jones, Kathleen Willey, and Juanita Broaddrick.

The ladies reiterate their stories and strong beliefs that Hillary Clinton defended her husband's behavior and denigrated them in the process. The panel is soon joined by Kathy Shelton, a rape victim at twelve years old whose assailant was represented by Mrs. Clinton when she worked as a public defender in Arkansas.

Donald Trump refuses to answer questions about his tape situation in the press conference, focusing all attention on the four women who are angry with Hillary Clinton. The Clinton campaign tells the press the stunt is "an act of desperation."

Trump's decision to replay the Clinton saga is aimed not so much at voters as at the Republican establishment, which may abandon him. His strategy is to make it difficult for GOP big shots to throw the election to Hillary Clinton, a woman reviled by millions of Republican voters.

Donald Trump also understands that conservative talk radio and some TV commentators who support him will embrace the press conference by making a stark contrast between his "words" and the actual misdeeds of the Clintons.

From left, Kathleen Willey, Juanita Broaddrick, and Kathy Shelton wait for the presidential town hall debate between Democratic presidential nominee Hillary Clinton and Republican presidential nominee Donald Trump at Washington University in St. Louis, October 9, 2016.

Trump is, in effect, providing a new narrative to his media supporters that goes like this: "Yes, I said offensive things. But the Clintons *did* terrible things to the women you see before you, and they
have gotten away with it."

After the press conference, the four women are seated prominently
at the debate, guaranteeing national TV coverage. Some believe their
presence in the auditorium has rattled Hillary Clinton.

If you examine Donald Trump's debate strategy without emotion,
his plan was effective. And it was *his* plan. He designed the scenario
himself and carried it out. The result was that he somewhat diminished
the *Access Hollywood* thing and reminded wavering Republicans that
defecting from him was a gift to a devil named Hillary.

The debate structure itself features questions from the two moderators, Martha Raddatz from ABC News and Anderson Cooper from
CNN. But there are also audience queries from preselected folks.

Both Raddatz and Cooper are perceived to be liberal, and they
are. It is simply inconceivable that either of them voted for Donald
Trump.

I worked with Martha at WCVB-TV in Boston. She is an excellent reporter who rarely lets her personal belief system influence her
presentation.

Anderson Cooper is less disciplined but generally does not seek to
be unfair. At CNN, he *must* present a liberal program, and so he does.

At one point in the debate, Candidate Trump told the world that
"it's three against one," meaning he was opposed by not only Hillary
but also the two moderators. Trump was angry because Raddatz and
Cooper did not ask candidate Clinton about the email situation.

When the focus turned to Trump, Anderson Cooper was the
doomsayer, quickly asking the candidate if his comments on the scandalous tape indicated "sexual assault." That was a question designed
to get attention, much like the Megyn Kelly controversy.

Mr. Trump, however, was ready, quickly replying that his offensive comments were "locker room talk." Trump then kicked it back
to Hillary: "She brings up words that I said eleven years ago—I think
it's disgraceful, and she should be ashamed of herself, to tell you the
truth."

For her part, Mrs. Clinton completely avoided any defense of her husband and her support of him. Instead, she tried to keep the focus on Trump, running down a list of his most egregious statements.

Responding, Donald Trump accused Hillary Clinton of a variety of crimes, for example, destroying her private emails in the face of an FBI investigation. He then pledged that, if elected president, he would appoint a special counsel to investigate her and said she'd likely wind up in jail.

Not to be outdone, Hillary responded, "Okay, Donald, I know you're into big diversion tonight—anything to avoid talking about your campaign exploding and the way Republicans are leaving you."

Finally, Trump told the world that Hillary "has tremendous hate in her heart."

It was an exhausting ninety minutes, and at the end a question from an audience member suggested that each of the candidates say something good about the other.

Hillary complimented the Trump children. Trump said Mrs. Clinton was persistent: "she doesn't give up."

Then Donald Trump extended his hand, and Hillary shook it.

With hate in her heart?

T T T

Sixty-six million Americans watched the second debate, down about sixteen million viewers from the first one. That's interesting because with the *Access Hollywood* tape, there was scandal, and that usually leads to a bigger audience.

Most pundits and reporters totally missed the most important story in St. Louis. With his campaign tottering, Donald Trump pulled off a bold strategy to avoid defeat before a single vote was cast. His audacity, going on the offensive, had worked again.

Thus, candidate Trump lived to fight another day. Two debates down, one to go.

Las Vegas beckons.

CHAPTER THIRTY-SIX

LAS VEGAS, NEVADA

OCTOBER 19, 2016

LATE AFTERNOON

America's premier party town welcomes gamblers above all others, and the gambler-in-chief has arrived.

Donald Trump can easily see a hotel bearing his name just off the famous Las Vegas Strip. It's another sweet deal for him: no direct involvement, the company that owns the building paying Trump millions simply for the privilege of using his name.

There is no casino inside the hotel, but it is a first-class operation. You would be comfortable staying there even if you didn't approve of Trump. The food is good, the grounds spotless, affluence everywhere.

This is what candidate Trump is selling as he prepares for his third and final debate against an increasingly dour Hillary Clinton. Well-managed success for the entire country is what Trump constantly promotes. "Make America Great Again." Don't believe the candidate? Check out that hotel with his name on it.

But Donald Trump may not get the chance to impose "greatness" on the nation. Just this morning, a poll was released that cannot please the candidate. With less than three weeks until the election, Trump is running well behind Hillary Clinton, according to the national survey taken by Quinnipiac University in Connecticut.

It is Clinton 47 percent, Trump 40 percent among "likely voters."

There is, however, another significant question in the poll: Is the news biased against Trump? Fifty-five percent say, yes, it is; 42 percent believe it is not.

So, potential voters are paying attention.

The data on the press suggests a certain amount of sympathy for candidate Trump. If voters despised him, they would not see negative coverage as "unfair." Many folks believe American media power is now being used to help Hillary and the Democrats. Fair play is a traditional American attribute, but it is becoming increasingly obvious that when it comes to covering Donald Trump, the press is not in the fairness business.

While the Clinton campaign is happy with its lead in the polls, there are a few disturbing signals. Hillary's trustworthy poll numbers are averaging around 30 percent, and her "likability" is very low as well. Just about every presidential poll confirms that.

In addition, there is uncertainty about African American support, which could be the deciding factor for the Democrats in Michigan and Pennsylvania. Four years ago, black voters turned out in record numbers to back Barack Obama's reelection. In this campaign, more than a few observers believe Hillary Clinton is not really connecting with African Americans, as hard as she might try.

Nevertheless, as the two candidates take the stage at the University of Nevada, Las Vegas, the numbers indicate ultimate success for candidate Clinton.

Her White House dream may be just a few weeks away.

TTT

THE THIRD DEBATE is dull, perhaps because just ten days ago, Trump and Clinton tore each other up in St. Louis.

Tonight, Fox News anchor Chris Wallace tries to keep things moving, but the truth is that Americans have heard it all before and the political rhetoric is getting tiresome.

Yes, yes, yes, we know Hillary supports "reproductive rights."
Sure, sure, sure, Donald will make great deals that will lead to prosperity.

We. Get. It.

There are less personal attacks this evening, although candidate Trump calls Hillary a "nasty woman" after she implies that he dodges taxes.

Sensing that the debate is a nothing, Donald Trump throws one verbal hand grenade, knowing it will be the only thing people will remember from the drowsy proceedings. When asked if he will accept the result of the upcoming election, Trump instantly becomes a provocateur: "I will tell you at the time. I will keep you in suspense."

Vintage Trump. He understands perfectly what will happen next. Social media will explode, cable news will yammer on about it for days. The news cycle will be Trump, more Trump, and, finally, Trump.

Was Hillary even at the debate?

It's exactly like getting paid for lending his name to a hotel. His brand is in lights.

What many Americans still do not understand is that Donald Trump does not care if you dislike what he says or what he stands for. He does not spend time analyzing pros and cons. He wants action, reaction, and victory. He believes notoriety leads to winning. There are millions of Americans who respect decisiveness and simplicity. Trump has designed the MAGA hats for them.

That's right! Make America Great Again! 'Cause it's not that great right now.

But as the Nevada desert cools down from the night air, time is growing short. Donald Trump has used controversy and bold behavior to get close to the mountaintop. He has almost pulled off the most stunning political power play in American history. Whatever the vote turns out to be, he has done an amazing thing.

He now needs to close the deal. But he's running behind. Something more will have to happen if Donald Trump is to win the White House.

And although he cannot possibly know it on the Nevada stage, that something more is on the way.

CHAPTER THIRTY-SEVEN

WASHINGTON, DC

OCTOBER 28, 2016

FRIDAY MORNING

The Federal Bureau of Investigation is the nation's most respected law enforcement agency. That is, it was until it ran headlong into the duet of Hillary Clinton and Donald Trump. Now no one really knows how much damage the Bureau will eventually suffer after all the investigations of it are complete.

It was the revelation that Secretary of State Clinton used her private email server to conduct State Department business that began the FBI's spiral downward. President Obama and Attorney General Loretta Lynch clearly wanted the investigation wrapped up quickly for political reasons—Mrs. Clinton was poised to take over for Obama if she could defeat Donald Trump.

But then things began to get "complicated." Hillary Clinton had no defense; she did it. Her explanation was that she used her personal email account for "convenience."

Then Loretta Lynch met privately with Bill Clinton in Arizona, putting the Justice Department in a very bad place. The attorney general said that she and the former president discussed "grandkids." Except for an alert Phoenix reporter, that inappropriate thirty-minute conversation would have remained clandestine.

Even after public exposure of the meeting, Loretta Lynch did not recuse herself from the federal investigation into Mrs. Clinton, as she should have. The assumption on the part of some law enforcement analysts is that her boss, Mr. Obama, wanted her to stay on the case.

In July, as mentioned earlier, FBI director James Comey went public saying Hillary had screwed up, but not enough to be prosecuted in the opinion of the FBI, which never should have rendered an opinion. The Bureau was mandated to turn over whatever evidence it had compiled to the attorney general, who, by job description, is tasked with the prosecution calls on high-profile cases.

But, again, it certainly looks like President Obama did not want to go through the regular chain of command in Hillary's case.

Was the fix in? More evidence would have to be forthcoming in order to answer that question.

What is certain is that Director Comey is more of a bureaucrat than a crime fighter. A lawyer out of the University of Chicago, Comey was appointed FBI chief by President Obama in 2013. By his own statement, he believed Hillary Clinton would defeat Donald Trump in the election.

Soon after he allowed candidate Clinton to avoid further legal scrutiny, the six-foot-eight Comey was part of a group that informed President Obama that Russian hackers had compromised a vast amount of emails from the Democratic Party. That was the first WikiLeaks dump.

Again, Mr. Obama chose to keep that information quiet, and Comey was directed to investigate the Trump campaign to see if it was working with the foreign hackers, certainly a legitimate probe by the FBI.

But, as we now know, Comey's top investigators were not neutral fact finders. They were anti-Trump partisans. Thus, the Bureau is now diminished, with possible indictments looming.

TTT

JAMES COMEY KNEW all that when he decided to insert himself into the presidential race yet again.

With eleven days left until the vote, Comey revisited his July statement in a letter to some members of Congress. In effect, he was saying that new evidence had surfaced in the Hillary Clinton email case.

"The FBI has learned of emails that appear to be pertinent to the investigation. I am writing to inform you that the investigative team briefed me on this yesterday, and I agreed that the FBI should take appropriate investigative steps designed to allow investigators to review these emails to determine whether they contain classified information, as well as to assess their importance to our investigation."

What Director Comey failed to tell the public is that the new "pertinent" emails were captured on a computer owned by the notorious former congressman Anthony Weiner, whom the FBI had nailed on child-sexting felonies.

Weiner was married to Huma Abedin, Hillary Clinton's close adviser. Apparently, the couple shared email accounts.

Even with the Weiner revelation kept quiet, there was consternation in the media. Realizing that their chosen candidate was now in jeopardy, the vast majority of the national press immediately condemned Comey.

On the other side, the conservative media convicted Hillary of high crimes and demanded her withdrawal from the race.

For Donald Trump, Comey became a member of the Magi, bringing gifts of great value. The candidate opined, "I have great respect for the fact that the FBI and the DOJ are now willing to right the horrible mistake they made."

Of course, the Clinton staff immediately sought to downplay the FBI reveal. But all the king's horses and CNN couldn't put the Clinton campaign back together again.

A few hours after Comey put out his letter, a leak pinpointed Anthony Weiner's tangential involvement, and things got even worse. To this day, Hillary Clinton believes James Comey cost her the election, and she said so in a book she wrote after the election.

As the Trump campaign celebrated and the national press gnashed its collective teeth, the question became "Why did Comey do it?"

The answer is simple: to cover his butt. That's what bureaucrats do. A shrewd political player, James Comey knew that if Hillary Clinton were elected president and it later came out that he did not disclose the new email information, especially with the villain Weiner involved, he would be ruined. His July exposition had already put him in an ideological kill zone. He had to get out in front; it was survival.

But the chaos was not over for James Comey, who actually thought he would get through the political mess with his job intact.

With all eyes on the FBI, Comey had another moment of reckoning coming up. This one would take Donald Trump by surprise.

CHAPTER THIRTY-EIGHT

WASHINGTON, DC

NOVEMBER 6, 2016

SUNDAY AFTERNOON

Donald Trump is closing in fast. With just two days until the nation votes for president, Trump is now two percentage points behind Hillary Clinton, according to the RealClearPolitics polling average. The same outfit has 216 electoral votes "safe" for Hillary, 164 solid for Trump.

Two hundred seventy electoral votes are needed to win.

Nevertheless, the media and the Clinton campaign, sometimes actually working together, as we saw when CNN's Donna Brazile slipped Hillary debate questions, still believe their candidate will prevail, perhaps by a large margin. The forecast from the political website FiveThirtyEight gives Donald Trump a 35.7 percent chance to win. Hillary Clinton's chances stand at 64.2 percent.

On television, I said that my analysis showed Mrs. Clinton fading and that she could well lose on Tuesday. I based my belief on her tepid campaign appearances and slippage in the polls.

To me, Hillary Clinton was just hanging on, while Donald Trump had some momentum. Trump's voter turnout is pretty much guaranteed because his supporters are so rabid. It's hard to tell which emotion is stronger: the enthusiasm for Trump or the loathing for Hillary.

On Mrs. Clinton's side, there is little emotion. "She's not like you. She was never like you."

Then a knock at the proverbial door. A tall man once again is on the porch with another letter. But it's Sunday, not a time when federal employees are usually on the job. Couldn't it wait until Monday?

No, it could not.

James Comey is back with an additional message for congressional leadership.

"I write to supplement my October 28, 2016, letter that notified you the FBI would be taking additional investigative steps with respect to former Secretary of State Clinton's use of a personal email server. . . .

"Based on our review, we have not changed our conclusions that we expressed in July with respect to Secretary Clinton."

Wow, that was fast. Nine days. Hillary Clinton is not guilty of a crime again.

But instead of joy, outrage erupts in the left-wing precincts. Senator Dianne Feinstein puts forth: "Today's letter makes Director Comey's actions nine days ago even more troubling."

No love for James Comey on either side. That's what you get when you blend politics with law enforcement.

Donald Trump doesn't really care what James Comey says. The candidate has convicted Hillary of far worse than an email rap. "Hillary Clinton is guilty," Trump tells supporters shortly after Comey's exposition. "The FBI knows it."

Meanwhile, the pro-Hillary press is going into full-tilt attack mode. The uber-left *New Yorker* magazine sums it up: "There has always been a radical imbalance in measuring Clinton's email practices against Trump's raw bigotry and authoritarian-minded contempt for the rule of law."

Sure. A possible national security breach by a high-profile secretary of state could never stand up to alleged "raw bigotry."

The Sunday-with-Comey thing continues to bother me. Did

Comey's FBI agents sit around on an autumn Saturday summarizing their conclusions? The actual letter is a short statement that could have been written in less than an hour. Comey's timing seems contrived to me.

I could be wrong. I have no evidence. But I do know the White House was growing increasingly worried about the vote.

Which would be on Tuesday.

Hillary already has her victory outfit picked out.

CHAPTER THIRTY-NINE

NEW YORK CITY

NOVEMBER 8, 2016

ELECTION DAY

Biggest news day in four years, and I am not covering anything until 8 p.m. That's because until most of the polls close, Fox News wants reportage, not *O'Reilly Factor* commentary. I completely understand: let the voters cast their ballots for president with clear heads. There's been more than enough preelection opinion.

Over at CNN, however, it's a different story, and the candidate graphics illustrate it best. Two tight headshots will appear on the screen all day and into the night. To the left, Donald Trump frowning with squinty eyes. The subliminal message: mean guy. To the right, Hillary Clinton shown smiling with dimples. The message: nice mom.

Most of the polls are predicting a Hillary win, and the national media are already in a celebratory mood.

So is the Clinton campaign.

With the voting about to begin, the contrast to the Trump campaign is striking.

T T T

IT WASN'T UNTIL 3:23 this morning that Hillary Clinton's campaign jet touched down at Westchester County Airport, north of New York City. The entire day before the vote had been quite a ride, with four events starring Hillary and her mega-famous entourage: Bruce Springsteen, Lady Gaga, Beyoncé, Jay-Z, and Jon Bon Jovi all appearing at various places, igniting Clinton pep rallies.

Mrs. Clinton wrapped up her campaigning after midnight in Philadelphia, where Barack and Michelle Obama gave her hugs as Bill and Chelsea Clinton looked on.

There was champagne on the short flight home and, as Robert Duvall said in *Apocalypse Now*, "the smell of victory."

T T T

DONALD TRUMP WAS also up late (because he's always up late). He had done five rallies on Monday and was finishing in Grand Rapids, Michigan, which Hillary had also visited.

But no famous people trailed Trump, and there was no champagne because he doesn't drink. At 1:49 a.m., he was still telling supporters he would "drain the swamp."

The swamp had turned in hours ago.

T T T

AT 8:22 THE next morning, Donald Trump, who may be a vampire, was speaking by phone to Fox and Friends: "If I don't win, I will consider it a tremendous waste of time, energy, and money."

T T T

AT 9:06 A.M., Hillary Clinton was dressed, made up, and voting at the Douglas Grafflin Elementary School in Chappaqua, New York, where she lives some of the time. Her other residence is in Washington, DC.

Mrs. Clinton seemed confident, telling reporters, "I know how much responsibility goes with this. So many people are counting on the outcome of this election and what it means for our country."

It would be another busy day for candidate Clinton. She had already chosen her victory speech outfit, a white pantsuit, and her writers had worked up two "we won" speeches. Hillary had to select the one she preferred.

T T T

SHORTLY AFTER NOON, Donald Trump and his wife, Melania, cast their ballots at New York City Public School 59, a few blocks from their Trump Tower home. According to the *New York Times*, some voters standing in line booed the Trumps, and one woman yelled a profanity.

When asked if that lady worked for the *New York Times*, no answer was forthcoming.

T T T

THE CLINTON CAMPAIGN had rented the mammoth Javits Center for its anticipated victory party. Lost was the irony that a young Donald Trump had sold New York City the land upon which the Javits Center was built.

According to the *Hollywood Reporter*, the Clinton people wanted a major fireworks display over the Hudson River to erupt when Hillary won, but the NYPD said no for security reasons.

There was, however, some big-name talent set to appear that evening at the Clinton bash, including pop star Katy Perry. Doors would open at 6 p.m.

Meanwhile, Hillary Clinton stayed in her Chappaqua home, doing a few get-out-the-vote radio interviews and studying her victory speech.

T T T

BY CONTRAST, THE Trump campaign had rented a ballroom in the pedestrian New York Hilton Midtown Hotel. Not much was planned. The only famous person booked was former *Apprentice* contestant Omarosa Manigault.

There was a pretzel guy in front of the hotel.

T T T

DONALD TRUMP SPENT much of Election Day in the "war room," located on the fourteenth floor of Trump Tower, or in his private office on the twenty-sixth floor. Advisers Steve Bannon, Stephen Miller, Kellyanne Conway, Reince Priebus, and Jared Kushner, along with Don Jr., Ivanka, and Eric Trump, were mostly in the fifth-floor "vote count room."

"It was business as usual," Don Jr. told me. "We always expect success and never talk about failure. My father thought they might pull something. Even though we were all beaten down [from campaigning,] we were still at war. Nobody relaxed. We were like caged animals."

TTT

AT 5:50 P.M., Hillary Clinton departed Chappaqua for the one-hour drive to Midtown. At about the same time, CNN White House correspondent Jim Acosta was tweeting doom for Trump. Folks were lined up for blocks waiting to get into the Javits Center to celebrate that doom.

TTT

AT 7 P.M., the *Hollywood Reporter* estimates there are just fifty people in the Trump room at the Hilton.

The pretzel guy has left.

TTT

AT 8 P.M., the real election coverage begins. Charles Krauthammer, the perspicacious writer and commentator, is convinced Trump is going to lose. Although conservative, Charles wants that outcome. So, I open Fox News's prime-time programming dueling with him:

O'REILLY: [Trump] is not underperforming. Would you cede me that?

KRAUTHAMMER: Look, Bill, underperforming in this election is not reaching 270 . . . The fact is that he has to carry the big three swing states, Florida, Ohio, North Carolina, to penetrate the blue wall. Right now, that looks like a distant prospect.

O'REILLY: Which state do you think Hillary Clinton will take out of those three?

KRAUTHAMMER: I think it's likely she takes Florida and it's a toss-up she takes North Carolina. Ohio, I think she has the edge.

O'REILLY: Where do you think her strength is going to come in Florida? ... The northern counties in the Central Time Zone remain to be counted. And that's Trump territory.

KRAUTHAMMER: She has a two percent lead now, and that's substantial.

O'REILLY: So, you're going to predict Clinton is the next president?

KRAUTHAMMER: If you force me, I'll take it.

T T T

HILLARY CLINTON LOST Florida and Ohio and North Carolina. In all, she was defeated in thirty states. Charles and most other pundits were stunned, but not Kellyanne Conway. At about 9:30 p.m., she told her boss, Donald Trump, that he would win. That was based upon exit polling.

Trump answered with his usual "Let's see what happens."

T T T

IT IS NOW 12:30 a.m. on November 9, and the race still has not been called. The *Hollywood Reporter* placed a correspondent at Hillary's victory party who filed this.

"Inside the media room, reporters slammed their tables at yet another Trump [state] victory. While many gathered outside for a much-needed cigarette break, guests began to quietly exit the venue, gloomily bidding their friends goodbye before going their separate ways. . . .

"[Hillary supporters are] describing themselves as 'heartbroken,' 'disappointed,' 'confused' and 'in shock.'"

Note the line "reporters slammed their tables." Reporters are supposed to be neutral. But when it comes to Donald Trump, they are not and never will be.

On television, the comments became personal and brutal. CNN analyst Van Jones described Trump's strong showing in racial terms. "This was a whitelash against a changing country."

T T T

IT IS ALL over at 2:20 in the morning. John Podesta, Hillary's campaign chairman, steps onto the stage at the Javits Center, telling the remaining crowd to go home. Hillary Clinton will not be speaking until tomorrow.

"We are so proud of her," Podesta says. "She's done an amazing job and she's not done yet."

But she is done.

T T T

AT 3 A.M., Vice President–elect Mike Pence, usually in the Land of Nod long before this, takes the microphone at the Hilton Hotel to introduce President-elect Donald Trump. It has been 511 days since Mr. Trump declared his candidacy. He has accomplished the unthinkable.

Donald Trump's victory speech is conciliatory, beginning with mention of his opponent.

"I've just received a call from Secretary Clinton. She congratulated us on our victory, and I congratulated her and her family on a very, very hard-fought campaign.

"Hillary has worked very long and very hard over a long period of time, and we owe her a major debt of gratitude for her service to our country."

The new president then goes on to say many words, but one sentence sums up his victory: "The forgotten men and women of our country will be forgotten no longer."

T T T

BEFORE LEAVING TRUMP TOWER to deliver his victory speech, Donald Trump received a congratulatory call from President Obama. Mr. Obama did most of the talking.

The moment was witnessed by his eldest son, Don Jr. "My father does not show emotion," he said. "The magnitude of this had not yet hit him. Everyone around him was saying, 'I can't believe we won.' But he said very little. He just continued to watch the coverage."

T T T

THE AGONY OF defeat for Hillary Clinton was something that only she can describe. After the election was called for her opponent, she stayed overnight in Manhattan. The next day, she delivered a short concession speech, asking her supporters to give Donald Trump "a chance to lead."

Ten months later, she told David Remnick, the editor of the *New Yorker* magazine, this: "At every step I felt that I had let everyone down. Because I had."

So it is that the American people had elected Donald J. Trump to lead them. But that did not sit well with some very powerful people.

And some of those people had a plan.

CHAPTER FORTY

LONG ISLAND, NEW YORK

APRIL 19, 2019

GOOD FRIDAY MORNING

It's been another turbulent week in America as the Mueller Report is now public and the usual hate-or-love-Trump debate is raging. The president believes he's been exonerated from allegations that his campaign colluded with Russia.

However, the Trump haters—"the Resistance," as they still call themselves—continue to see a corrupt president who should be removed from office.

The intensity of the ongoing brawl stems from long before the 2016 ballot. Donald Trump became the fifth president in U.S. history to lose the popular vote but gain the office. However, in the state of California, which is now in a one-party situation, Trump lost by more than 4 million votes.

Take the Golden State out of the mix, and the election was decisive for Donald Trump, who convinced almost 63 million Americans to vote for him.

How did that happen?

Mr. Trump is the first president without any previous experience in public service. He is a man of self-interest, confidence, and unshakable determination.

His flaws were brightly illuminated by a partisan press, which became heavily invested in not only Trump's defeat, but also his complete destruction.

As part of that effort, the national media followed Hillary Clinton's lead and diminished Americans who had dared support Donald Trump. The "deplorables" brand, and the scorn that goes with it, was deeply felt by millions of voters.

That was *the* most important element in Trump's victory because it solidified his support. No matter what the Democrats or the press said about *their* candidate, he was better than his detractors. And that mind-set remains to this day.

Crude language, exaggerations, bombastic tweets—none of that really matters. Millions of Americans believe they themselves have been directly attacked by arrogant elitists. On Election Day, those Americans cast payback votes.

To this day, much of the media does not understand what happened, and that failure to grasp reality extends into serious situations like the investigation into how Russia intruded on a U.S. presidential election.

Instead of the entire nation being galvanized against the naked aggression of Vladimir Putin, the Mueller Report is almost exclusively a Trump thing, with the president's supporters dismissing the allegations because they don't trust "the swamp" or believe the media, and the Hate Trump cadre totally denying Mr. Trump due process and demanding his departure, even though Robert Mueller put forth evidence deemed inconclusive by the Justice Department.

Instead of "getting it"—understanding that Donald Trump is president because the media allied itself with Hillary Clinton—the press is unrepentant and clueless as to how they actually empower the president.

A look back by the *New Yorker* magazine vividly makes that point. "[Hillary] lost because she could never find a language, a thematic focus, or a campaigning persona that could convince struggling working Americans that she, and not a cartoonish plutocrat, was their champion. She lost because of the forces of racism, misogyny, and nativism that Trump expertly aroused. And she lost because of external forces (Vladimir Putin, Julian Assange, James Comey) that were beyond her control and are not yet fully understood."

So, there it is, and based on a number of statements she made after the vote, Hillary Clinton might agree with most of that very liberal and shortsighted analysis.

But here's the truth. Mrs. Clinton was never a champion of working Americans in any way. There were no "forces of racism and misogyny" that mattered a whit on Voting Day. Barack Obama was elected twice. Oprah Winfrey is the most successful celebrity in history.

And calling Donald Trump "cartoonish" implicitly insults the nearly 63 million Americans who voted for him.

Here's the final word on President Trump's triumph. Despite all Trump's bedrock support, it happened because African Americans did not rally to Hillary Clinton's cause. Although she carried 88 percent of the black vote, 7 percent fewer African Americans showed up at the polls than in 2012.

About 765,000 black voters simply stayed home. Had they turned out for Hillary at an 88 percent rate, she most likely would have won in Pennsylvania and Michigan, and would be in the White House right this moment.

Facts like that are routinely ignored by an American press, which often rejects truth if it does not fit into their ideological narrative. Just turn on your television set. It's right there before your eyes, on both sides of the Trump equation.

TTT

So, NOW WHAT? A complicated, politically inexperienced man is in charge of the most powerful nation on earth. With a steep learning curve that would be daunting for any human being, President-elect Trump will be under constant pressure. The American media has basically set itself up to denigrate the Trump administration. Therefore, the new president's accomplishments will be routinely ignored and his controversies declared "bombshells."

Donald Trump is facing a special prosecutor, Vladimir Putin, vast illegal immigration problems, Little Rocket Man, and the Chinese government setting out to dominate the world economically.

Other than that, things are calm at the White House.

Well, that's not entirely true. Donald Trump now lives there, and it's never calm when he's in any building. After nearly three months in office, many Americans are asking questions: Will things ever calm down? Will the president ever be allowed to lead?

A look back to Inauguration Day just might hold the answer to those questions.

PART THREE

PART THREE

CHAPTER FORTY-ONE

_____

WASHINGTON, DC

JANUARY 20, 2017

INAUGURATION DAY

Donald Trump's campaign for reelection in 2020 begins the day he takes the oath of office as the forty-fifth president of the United States. There is no rest for the new chief executive; he is incapable of that. Mr. Trump already has his eye on his legacy and thus remains in campaign mode, as outgoing president Barack Obama will soon find out.

As per tradition, last night the Trump family rested at the Blair House, across the street from the White House. Blair is essentially a presidential guest residence consisting of about eighteen thousand square feet of living space spread across four buildings flanking Lafayette Park. Most human beings are awed by Blair. However, most folks did not build Trump Tower.

Today, Americans and the world will again witness a peaceful change of power in the most powerful nation on the planet. But drama will unfold. After all, Donald Trump is involved.

To understand exactly how the incoming president really sees America, you must realize his view of life in general. Donald Trump assesses the world in just two colors: black and white. Gray does not exist. Other colors are irrelevant to him.

He is also a "no" person, at least outwardly—no doubt, no fear, no apologies, no retreat. He will fight most battles aggressively, even the small skirmishes that many folks would ignore.

This confrontational style is a major departure from that of presidents of the past, most of whom employed some element of caution in their public dealings. Caution and Donald Trump seldom interact.

President Trump is also not a "people person," although he respects the goal of Americans who desire to achieve prosperity. He is more comfortable interacting with crowds rather than individuals. The new president sincerely wants to deliver economic opportunity and is angered by policies that restrain that goal. This is Trump's core political strategy: to drive economic expansion that will translate into better lives for all Americans.

Except for his enemies, of course: no quarter for them unless they recant their anti-Donald posture.

One important aspect of the new president's thinking is that every group should participate in material success. He sees more prosperity for minorities as a gold star for him, a sterling achievement, as most other presidents could not deliver that. Thus, President Trump is personally invested in helping poor and working Americans, a fact that will be ignored by his detractors, who have intentionally distorted his demographic outlook—and even worse, branded him racist for political reasons.

As he prepares to lead the nation, the new president already has a number of major "transactions" on his mind in order to accomplish his goals and ensure his place in history. Joe Biden entitled his biography *Promises to Keep*, and Donald Trump espouses the same commitment.

There is an ancient rule in sub-Saharan Africa: never get between a hippopotamus and water. In the new administration, the adage has become "never get between Donald Trump and his promise." The new president will be relentless in promoting his stated national view, and those who oppose it will be harshly confronted, including, very shortly, the outgoing president.

Finally, Donald Trump has learned many things during his arduous campaign, lessons about ultimate success. Advisers told him to be more "diplomatic." They opined that he should not use personal insults. They suggested that he court the media and cut back on Twitter.

Trump totally rejected all that advice.

Trump was elected president of the United States.

So, now, as he prepares to take the Presidential Oath of Office in a few hours, the question becomes: Will Donald Trump modify his behavior, and conduct himself in a more traditional way?

Will he act "presidential"?

The answer to that question will become clear as Inauguration Day unfolds.

T T T

PRESIDENT-ELECT TRUMP AND his wife, Melania, are up well before dawn on this overcast Friday. They will be groomed from hair to heel, as the world will be watching their every move during the historic proceedings.

The entire Trump family, soon to be awakened, will attend a number of events, including the most important: the swearing-in ceremony at noon in front of the Capitol Building.

In preparation for the day, President Obama's top adviser, Valerie Jarrett, set up a private meeting with Trump confidante Kellyanne Conway. The two women discussed how to make the transition as smooth as possible, knowing the media would be anxiously seeking some kind of confrontation.

According to Conway, President Obama directed his staff to be "good" to the incoming Trump people, and so they were.

T T T

As DAWN BREAKS on the biggest day of his life, Donald Trump is already restless. He has much on his mind. He rarely drinks coffee or eats much in the morning. Instead, he tweets.

At 7:15 a.m., the first Trump tweet goes out: "It all begins today! I will see you at 11 a.m. for the swearing-in. THE MOVEMENT CONTINUES—THE WORK BEGINS!"

There is a reason for that tweet. The new president wants huge TV ratings when he takes the oath. He also anticipates a record crowd watching in person on the Mall. Later in the day, he will tell the press the turnout will be "unbelievable, perhaps record-setting."

That point of view will become President Trump's first controversy in office.

A little past 8:30 a.m., members of the Trump team, Kellyanne Conway, Reince Priebus, and Hope Hicks, arrive at Blair House. Stephen Miller and Steve Bannon have written the Inaugural Address, and Donald Trump is editing the words with a blue Sharpie. This is standard procedure. But unlike with many other speeches, Trump has rehearsed this one again and again, adding and subtracting words. In the end, it is almost entirely his speech.

Ten minutes later, the Trumps leave Blair House to attend a prayer service at St. John's Episcopal Church, a tradition for incoming presidents.

At 9:30 a.m., President Barack Obama also takes to Twitter, a rarity for him. "It's been the honor of my life to serve you . . . I won't stop; I'll be right there with you as a citizen, inspired by your voices of truth and justice, good humor, and love."

The wording is standard political fare, something the new president will avoid. He will use Twitter as a cudgel.

At 9:55 a.m., the Trumps arrive at the White House to greet the outgoing Obamas.

The meeting was gracious, with Michelle Obama hugging Melania Trump as the new First Lady gave her a gift; President Obama leaving a personal letter to Donald Trump in the Oval Office; and of course, the official White House pictures memorializing the event.

But then something strange happens. The two men disappear for more than an hour. According to close Trump associate Steve Bannon, Trump and Obama hit it off. In fact, Mr. Obama briefed Mr. Trump, telling him that North Korea would be his biggest problem

The president-elect and Melania are greeted by President Barack Obama and First Lady Michelle upon arriving at the White House on Inauguration Day.

and that hiring General Michael Flynn as a national security adviser would be a big mistake.

In hindsight, the Flynn advice was solid.

Donald Trump emerged from the talk with a positive feeling for Barack Obama personally. But it did not change Trump's negative opinion about his predecessor's governance.

Before leaving the White House for good, the Obamas are presented with two American flags: the first flew over the White House on the first day of Mr. Obama's tenure in January 2009. The second flag flew this morning.

It is now after 11 a.m., and the two presidents enter a black limousine, which will take them to the Capitol for the swearing-in ceremony. A light rain is falling. At the Capitol, the two men will separate for good. Donald Trump, his wife, and five children will be ensconced in a Capitol office until he takes the outdoor stage.

Donald Trump Jr., the soon to be new president's oldest son, speaks privately with his father.

"He never shows emotion, but he was in awe of what was happening. He said to me, 'Now we'll find out who our friends are.' He wasn't nervous about his speech because he's a game-time player, but he was focused on it. He planned to stick it to the establishment. He was also concerned about the size of the crowd, because we were hearing the Park police were keeping people away."

Kellyanne Conway was involved in crafting the tone of the new president's speech, along with Bannon and Miller.

"We wanted to combine the tough Trump with the uplifting Trump," Conway told me. "Winning finalizes all sentences, but we did want to make a patriotic appeal for cooperation. The final wording was done by the president, who believed his ideas had to be restated."

It is 11:55 as Vice President Mike Pence is sworn in by Supreme Court justice Clarence Thomas.

Then Donald Trump takes the oath as it is administered by Chief Justice John Roberts.

At noon, the Associated Press sends this dispatch to the world: "Donald Trump is now the 45th president of the United States. He's just taken the oath of office on the West Front of the Capitol.

"The combative billionaire businessman and television celebrity won election in November over Hillary Clinton, and today he's leading a profoundly divided country—one that's split between Americans enthralled and horrified by his victory.

"The unorthodox politician and the Republican-controlled Congress are already charting a newly conservative course for the nation. And they're promising to reverse the work of the 44th president, Barack Obama."

I believe it is fair to point out that the folks who run the Associated Press are among those "horrified" by Donald Trump's ascension. The dispatch is not inaccurate, but it lacks one kind word about a man who pulled off the most stunning campaign achievement in U.S. history.

Not one kind word.

T T T

It is 12:05 when President Trump begins his Inaugural Address. It lasts just fifteen minutes, considerably shorter than President Obama's two previous speeches in the same setting.

The new president thanks the four prior chief executives in attendance: Jimmy Carter, Bill Clinton, George W. Bush, and Barack Obama. He acknowledges that the Obamas have been very "gracious" handling the transition.

Then Mr. Trump lets it rip:

- The president says that the transfer of power is not to him but "Washington," giving power back to the people.
- He says the nation has deteriorated badly but "this American carnage stops right now."
- He pledges to protect the borders.
- He promises to eradicate "radical Islamic terrorism."
- President Trump then takes a swipe at President Obama: "From this day forward, a new vision will govern our land. From this day forward it's going to be only America first."

Barack Obama shows no reaction, but Michelle frowns. However, Trump's words should come as no surprise. The new president believes the Obama administration has been a "disaster."

However, it may be President Bush who has the strongest external reaction. According to a reporter citing anonymous sources, Bush says this about the speech: "That's some weird shit."

At 12:30, President Trump says his leadership will begin a new national pride that will "heal our divisions."

At about the same moment, the Associated Press sends out a dispatch describing Mr. Trump's view of America as "dark."

Let the healing begin.

T T T

The Clintons and Bushes on the platform at the U.S. Capitol in Washington, DC, on January 20, 2017, before the swearing-in ceremony of President-elect Donald Trump.

President Trump takes the oath of office during the presidential inauguration ceremony at the U.S. Capitol in Washington, D.C., January 20, 2017.

IMMEDIATELY AFTER THE speech, the Obamas hop on a helicopter bound for Joint Base Andrews, in Maryland. From there they will fly to Palm Springs, California, for a vacation.

At about 1:50 p.m., President Trump arrives at the inaugural luncheon, where he shakes Hillary Clinton's hand. Lobster, beef, and shrimp head the menu.

Donald Trump likes shrimp.

After lunch, the parade begins. Then it's back to the White House to announce cabinet appointments. Later, the president and First Lady will attend three inaugural balls.

T T T

MEANWHILE, ON TELEVISION, the "whose crowd was bigger" controversy is wasting the time of the American people.

The National Park Service no longer estimates crowds, but based on subway ridership and other evaluations, it appears that President Obama's First Inaugural Address had more in-person attendees than President Trump had.

Photographs taken at the National Mall show the crowds attending the inauguration ceremonies to swear in U.S. President Donald Trump at 12:01 p.m. (left) on January 20, 2017 and President Barack Obama (right) sometime between 12:07 p.m. and 12:26 p.m. on January 20, 2009.

Same thing with TV ratings: Obama, thirty-nine million in 2009; Trump, thirty-one million in 2016. But many more Americans watched today's proceedings online, leading Trump spokesman Sean Spicer to say the new president's total audience was the largest ever to witness an inauguration.

Maybe it was.

Who cares?

Reporting on television, I certainly didn't. But NBC News and CNN cared deeply. So did President Trump. Perhaps the only time those forces have had anything in common.

TTT

THE WHITE HOUSE is now the Trump domicile. The president's grandchildren race through the large rooms, having a blast. There is fried chicken, burgers, fries, anything they want.

In one of his few private moments, the new president says to his eldest son, "I wish my mother and father were alive to see this."

Donald Trump rarely shows emotion, and neither does Melania, but Trump is very aware of the history in this house. He believes he has earned the top job and is sincere about rejecting the Washington establishment and working for the folks.

That attitude and Mr. Trump's basic confrontational demeanor will spawn the "Resistance," an alliance of media and political power. And as the new president dances to Paul Anka's "My Way" at two inaugural balls, he does not really know what awaits him in the anti-Trump precincts. Naïvely, he believes the press will give him a chance to prove himself.

If he knew on his first day in power what was brewing, he would not be dancing.

He would be planning for the worst.

Because the worst is heading his way.

CHAPTER FORTY-TWO

THE WHITE HOUSE

MAY 17, 2017

LATE AFTERNOON

It has been a rough four months for President Donald J. Trump. Beginning with the release of a salacious, unverified "Russian dossier" by a far-left internet site on January 10, to the appointment today of a special counsel to investigate alleged "Russian collusion" involving the Trump campaign, the president has not had one day of rest on the job. Even though the "dossier" people were paid in part by Hillary Clinton's campaign, surely a red flag, the media Trump-haters have convicted the president of a variety of crimes and bash him nightly on cable news.

The negative coverage is unrelenting and unseemly, lacking any fairness whatsoever. Anonymous sources rule, late-night political zealots mock, the opposing party plans for impeachment.

Harrowing does not come close to covering it.

The president is genuinely perplexed by the "dossier" thing. As the *Washington Post* reports, the Democratic National Committee and the Clinton campaign hired a partisan group called Fusion GPS to dig up dirt on then-candidate Donald Trump. The group did what it was ordered to do; the problem is that much of the dirt is not true. Nevertheless, defamatory suggestions of prostitutes and shady deals got into the public discourse, and no one was held to account.

Donald Trump has never experienced this level of hatred. As a wealthy businessman, he could wall himself off from critics, sit high above them in Trump Tower. He ran his company without challenge. He mostly did what he wanted to do.

But sitting in the Oval Office, the president realizes that part of his life is over. His enemies are making him suffer every day. Studies show that more than 90 percent of the network nightly news coverage is against him. That constant negativity is taking a toll on his well-being.

As always, Donald Trump is fighting back, branding many media operations "fake news" and lashing out against those who despise him. This just fuels the hatred, which has now spread to the neighborhoods of America.

It is a political civil war.

Trump's handpicked attorney general, former Alabama senator Jeff Sessions, has been a major disappointment to the president. Facing a federal investigation into Russia's interference in the presidential election, Sessions chose to recuse himself because he had a few social conversations with Russian officials in Washington during the election cycle.

That infuriated Donald Trump, who was counting on Sessions to oversee the collusion investigation. Now things are out of control after Assistant Attorney General Rod Rosenstein offered the job of investigating the mess to Robert Mueller, a former FBI chief.

There is no present FBI director because President Trump fired James Comey eight days ago. Mr. Trump did not trust Comey, who had saved Hillary Clinton from indictment in the email investigation, and he does not trust Special Counsel Mueller.

But the chief executive is powerless to stop the intense intrusion into his ability to govern, and that is embittering him. He labels the investigation a "witch hunt" as his personal frustration mounts.

The columnist Victor Davis Hanson, generally a Trump supporter, provides an interesting overview as to how the "dossier" and Russian allegations were used by the Trump-haters to try to destroy the president.

The first strategy, according to Hanson, was to create doubt that Trump's victory was "legitimate," the spin being that without Putin's help, the president would have lost to Hillary Clinton.

This assertion unsettled Donald Trump, to say the least.

The second line of anti-Trump attacks was personal, as Professor Hanson describes:

> Both politicos and celebrities tried to drive Trump's numbers down to facilitate some sort of popular ratification for his removal. Hollywood and the coastal corridor punditry exhausted public expressions of assassinating or injuring the president. . . .
>
> Left wing social media and mainstream journalism spread sensational lies about supposed maniacal Trump supporters in MAGA hats. They constructed fantasies that veritable white racists were now liberated to run amuck insulting and beating up people of color as they taunted the poor and victimized minorities with vicious Trump sloganeering. . . .

In the face of the constant attacks on him and his supporters, Donald Trump has made mistakes. He vents at staff, discusses taking actions that could harm the nation, and becomes even more distrustful of human beings in general.

On Air Force One about eighteen months after the Mueller appointment, as the press continued its daily attack barrage, I asked the president about the situation:

O'REILLY: **What is your level of disappointment? Because the free press is a very important part of this country. The Founding Fathers gave us special privileges.**

PRESIDENT TRUMP: **Well, it's not a free press; it's a largely corrupt press. It's not even inaccurate; it's downright corrupt what they do. It's amazing how it's all gone down, because most people would think, Bill, that the press is honest.**

O'REILLY: **Is the press treating you the same way it treated [Richard Nixon]?**

PRESIDENT TRUMP: **I think they treat me much worse ... They treat me much worse than anybody who's ever been in office. And it's fake news.**

▼▼▼

PRESIDENT TRUMP'S PREDICAMENT as he tries to establish some authority in his first months in office directly impacts the American people. Eventually, the world would learn from Robert Mueller that there was no "collusion" between the Trump campaign and the Russians. But the damage Donald Trump is sustaining on a daily basis is hurting him both personally and on the job.

Victor Davis Hanson is perceptive on this again: "The [Mueller] team soon discovered there was no Trump-Russian 2016 election collusion—and yet went ahead to leverage campaign subordinates on process crimes in hopes of finding some culpability in Trump's past 50-year business, legal, and tax records. The point was not to find out who colluded with whom (if it had been, then Hillary Clinton would be now indicted for illegally hiring with campaign funds a foreign national to buy foreign fabrications to discredit her opponent), but to find the proper mechanism to destroy the presumed guilty Donald Trump."

Hanson's analysis can obviously be challenged. The fact is, some of Trump's associates did lie to federal investigators. But the columnist's opinion is also held by President Trump to this day.

▼▼▼

So IT IS that Donald Trump's world has devolved into constant conflict, a situation that would drain any human being. But Trump has one sustainable weapon at his disposal: power.

And he will soon use it to attempt to neutralize his legion of enemies.

CHAPTER FORTY-THREE

WASHINGTON, DC

JUNE 26, 2017

LATE MORNING

It is a good day for President Trump. The Supreme Court has just ruled that his so-called travel ban limiting people from seven Muslim nations from coming to the United States is legal.

As part of his foreign policy vision, Mr. Trump divides the Muslim world into good and bad. If a nation provides assistance to his administration, like Jordan or Egypt, it is good. If a country causes problems, like Iran or Somalia, it is bad.

President Trump could not care less about the Islamic faith or local overseas politics. To him, you either help or hurt America, and that's how he makes his determinations on policy. Above all, he does not want a replay of 9/11 on his watch.

Above all.

Trump's Executive Order 13769, executed just seven days after he took office, restricted citizens of Iran, Iraq, Libya, Somalia, Sudan,

Syria, and Yemen from entering the United States for ninety days. It also cut back refugee acceptance.

No doubt, the president wanted to send a message to the world and to his base at home that there was a "new sheriff in town," one who would be tough on disorderly Muslim countries. If the CIA believed some Islamic nations were not cooperating in profiling travelers, well, the president would stop visitors from those countries.

Immediately, his detractors accused him of racism.

It took less than a week for a federal judge to place a restraining order on the new president's action, but today, the Supreme Court ruled 5 to 4 that the executive order was constitutional and could go into effect.

Emboldened by the decision, the White House almost immediately released a warning to Syria, bluntly stating that America would punish the Assad regime if it continued to use poison gas on rebels.

That is what President Trump wanted to do all along: punish Bashar al-Assad. President Trump believes Barack Obama's failure to carry out his very public "red line" threat against Syria showed weakness to the world.

The new president is determined *never* to show weakness. To him, that's not part of "making America great again."

While the partisan cable news shows debated Trump's alleged racism, a new American foreign policy was unfolding. President Trump has a strong belief that the United States leads the world economically and morally. He wants other nations to deal fairly with America and has strong opinions on what is equitable and what is not.

Mr. Trump digested President Obama's private warning that North Korea would be a grave threat. The new president saw that as a challenge, and so the courting of dictator Kim Jong-un began.

President Trump believes he can make smart deals with almost anyone: Putin, the Chinese, the emotionally disturbed Kim. He will overlook atrocities and even flatter despots in order to get those "good" deals. In Trump world, the end almost always justifies the means.

But if a foreign leader or anyone else resists Trump's vision, his reaction is glacial. Hello, Angela Merkel.*

Many world leaders were stunned by the new president's blunt management style, the complete opposite of that of the pliant Barack Obama. And it is fair to say that inside the White House, Mr. Trump's way of doing business was far different than how Mr. Obama handled things.

T T T

DONALD TRUMP IS a creature of habit; he embraces routine. He begins his day shortly after 5 a.m. by turning on the television set and watching news in his private residence on the second floor of the White House. He is usually by himself at this point.

Early morning is tweet time for the president. During the working day, he dictates tweets to trusted aide Dan Scavino, who corrects his grammar and confers with his boss about messaging.

But after awakening, it is Trump's thumb exclusively pounding his message out, often after he's heard something on the news.

The president does not drink coffee or eat much before noon. Instead, he begins his Diet Coke consumption. He can drink up to fifteen bottles a day. Always with ice, in a glass. Never, ever out of a can. The soda must come from a bottle.

There is a business office in the residence, and it is here the president makes calls to foreign leaders, politicians, and friends before he comes downstairs to the "Oval." Besides his wife and son Barron, the only person around the residence is Donald Trump's "body man."

Most presidents have them—men responsible for getting the chief executives what they need. It is a trusted and largely nonvisible position.

President Trump does his own grooming and is meticulous in his dress. Since entering the White House, he has gained a considerable

---

* President Trump has little use for the German chancellor. He believes she does not pay her fair share of NATO expenses and is foolish for cooperating with Russia on a natural gas pipeline, among other things.

amount of weight. However, he does not diet or exercise much, believing that any significant weight loss would change the look of his face, which he does not want.

At eleven, President Trump strolls into the West Wing of the White House to begin his official day, which is laid out for him by his chief of staff, who is usually on the job quite early. The West Wing is essentially a series of narrow corridors flanked by small- to moderate-size offices.

The legendary Oval Office is functional but not grandiose. Most meetings are held in nearby conference rooms. The president's schedule is tightly time-controlled, but he can elongate any conversation at any time.

President Trump likes to use the small lunch room off the Oval Office to read newspapers and watch the news when he is not otherwise occupied. This is called "executive time" on the official White House schedule. He often eats lunch there at around 12:30, usually comfort food like steak, burgers, or shrimp salad. The White House kitchen accommodates rapidly.

On top of the Resolute desk in the Oval is a small box with a red button on its side. When Donald Trump pushes that button, a Diet Coke in a glass with ice appears almost instantly.

On most Mondays, President Trump has lunch with Vice President Pence, a man he trusts. The two exchange ideas and gossip and often strategize about how to deal with the hateful media.

Mr. Trump is not feared by his staff; nor is he moody. He occasionally shows anger when he feels someone is doing something stupid or has betrayed him. He does vent against the press often.

While in the West Wing, Donald Trump, like President Ronald Reagan, never removes his suit jacket.

At six o'clock in the evening, the president answers phone calls that have come in during the day. Sometimes he'll call some staff in to talk about pro football or something in the news. This is relaxing for Mr. Trump.

He usually departs at seven to eat dinner in the private residence with Melania and Barron, their thirteen-year-old son. Unlike the

From left, Cardinal Timothy Dolan, archbishop of New York; Republican presidential nominee Donald Trump; and Melania Trump listen as Democratic presidential nominee Hillary Clinton speaks during the Alfred E. Smith Memorial Foundation Dinner at the Waldorf Astoria, October 20, 2016, in New York City.

Obamas, the Trumps rarely go out to dinner or socialize unless it is government related. After dinner, Mr. Trump often watches the cable news opinion shows.

Donald Trump has no hobbies other than golf and is not an avid book reader or movie watcher. The only film the staff can remember him viewing is *Midnight Express*, the 1978 story of a young American imprisoned in Turkey on drug charges.

From time to time, the president will invite media people into the White House in an attempt to "win them over." This frustrates some of his advisers, who believe the president is naïve in this area and that the outreach is a total waste of time. But Donald Trump firmly believes that he has vast powers to persuade people to see things his way.

If a conversation is going well, the president may take his guests upstairs to the Lincoln Bedroom and show them Abraham Lincoln's handwritten Gettysburg Address.*

T T T

MELANIA TRUMP IS rarely seen in the West Wing except on travel days. Her office is in the East Wing, and her staff is very loyal and quiet. She has, perhaps, the lowest profile of any modern-day First Lady but does have her husband's ear. Every person in the White House knows not to get on the wrong side of Melania, although in general she is easygoing.

President Trump adapted quickly to life in the people's house, but six months after his election, he remains frustrated by his enemies and the slow pace of implementing his agenda. Unlike his past life, when he could dictate the action that he craves, now he is stymied by Congress, the courts, and the oppositional media.

Perhaps Mr. Trump's greatest annoyance is the southern border, where things remain almost out of control.

And are about to get much worse.

---

* After interviewing President Obama at the White House, he was kind enough to walk me up to the Lincoln Bedroom and show me the address. Having written *Killing Lincoln*, I found this a very special moment in my life.

CHAPTER FORTY-FOUR

PHOENIX, ARIZONA
AUGUST 22, 2017
EVENING

Presidents are human beings like everyone else, and they have their obsessions, things that mean a lot to them. For example, Teddy Roosevelt was fixated on controlling corporate monopolies, preserving wild land, and engaging in acts of personal heroism.

Ronald Reagan was obsessed with defeating communism, George W. Bush with exacting retribution for the terrorist attacks of 9/11.

President Donald Trump also has specific things that drive him in the policy arena. His mind is sharp, but his concentration is limited. He absorbs information quickly, but it is only with topics that interest him that he becomes truly engaged.

The four pillars of Trump's presidency are these: improving the economy, stopping illegal immigration, defeating Islamic terrorism, and preventing foreign nations from exploiting America financially.

Donald Trump is fanatical on those things; everything else is secondary.

By contrast, President Obama's passion was using the federal government to directly improve the economic circumstance of the "have nots" by providing subsidized health care access and redistributing wealth through a variety of entitlement programs.

Imposing "social justice" by federal regulation was also an Obama obsession.

All else was all else.

The visions of Presidents Trump and Obama could not be farther apart. Same thing with their demeanors. It is somewhat amazing that a country could elect these two polar opposites as leaders in the span of four years.

ＴＴＴ

IT IS ANOTHER scorching day in Arizona, and President Trump's presence here is making things even hotter. This morning he visited border officials in Yuma, where illegal immigration has been partially checked. Later he will hold a rally in Phoenix.

In 2006, under President Bush, there were just five miles of border fence in Yuma. Eleven years later, there are sixty-three miles of barrier in the sector, and migrant apprehensions have dropped 80 percent.

This is what Donald Trump has come to see and hear. Building a border wall is a signature issue for him, and he well understands that his core supporters expect him to put the wall up.

But there is fierce opposition to any tough measures to impede illegal immigration, including the wall. Many Democrats in Congress need the votes of Hispanic Americans, and most Hispanics are registered Democrats. The more migrants, the better, is the thinking in liberal precincts.

As with Muslims, President Trump does not have disdain for individual Latin American people. His business operations hire plenty of them. He does not think Hispanics are "bad" or not worthy of respect.

But Mr. Trump does not respect countries like Mexico, Honduras, and El Salvador, where corruption and violence rule. He does not believe that the United States has an obligation to accept millions of migrants who will, at least initially, have to be publicly supported.

Mr. Trump is also a "law and order" guy who is furious that federal immigration law is not being obeyed in places like California. He does not oppose immigration, but he demands that it be legal and regulated. He wants achievers to come to America, not those who might be dependent. The president promotes "merit-based immigration."

That core belief puts him in conflict with liberal thinkers, some of whom are demonstrating against Donald Trump right now. In fact, the Phoenix Police have fired tear gas canisters at those aggressively protesting outside the convention center.

Inside, about fifteen thousand people are attending the "Make America Great Again" rally. The president will speak for one hour and fifteen minutes, saying, among a number of other things, that he might shut down the government if Congress does not allocate money for a border wall. That statement will be realized.

President Trump also continues to put forth that "Mexico will pay for the wall." But this is rhetorical sleight of hand. The government in Mexico City would, under no circumstances, give the United States cash for a barrier; that is obvious.

The president, however, plans a tax on Mexican imports that would bring in revenue, thus offsetting the cost of the wall. Hence his assertion that Mexico will "pay."

The Hate Trump media, of course, is invested in portraying the president's immigration policy as racist. Just like the "travel ban." Just like the Obama birth certificate deal. This is a cheap line of attack but an effective one; millions of Americans are buying it.

It is true, however, that President Trump divides the world and its leaders into winners and losers.

He has never felt a responsibility to the losers.

T T T

THROUGHOUT LATE SUMMER and autumn 2017, President Trump ramps up his agenda. In September, he speaks to the United Nations, calling the despotic leader of North Korea "Little Rocket Man" (Elton John cringes), denouncing Iran, and praising Jordan for accepting refugees from Syria in the fight against ISIS.

He meets with a variety of world leaders, and his days are full of action, which he likes a lot. Many Diet Cokes are consumed.

Meanwhile, the Russian collusion investigation continues to burn, and nearly every day the press drops another "bombshell," citing anonymous sources that claim Trump attended satanic rituals with Putin or something.

Despite the distractions, Donald Trump maintains his routine, using Twitter to hit his enemies, seeking approval among his base.

But President Trump knows there is one thing, above all, that he must accomplish if he has any hope of getting reelected.

And that one thing is about to drop.

CHAPTER FORTY-FIVE

WASHINGTON, DC

DECEMBER 22, 2017

MORNING

Humbug! says the *New York Times*, the *Washington Post*, the *Los Angeles Times*, *USA Today*, NBC News, CNN, and the rest of the anti-Trump media. The new tax law will ruin the economy, drive more income inequality, and is an actual threat to America!

President Donald Trump has just signed the Tax Cuts and Jobs Act, his signature campaign issue (along with the wall). Not one Democrat in the House or Senate voted for it. Warren Buffett and Bill Gates also opposed it, as did billionaire Michael Bloomberg, who called the bill "an economically indefensible blunder."

All the detractors would be proven wrong.

As he prepares to fly to Palm Beach, Florida, for Christmas, President Trump is outwardly cocky, but surely he knows how close he has come to Armageddon. His tax revision bill passed in the Senate by just two votes.

The president had already seen his campaign promise to expunge Obamacare fail by one vote, Senator John McCain's, and if his tax vision had been defeated, his entire administration would have been in great jeopardy. That's because Mr. Trump is counting on a much lower corporate tax rate to electrify the economy. Now he has it.

The American left is in a fury over the new law because it drops the corporate tax burden from 35 to 21 percent, opens up Alaska's Arctic National Wildlife Refuge to oil drilling, and removes the "individual mandate" from the Affordable Care Act that forced Americans to buy premiums or be punished by the federal government. This was a centerpiece of Obamacare.

With the stroke of a pen, Mr. Trump has destroyed three of the sacred scriptures of liberalism: high business taxes, limiting fossil fuels, and adoring Barack Obama.

Although he does not yet realize it, the new tax law is the final indignity for President Trump's opposition. From now on they will become even more ferocious, stepping up the campaign to remove the president from office. Many who despise Trump are convinced that Special Counsel Mueller will find felonious activity on the president's part during the campaign, and that will lead to impeachment and conviction.

They will be proven wrong as well.

But for now, the Christmas season is open season on President Trump. According to much of the national media, he is brutalizing the poor. He is also adding to climate change danger and damaging the planet. And perhaps worst of all, he has disrespected the sainted Barack Obama.

Trump. Has. To. Go.

As he boards Air Force One, President Trump is likely not thinking about any of that. He is not a man who dwells on the possible unintended consequences of his actions. He is certain that he finally has a "huge" win, and if his economic view is correct, his supporters and detractors will soon have more money in their possession.

For the president, this is the ultimate deal, the one that will ensure his place in history.

T T T

IT HAS BEEN nine years since the American economy was a source of hope for working people. In 2007, years of corporate greed and hidden criminality in the home mortgage area subverted the entire economy, leading to a massive recession. It all happened during President George W. Bush's second term, and doomed the Republican Party. The best illustration of what exactly occurred can be found in the book (and later the movie) *The Big Short*.

Senator Barack Obama's charisma totally overwhelmed his challenger, John McCain, in the 2008 presidential election. Mr. Obama took office along with a Democratic congress. The new president believed that strict new government regulations and strong federal control of the private marketplace would bring the economy around.

Barack Obama was wrong.

Perhaps the best assessment of what happened on Obama's watch comes from Martin Regalia, the former chief economist at the U.S. Chamber of Commerce.

"Since mid-2009, the economy adjusted for inflation has grown at a 2.1 percent annual pace . . . the worst economic recovery in the post–World War II era. . . .

"The average length of time that the economy has taken to regain its long-run potential in the eight post–[World War II] recoveries has been 11.5 months . . . fully six years after the end of the [Bush the Younger] recession, our economy has yet to regain its potential. . . .

"[Income] inequality as measured by the Gini coefficient actually increased more during the Obama years than during the Bush administration."

Mr. Regalia's analysis was written with two years remaining in President Obama's second term. Things did not get much better.

That's one of the main reasons that almost 63 million Americans voted for a billionaire populist for president. Donald Trump promised economic prosperity. Many folks believed the promise.

That belief bore out.

TTT

DESPITE TEMPERATURES IN the seventies, Christmas at Donald Trump's Mar-a-Lago resort on Florida's Atlantic coast is as festive and traditional as most places in America.

The main building is tastefully decorated, and the palms are decked with boughs of holly. Secret Service agents ring the property, and every time the president leaves the premises, traffic is diverted.

That definitely cuts into the "goodwill toward men" deal for the affluent people celebrating the birth of Jesus in Palm Beach.

It is hard to imagine Donald Trump singing Christmas carols or doing last-minute shopping. He does occasionally greet club guests and often dines in the public areas with friends. In the morning, upstairs in the lavish mansion, the president takes calls from around the world, and consults with his advisers on a secure phone.

The truth is that President Trump is always working, even when he's on one of the many golf courses he owns. There is always something occupying him. That's why he enjoys being president: there is always action, challenges, the specter of a new deal.

In his real estate empire, Trump usually had to seek the action. Now, running the most powerful country on earth, he finds that the drama comes to him.

As he ticks off the Christmas vacation days in Florida, Donald Trump knows very well that the upcoming year, 2018, will likely make or break him.

There will be plenty of action and confrontation.

Happy New Year, indeed.

CHAPTER FORTY-SIX

THE WHITE HOUSE
JANUARY 4, 2018
AFTERNOON

This will not be a good year for President Donald Trump. Although he is still feeling strong from his big tax-cut win in December, things will soon begin to spiral downward. Today, the president will ask Congress for $18 billion to build 316 miles of new border fence and reinforce 400 other miles of barrier.

He will not get the money.

About a week from now, an adult-film actress named Stormy Daniels will say she received $130,000 to keep quiet about a long-ago tryst with Donald Trump. The woman will be in the news for months.

Also this year, President Trump will ask Kim Jung-un to drop his nuclear weapons program. Mr. Trump will travel all the way to Singapore to meet with the North Korean martinet. The president will not seal the deal with Kim.

After that, Donald Trump's personal lawyer, Michael Cohen, will betray him and eventually plead guilty to eight felonies. The story will generate news coverage that borders on hysteria.

Mr. Trump's television protégée Omarosa will also betray him in pursuit of book sales.

The president's handpicked attorney general, Jeff Sessions, will infuriate him over the Russian investigation and will resign under pressure in the fall.

Another woman, Karen MacDougal, will embarrass the president with affair allegations, and the *National Enquirer* will admit to being involved in hush money payments. More hysteria.

Illegal alien crossings at the southern border will surge as vicious people smugglers figure out how to scam U.S. asylum provisions. President Trump will send troops to the border.

Mr. Trump's nominee for the Supreme Court, Brett Kavanaugh, will be accused of sexual misconduct in his youth, leading to a bitter round of Senate hearings where the constitutional right of "due process" is battered. Although the FBI could find no evidence of any wrongdoing by Kavanaugh, he is barely confirmed by the Senate. He and his family absorb enormous punishment in full view of the country—his accuser, Christine Blasey Ford, is also heavily criticized by conservatives.

But the lowest point in 2018 for the beleaguered president will come in the midterm election, when Republicans will lose their majority in the House of Representatives. This will allow Nancy Pelosi, who loathes Donald Trump, to once again assume the powerful position of House Speaker.

At this point in history, Mrs. Pelosi is heavily invested not only in defeating Donald Trump for reelection in 2020, but also in personally destroying him. Thus, President Trump will get almost no cooperation from the House, and most meaningful legislation will stall. That will frustrate many American voters, which is part of Nancy Pelosi's plan. The other strategic aspect embraced by the Speaker is to create as much chaos for the White House as possible. With Special Counsel Mueller's Russian-collusion investigation inviting daily anti-Trump speculation from the media, Mrs. Pelosi's desire to cripple Donald Trump's presidency will quickly gather significant momentum.

T T T

Speaker of the United States House of Representatives Nancy Pelosi (Democrat of California) shows off the gavel after accepting it from United States House Minority Leader Kevin McCarthy (Republican of California) as the 116th Congress convenes for its opening session in the House Chamber of the Capitol in Washington, DC, on January 3, 2019.

FOR PRESIDENT TRUMP, this year will be one of bitter confrontation. He will continue to denounce the Mueller investigation as a "witchhunt" and "fake news," and publicly condemn the entire process.

Behind the scenes, however, Mr. Trump will maintain some semblance of discipline. Although he is bitter about his election and governance being tainted by allegations that he deems false, he apparently does not use his power to directly inhibit Robert Mueller's investigators from fact gathering. That will save Donald Trump from a Nixonesque scandal.

Talking with acquaintances, including your correspondent, the president vents hard about the unfairness of the Russian situation.

He is incensed that the press is torturing him with allegations, using unproven scenarios to try to weaken and humiliate him.

Mr. Trump truly believes the American media are "the enemy of the people." But he continues to speak with his primary tormentors, believing he might be able to persuade them to treat him more fairly. That seems at odds with his almost daily attacks on the media. In fact, on May 9, President Trump will tweet:

"The Fake News is working overtime. Just reported that, despite the tremendous success we are having with the economy & all things else, 91% of the Network News about me is negative (Fake). Why do we work so hard in working with the media when it is corrupt? Take away credentials?"

As we will see, President Trump will not banish the media, most of which rivals Nancy Pelosi and Hillary Clinton in terms of disdaining all things Trump. In fact, if you had to generalize about how most press people assess Donald Trump, Mrs. Clinton's public words sum it up:

"I think the president and his administration pose a clear and present danger to our democracy. I hoped, back on the day after the election, that I wouldn't be sitting here, all these months later, feeling compelled to say that with a sense of urgency.

"[Donald Trump] is immature, with poor impulse control; unqualified for the position that he holds; reactive, not proactive; not strategic, either at home or on the world stage."

To be fair, that view can be factually challenged. As the year 2018 draws to a close, the American economy is doing better than at any time during the Obama administration. ISIS, which had exercised horrifying power while Hillary Clinton was secretary of state, is almost defeated. And minorities in America are far better off in the job market than they were under Presidents Clinton and Obama.*

Surely, the American economy's dramatic rise was not "reactive," but the result of new benefits targeted to the corporate world, which then expanded investment and hiring.

---

* In April 2019, black unemployment stood at 6.7 percent. Until Donald Trump took office, this statistic had never been below 7 percent in the forty-five years since the Bureau of Labor Statistics began separating unemployment numbers by race.

Few press vehicles will point those things out, and Hillary Clinton certainly will not.

But is all the "negativity," to use Donald Trump's own words, affecting the president's psyche? No, according to his son:

O'REILLY: [Your father] seems to be fed up . . . The media is ingrained in America.

TRUMP JR.: Yeah, but they don't represent America. They represent their small bubble interest. People are influenced by them . . . but I think his resolve is strengthened to combat that even more.

O'REILLY: Have you seen a personality change?

TRUMP JR.: No, not even a little bit.

T T T

President Donald Trump and First Lady Melania Trump greet members of the U.S. military during an unannounced trip to Al Asad Air Base in Iraq on December 26, 2018, the president's first visit to U.S. troops deployed in a war zone since his election two years prior.

THERE WILL BE no Christmas in Palm Beach this year because the government has been partially shut down over border wall money. So, the president and his family celebrate the federal holiday in the White House.

Then, President and Mrs. Trump make a surprise visit to Iraq to extend Christmas greetings to American troops stationed in that difficult country.

So, as 2019 approaches, Donald Trump has many things weighing on him. The Mueller Report will soon be released, and there is uncertainty for the president there.

Some Democrats are preparing to announce they will run against him in 2020, and the press is as angry with a president as it's ever been. Richard Nixon was mercilessly hammered during Watergate, but he didn't have to deal with a twenty-four-hour news cycle that doesn't even stop on Christmas.

'Tis the season to be jolly.

A cynic might say, "Yeah, sure."

CHAPTER FORTY-SEVEN

THE WHITE HOUSE
JANUARY 20, 2019
AFTERNOON

The third year of the Trump presidency begins with day thirty of the partial government shutdown. Five days from now, on Friday, the shutdown will end when President Trump okays a deal that will fund the government for three weeks so a compromise can be sought over federal funding for a part of Mr. Trump's proposed wall on the southern border.

Predictably, no compromise will be reached as congressional Democrats remain steadfast against a new barrier. President Trump will then declare a national emergency on the border and seek money for the wall elsewhere in the federal budget.

The border controversy and shutdown illustrate perfectly the deep divide between Donald Trump and his opposition, including the national media.

In ordinary times, Congress would likely have been able to forge a compromise on the illegal immigration issue. But of course, these are not ordinary times. Policy has become personal; disagreement has turned into hatred.

A vivid example of this will occur twelve days from now, when the publisher of the *New York Times*, A. G. Sulzberger, and two of his White House reporters meet with President Trump in the Oval Office.

The *Times* opinion pages have brutalized Donald Trump from the beginning of his political adventure, and its hard-news operation often uses anonymous sources to put the president in a negative place.

Very few positive Trump stories appear in the *New York Times*.

In response, the president has labeled the *Times* "fake news" and has harshly criticized the newspaper. This has apparently upset Mr. Sulzberger, who believes Mr. Trump's negative words are putting journalists in danger.

At the Oval Office meeting, Sulzberger will say this: "Tough coverage is part of occupying the most powerful seat on earth . . . [S]peaking for the *Times*, you know my enduring commitment [is that] we will treat you fairly and accurately."

The president answers that he appreciates the publisher's words but then unloads.

"I have great respect for the press—but when I won the election and I know, and I'm not going to say that you apologized [to your readers,] but they did a whole big thing . . . and there were those who say that it was an apology. I was treated really badly during the election. That's the good news. The bad news is I'm treated even worse [now]. I'm treated bad."

Most Trump supporters would agree with the president's assessment of the *New York Times*, but its publisher, whose family owns the paper, does not.

And as old Rudyard Kipling once opined, "Never the twain shall meet."

T T T

ON APRIL 18, 2019, the Mueller Report on the investigation into the Trump Organization's allegedly working with Russia to undermine

Hillary Clinton during the 2016 election campaign was released. After almost two years and $30 million spent, the investigation concluded that there was no collusion between the Trump campaign and Russia. In addition, allegations of obstruction of justice remain dubious. After reading Mueller's report, Attorney General William Barr declared in a letter to Congress that "to obtain an obstruction conviction, the government would need to prove beyond a reasonable doubt that a person, acting with corrupt intent, engaged in obstructive conduct with . . . In cataloguing the President's actions, many of which took place in public view, the report identifies no actions, that in our judgment, constitute obstructive conduct."

T T T

THE DAY AFTER the Mueller Report was released, the *New York Times* issued a scathing editorial against President Trump: "The real danger the Mueller Report reveals is not of a president who knowingly or unknowingly let a hostile power do dirty tricks on his behalf, but of a president who refuses to see that he has been used to damage democracy and national security."

A skeptic of the *Times* might point out that writing that President Trump might have "knowingly" let Russia work on his behalf directly contradicts the conclusion of the Special Counsel.

As a newspaper publisher once promised with an "enduring commitment," fairness and accuracy are vital.

T T T

THE MUELLER REPORT did not change many minds in the anti-Trump community and led to some very bizarre displays on both sides. One of them by the Trump reelection campaign, which began selling shirts and drinking mugs emblazoned with "Collusion Delusion."

The president trumpeted total exoneration, but this was like kicking a beehive. Democrats attacked on all fronts, using House committees and media surrogates to cast doubt on the Mueller findings and to trash perceived Trump supporters like Attorney General William Barr.

In fact, anyone associated with the president was hammered.

For example, economist Stephen Moore was nominated by Mr. Trump as a candidate for the Federal Reserve Board of Governors. Usually, that's a fairly easy appointment.

Not this time. Mr. Moore was viciously attacked in personal ways and finally withdrew his name. The *Wall Street Journal* editorialized this way:

> *Mr. Moore's real sin was helping to fashion the tax reform that Mr. Trump adopted as a candidate and that passed in modified form in 2017. The economic left might forgive Mr. Moore for being wrong. But it will never forgive him for being right that deregulation and lower rates would help the economy rise above the Obama years of malaise to a higher plane of 3 percent growth and the best market for workers in 20 years.*
>
> *Mr. Moore's critics at the* New York Times *and the* Washington Post *predicted a stock market crash and recession if Mr. Trump was elected and his plan implemented. Mr. Moore made the mistake of making them look bad.*

▼▼▼

AND SO IT is that the political and social civil war in America rages on, with one Donald J. Trump right in the middle of nearly every battle.

Various House committees, controlled by Democrats, attempt to deprecate the Mueller Report and cast the investigation as a condemnation of President Trump.

Yogi Berra was wrong when he said, "It ain't over till it's over."

This one will never be over.

▼▼▼

STILL, THE PRESIDENT seems to sometimes relish the fight that will only end when he leaves office. And even after that, the Trump legacy will resound throughout the United States of America.

We will never see the likes of him again.

And that will greatly please those Americans who believe Donald

Trump has harmed the nation. But most of all Trump's departure will be greeted with rapture by his media opponents, who are doing everything possible to see that he loses in 2020.

On April 26, 2019, the *Los Angeles Times* said this:

> *There can be no doubt that four more years of a Trump presidency would be a disaster for the country. He has proved himself an incompetent and ignorant chief executive. . . .*
>
> *Rather than appeal to what Abraham Lincoln called "the better angels of our nature," Trump has savaged the press and his political opponents, demonized immigrants and provided rhetorical aid and comfort to brutal police officers and white nationalists.*
>
> *So, yes, an important question for voters in next year's Democratic primaries must be: Can this candidate defeat Trump?*

A few days later, while the better angels were contemplating that assessment of the president, the U.S. government announced the lowest unemployment rate in fifty years.

The celebration was not universal.

AFTERWORD

MANHASSET, NEW YORK

MAY 29, 2019

LATE MORNING

Special Counsel Robert Mueller looks tense. He is reading an eight-minute statement reiterating that his two-year investigation has not produced evidence of the Trump campaign colluding with Russia during the 2016 election. Mueller says his report does not rule out that President Trump might have done something wrong in the obstruction of justice area, but he is not allowed to bring charges against a sitting president under the Constitution.

True, but Mr. Mueller is certainly able to cite criminal activity if he can prove it. Judge Kenneth Starr did that eleven times in his investigation of President Clinton in 1998. But there is no proof in Mueller's report that crimes were committed by President Trump.

Nevertheless, Robert Mueller is emphasizing that his investigators cannot say Donald Trump did NOT violate the law. Mueller then goes on to imply that Congress should resolve the question since the Justice Department, citing lack of evidence, has declined to take the case any further.

Is that fair of Mueller?

Individual Americans will have to decide for themselves. But it is clear today on television screens all over the world that Mr. Mueller has absolutely no use for Donald Trump and would not object to impeachment proceedings.

▼ ▼ ▼

APPROXIMATELY TWELVE HOURS after Robert Mueller finishes his short dissertation, the phone rings in my house. The White House operator asks me if I can speak with the president of the United States.

Uh, yes, I believe I can.

It has been nearly five months since I spoke with President Trump aboard Air Force One. Since that time, I have conversed with him three times about life, liberty, and the pursuit of happiness—mostly his happiness.

But now the time has come to get down to it. Has Donald Trump's view of America changed considering all that has happened in the past three years? Does he see his country the same way he did before he began his presidential odyssey?

That's where we begin.

O'REILLY: **Has this Mueller situation changed your view of America?**

PRESIDENT TRUMP: **It's made me more circumspect. It's changed my life. What I am going through, no other president has gone through and it's evil. But it's also made me stronger because I have to get through it.**

O'REILLY: **Why is the campaign against you happening, in your opinion?**

PRESIDENT TRUMP: **Let's take Mueller. He's my enemy. I turned him down after he asked me to head the FBI (after James Comey was fired). I said no. And years ago, he was a member of a golf club I owned on the Potomac. He called me asking for his deposit back. He said he was leaving the area. I think it was $15,000. But I said no because then I'd have to do that for all members. And** the conversation got heated, it was nasty if you want to know the truth.

O'REILLY: So you think it was personal with Mueller?

PRESIDENT TRUMP: This was an attempted overthrow, Bill. And if I didn't fire Comey we would have never known about it. It's wrong. This should never happen to another president.

O'REILLY: Has your love for your country changed?

PRESIDENT TRUMP: I've learned a lot. I think this Mueller investigation will go down as one of my great achievements.

O'REILLY: What?

PRESIDENT TRUMP: Because the corruption would have never been uncovered. All these powerful people trying to subvert an election, people wouldn't have known about it.

O'REILLY: Why do you think some powerful people want to hurt you?

PRESIDENT TRUMP: I don't know why they hate me. I guess it's because I'm an outsider. I did something no one else had ever done. It's about power. In New York, it's money, but the New York guys are babies by comparison. I've never seen anything like it. You think you can trust people and they turn around and hurt you. You can't trust anyone.

O'REILLY: Do you think the federal system is corrupt?

PRESIDENT TRUMP: The media is more corrupt. How can you win Pulitzer Prizes writing about stories that aren't true, using anonymous sources that tell lies? Shouldn't they have to give those prizes back? It's horrible. I mean I've rebuilt the military, we have the best economy, women and minorities are doing much better and still all I get are bad stories.

O'REILLY: Why do you think things are so devious?

PRESIDENT TRUMP: I think about it all the time. The *Washington Post* and the *New York Times* are the worst. Local news has actually been good to me. I think it comes from the top. Jeff Bezos (owner of the *Washington Post*) uses the paper to lobby. It's a business thing for him.

O'REILLY: What about the fake news branding?

PRESIDENT TRUMP: A big success because I have exposed them as corrupt. It used to be people trusted the media but they are so far down in the polls.

O'REILLY: How has the media hatred affected you?

PRESIDENT TRUMP: In one way it's positive. It shows that I can take it. Not many people could get through what I've had to take. Rudy Giuliani's a tough guy but he told me he doesn't think he could handle all the hate.

O'REILLY: What do you tell your thirteen-year-old son about America in the face of all this?

PRESIDENT TRUMP: You know he sometimes comes to me and says, "Dad, they are really coming after you. It's sad."

O'REILLY: What do you say to that?

PRESIDENT TRUMP: I always say: we just keep going forward, that's what we do. You know, the media doesn't care if they hurt families. They are the meanest people. But when I leave office, I'll have my revenge. Because many of them will go out of business. Without Trump, what have they got?

O'REILLY: So your love for America hasn't changed?

PRESIDENT TRUMP: I love my country but many things in it should not be happening and I hope no other president goes through this. It's bad for America.

TTT

DONALD TRUMP IS not going to change. He will not modify his behavior, stop tweeting, or begin wearing jeans. He'll stay the way he is until the grave.

Many of the 63 million Americans who voted for Trump in 2016 will not change, either. They have too much emotion invested in Mr. Trump. And they generally loathe his detractors.

Despite the almost daily controversies, citizens see how the president is governing and close to half the country approves of his job performance in any given polling week.

This is based on the healthy economy, I believe, not on ideology.

If you study the president you will not see much promotion of conservative principles. Vice President Pence is much more on the right than his boss is.

However, the president understands his base support comes from conservative Americans, therefore he will not alienate them. He will continue to choose traditional Supreme Court justices, back stronger laws against abortion, and defend the Second Amendment.

This is essentially why the American left hates Donald Trump. Some liberals make assertions about character and such but that's mostly bull. Liberal America, in general, supported President Clinton to the end of his administration.

No, the anti-Trump "Resistance" is mostly about social policy. And there are many ingredients in that stew. But the primary flavor is a belief on the committed left that America is an unjust country and Donald Trump is a major part of that injustice. That core anti-Trump belief is what spawned Robert Mueller and the ongoing attempts to oust Donald Trump from power.

However, the raw hatred that is on vivid display may actually work in President Trump's favor as he seeks reelection. Independent voters will decide who wins in 2020 and any overreach, say, a flimsy impeachment attempt by House Democrats, could well bolster the Republicans.

The most important question for the nation right now is this: Can President Trump win another term after all that has happened? It would be another stunning political story if he did—especially because he has the establishment media lined up against him in a way never seen before in this country. He is also facing a hostile House of Representatives that will continue to oppose him on all fronts.

And so it is that a man from Queens has achieved incredible power through guile, determination, and immense ambition.

But Donald Trump has paid a price for that power—a price he could never have foreseen.

Nor could any of us.

ACKNOWLEDGMENTS

As I wrote in the beginning of the book, getting the truth about Donald Trump was difficult. So, a very special thank-you to Martin Dugard and Makeda Wubneh, who helped me separate fact from propaganda.

Also, I owe a debt of gratitude to Bill Shine for primary source material, including access to the president himself. And thanks to Charles Lachman, executive producer of *Inside Edition*, for his help.

Finally, my team at Henry Holt led by Steve Rubin and Serena Jones is both professional and perspicacious. We've made history together.

ILLUSTRATION CREDITS

Page 101: Chester Higgins Jr./The New York Times/Redux

Page 108: Olivier Douliery/White House Pool (ISP Pool Images)/Corbis/ VCG via Getty Images

Page 109: Christy Bowe/Corbis via Getty Images

Page 134: Doug Mills/The New York Times/Redux

Page 147: David Becker/Getty Images

Page 157: Andrew Milligan/PA Wire (Press Association via AP Images)

Page 167: James Atoa/Everett Collection

Page 176: James Atoa/Everett Collection

Page 191: Danny Wilcox Frazier/VII/Redux

Page 205: Steven Ferdman/Everett Collection

Page 208: Justin Sullivan/Getty Images

Page 225: Brian Snyder/Reuters/Newscom

Page 255: Mark Wilson/Getty Images

Page 258 (top): Mandel Ngan/AFP/Getty Images

Page 258 (bottom): Xinhua/Yin Bogu via Getty Images

Page 259: Reuters Staff/Reuters/Newscom

Page 269: Brendan Smialowski/AFP/Getty Images

Page 281: dpa picture alliance/Alamy Stock Photo

Page 283: Saul Loeb/AFP/Getty Images

BILL O'REILLY is a trailblazing TV journalist who has experienced unprecedented success on cable news and in writing fifteen national number one bestselling nonfiction books. (There are currently more than seventeen million books in the Killing series in print.) Mr. O'Reilly does a daily podcast on BillOReilly.com. Also, his daily radio program, *The O'Reilly Update*, is heard on hundreds of stations across the country. He lives on Long Island.